K 920 GIG

THE FOUNDATIONS OF RESTITUTION FOR WRONGS

'Restitution for wrongs', or 'restitutionary damages', is the judicial award which compels the wrongdoer to give up to the victim the benefit obtained through the perpetration of the wrong, independently of any loss suffered by the victim.

The establishment of a civil trial in Roman law, which left compensation as the main response, and a widespread, loss-centred interpretation of the Aristotelian theory of corrective justice explain, but do not justify the difficulties encountered by modern attempts to account for restitutionary damages. Mistakes in the classification of this institution have complicated the picture.

To overcome some of these problems, this study considers the basic structure of restitutionary damages from different angles. In part one, the topic is analysed from a comparative perspective. Although the focus remains on English law, the German, the Italian and the Roman jurisdictions provide research data which, in part two, support the development of a theory of restitution for wrongs as corrective justice.

The Foundations of Restitution for Wrongs

Francesco Giglio

·HART·
PUBLISHING

OXFORD AND PORTLAND, OREGON
2007

Published in North America (US and Canada) by
Hart Publishing c/o
International Specialized Book Services
5804 NE Hassalo Street
Portland, Oregon
97213-3644
USA
Tel: +1 503 287 3093 or toll-free: (1) 800 944 6190
Fax: +1 503 280 8832
E-mail: orders@isbs.com
Website: www.isbs.com

Hart Publishing, 16C Worcester Place, Oxford, OX1 2JW
Telephone: +44 (0)1865 517530 Fax: +44 (0) 1865 510710
E-mail: mail@hartpub.co.uk
Website: http://www.hartpub.co.uk

British Library Cataloguing in Publication Data
Data Available

ISBN-13: 978- 1-84113-647-9 (hardback)
ISBN-10: 1-84113-647-6 (hardback)

Typeset by Columns Design Ltd, Reading
Printed and bound in Great Britain by
TJ International Ltd, Padstow, Cornwall

Preface

At this point, shortly before sending this monograph to the publisher, what surprises me most is not the fact that it has taken me the best part of eight years to complete it. Rather, I am baffled by the simple recognition that my manuscript would happily take another eight years to refine. I console myself with the twin thoughts that no book is perfect and that I am a slow thinker. In addition, I had to familiarise myself with very many different areas of law in various legal systems. But many friends and colleagues bear a share of responsibility in having compelled me into such a long period of reflection. I cannot believe how lucky I was, having so many people who read my ideas and demolished them, forcing me to start again. My small revenge is to involve them in my project by naming here at least some of them.

The late Professor Peter Birks must be the first. I must confess that, when I met him for the first time at All Souls College, I had just arrived in England from Germany and was not aware that I was speaking to one of the great masters of the twentieth century. Thus, I started talking of myself and of my great talent. As I had just finished my previous project in Germany on the law of unjust enrichment, I told him what that area of law was about. I am even more grateful to him for not having sent that arrogant Italian out of his rooms immediately than for having taken me as a doctoral student at Oxford University. More than anything, the hours spent in his Roman law seminars will always be in my memory.

At that time, Peter had two DPhil students working on similar projects, James Edelman and myself. Jamie was enviably much quicker than I in producing his doctorate. Even more annoyingly, his work opened up issues which I simply could not ignore. Although I disagree with most of what Jamie states, his monograph on *Gain-Based Damages* is a milestone which has compelled everyone else to re-think the whole subject of restitution for wrongs. Jamie is responsible for at least two years of the eight which have been necessary to complete this book. The forcefulness of his arguments accounts for the differences between my monograph and the doctoral thesis upon which it is based. In the best Birksian tradition, I changed my views on the nature of restitution for wrongs and developed a new approach which appears to me to be much more coherent with the principle of corrective justice.

I am terribly grateful to my friend and colleague John Murphy. He is the only person who has managed to read the whole manuscript – and not only once, but many times. His sometimes witty, but always sharp and useful comments have played a major role in the fine-tuning of my ideas and my prose. His contribution has been essential.

I have received much help from my DPhil examiners, Geoffrey Samuels and Kit Barker. After more than two hours of *viva voce* examination in December 2003, in which they gave me a really hard time, we parted good friends. Kit provided moral and factual support in the years after the examination, for which I shall always be indebted to him. Reading some of Geoffrey's work published in recent years, I have realised how our views diverge. Still, his examination was extremely fair. He encouraged me to develop new ideas and helped me in obtaining funding for my research.

Various other University of Manchester colleagues – both past and present – must also be mentioned: Robert Crier, Neil Duxbury, Andrew Griffiths, Joseph Jaconelli, Andrew McGee and the always-helpful Law Librarian Sue Bate. The School of Law of The University of Manchester and, in particular, its Head of Department, Andrew Sanders, deserve special mention. Andrew has trusted me and it is because of the valuable research time which my School granted to me that the book is ready after 'only' eight years.

My research has seen me wandering around many European universities, the libraries and institutes of which have offered me excellent refuge thanks to kind colleagues. Let me mention Guido Alpa at the Università degli Studi di Genova (now at the University La Sapienza in Rome), Helmut Grothe and Cosima Möller at the Freie Universität Berlin, and the Universität Osnabrück. In Osnabrück, Christian von Bar's European Legal Studies Institute has been one of my main ports of call. Undoubtedly, I would have had to make many more visits abroad if I had not had the privilege of researching at the Bodleian Library of the University of Oxford.

My theoretical position on restitution for wrongs as corrective justice owes much to Dennis Klimchuk. Although he does not always agree with me, his comments have been crucial in the shaping of my views. I am extremely thankful to him and many members of the School of Law of the University of Western Ontario.

My final thanks must go to my publisher, Richard Hart, who has believed in my project, placing science before profit. I hope to prove him wrong: science and profit can go together.

This book is dedicated to my wife, Nicola. She has brought love and *Vernunft* in my life and has given me a solid basis on which to conduct research and, more importantly, to enjoy the research-free time.

Contents

Table of Citations

von Bar	C von Bar, *Gemeineuropäisches Deliktsrecht* (München 1996), vol I, the paragraphs cited do not change in the English translation: *The Common European Law of Torts*, Vol I (Oxford, Clarendon 2000)
Birks, Restitution	P Birks, *An Introduction to the Law of Restitution* (revised edn, Oxford, Clarendon 1989)
Coleman, Risks	J Coleman, *Risks and Wrongs* (Cambridge, CUP 1992)
Edelman	J Edelman, *Gain-Based Damages* (Oxford, Hart 2002)
Fleming	JG Fleming, *The Law of Torts* (9th edn, Sydney, Sydney, Law Book Company 1998)
Kaser RP I	M Kaser, *Das römische Privatrecht, 1. Abschnitt, Das Altrömische, das Vorklassische und das Klassische Recht* (2nd edn, München, Beck 1971)
Kaser RP II	M Kaser, *Das römische Privatrecht, 2. Abschnitt, Die Nachklassischen Entwiklungen* (2nd edn, München, Beck 1975)
Larenz and Canaris	K Larenz and C-W Canaris, *Lehrbuch des Schuldrechts. Band 2: Besonderer Teil, Halbband 2* (13th edn, München, Beck 1994)
McGregor	H Mcgregor, *McGregor on Damages* (17th edn., London, Sweet & Maxwell 2003)
Monateri, Responsabilità	PG Monateri, 'Le Fonti delle Obbligazioni, 3, La Responsabilità Civile', in R Sacco (ed), *Trattato di Diritto Civile* (Torino, Utet 1998)
MünchKomm/	*Münchener Kommentar zum Bürgerlichen Gesetzbuch* (4th edn, München, Beck), H Oetker, §§ 249-255 (2001); V Emmerich, §§ 279-283 (2001); D Lieb §§ 812-822 (2004); H-J Mertens, §§ 823-829 (1997)
Palandt	O Palandt (ed), *Bürgerliches Gesetzbuch* (64th edn, München, Beck 2005)
Reuter and Martinek	D Reuter and M Martinek, *Ungerechtfertigte Bereicherung* (Tübingen 1983)
RGRK	Reichsgerichtsraten und Bundesrichter (eds), *Das bürgerliche Gesetzbuch, mit besonderer Berücksichtigung der Rechtsprechung des Reichsgerichts und des Bundesgerichtshofes* (12th edn, Berlin 1989)

Table of Cases

German Cases

Italian Cases

Introduction

'THE FOUNDATIONS OF Restitution for Wrongs' is a difficult choice as a title. It might sound pretentious and could pave the way to a useless broad-spectrum analysis. It is possible, if not to avert, to reduce the risk of being pretentious by explaining why this title has been chosen. In recent years, many judicial and academic doctrines have increasingly contributed to illustrate some aspects of restitution for wrongs; yet these efforts tend to concentrate on particular issues and are difficult to reconcile within a general framework. A wide-angle analysis would enable a more coherent approach to restitution for wrongs because it would consider the basic theoretical fabric of this topic. This is what I endeavour to do in the present study. To achieve my goal, I pursue two avenues: legal comparison and legal theory. The former offers the tools for a better understanding of English law through the evaluation of the responses given by other jurisdictions to two central issues: the identification of the party which should keep the wrongful profits and the consistency of restitution for wrongs with the law of obligations. Legal comparison, however, would struggle to explain why a certain allocation of wealth is, or should be, adopted by the legal system. Theoretical analysis is the proper place to deal with this question, which is increasingly attracting the interest of philosophers and theorists.

On the other hand, a detailed analysis of cases and theories would no doubt provide a large quantity of information. But it would jeopardise my aim of setting a general framework. Conversely, a too superficial investigation would deprive the analysis of any valuable content. For this reason, I shall stick to a few guidelines: to identify the structural elements of restitution for wrongs, explain why these damages should be awarded, and distinguish them from other heads of damages which take the benefit of the wrongdoer into consideration. The individuation of research targets is all the more important if one considers that restitution for wrongs can be tackled from many different viewpoints. In *Attorney-General v Blake*,[1] the House of Lords finally recognised that gain-based damages are part of the judicial tools. In the literature, James Edelman's recent monograph has provided a principled analysis of restitutionary damages, while Ernst Weinrib in a seminal article has powerfully opened the discussion on their theoretical basis.

The terms 'restitutionary damages' and 'restitution for wrongs' refer to the legal response which compels the wrongdoer qua wrongdoer to give up to the victim

---

[1] *A-G v Blake* [2001] 1 AC 268.

the benefit obtained from the perpetration of a wrong. A simple instance will clarify its context of application. Famous actor C employs D as a private secretary. In the employment contract there is an express reference to D's duty to respect her employer's privacy in any form. This notwithstanding, D writes a book on C's private life. The book sells very well and D's profits outstrip C's loss. C brings an action for damages. If the court were to award only compensation, C would not be worse off after the award than he was before the wrongful event took place. Yet, wrongdoer D would be better off, for she could keep the difference between what she has to pay as compensation and the proceeds of the sale of the book. A decision about restitution for wrongs is a decision about which party deserves that difference.

The foundations of this legal institution are multifarious. I do not intend to examine all aspects linked to them. As already intimated, the perspective from which the topic will be investigated is mainly comparative and theoretical. The comparison will cast light on the English concept of restitution for wrongs through an investigation of German and Italian law, but also Roman law. The theoretical analysis will pursue two main tasks. On the one hand, I shall explain how legal philosophy has shaped the matter at issue and how the academic lawyers have sought to accommodate the judicial doctrines in a coherent structure. On the other hand, I shall provide an account of the nature of restitutionary damages based upon corrective justice.

One of the central questions which I shall consider concerns the reason why restitution for wrongs is seen as exceptional or rejected altogether. There are many possible explanations. The identification of all factors which contribute to the mistrust surrounding restitutionary damages would have put my research skills under excessive strain. I have concentrated my efforts on two areas which, in my view, have played a central role: legal history and Aristotelian philosophy. In the search for the appropriate clues, the comparative-theoretical analysis reaches three main conclusions. First, there is no structural incompatibility between the law of damages of the legal systems under comparison and restitution for wrongs. If restitution for wrongs were to be introduced into the legal systems compared it would not conflict with any of their fundamental principles. Secondly, there are at least two reasons accounting for the suspicion with which the courts look at restitutionary damages. The first can be traced to a development of the Roman civil trial which eventually left compensation as the main legal response to all civil wrongs. The second lies in the influence which Aristotelian philosophy has exerted – especially through the Late Scholastics – on legal science. Thirdly, corrective justice does account for restitution for wrongs.

The theory of restitution for wrongs is caught within the larger debate on the role of non-compensatory damages. As this debate focuses primarily on exemplary damages, there is a risk of confusing restitution with punishment to the detriment of a correct understanding of the former. Yet, the temptation of the a fortiori argument, according to which whenever there is room for exemplary damages there is room also for restitutionary damages, must be resisted. Peter

Jaffey has argued 'the "quasi punitive" nature of disgorgement'.[2] However, restitution for wrongs is not a mild form of punishment. It is historically, structurally and conceptually independent of punishment. Furthermore, the importance of compensation within the law of damages and the debate on punishment tend to obscure the nature and function of restitution. I shall distinguish restitution for wrongs not only from compensation, but also from punishment for wrongs.

The semantic analysis which opens this study will introduce concepts which can be used both in a common law and in a civil law framework. Restitution for wrongs will be placed in the context of the law of obligations, which presents different issues of compatibility in each legal system compared. At this point, I shall give a closer look to some areas of the law of obligations where restitution for wrongs is or might be applied. The different approaches followed by the foreign legal systems contribute to identify the main characteristics of the English academic and judicial constructions. The ensuing theoretical examination will build upon the results of the legal comparison to illustrate the foundations of restitution for wrongs. Some instances of this head of damages are not recognised as such. In other cases, the judicial award seems restitutionary whereas in reality it is compensatory. A wide-range research on the foundations of restitution for wrongs helps to distinguish those awards which consider the defendant's gain, and yet are fundamentally compensatory, from the real instances of restitution. One such case is the violation of intellectual property rights. In many legal systems, it gives rise to a head of damages which targets the gain of the wrongdoer. And yet, this measure is not restitutionary, for it involves the violation of a proprietary interest of the victim, so that the victim obtains compensation for the loss inflicted to that interest. The difference between compensation and restitution will become clear through the examination of the impact of legal philosophy on legal analysis. It will emerge that most of the references to 'restitution' in Aristotle's successors, including Weinrib, concern cases of compensation.

This study evolves over nine chapters and a conclusion. The various issues will be progressively introduced, so that the reader will be able to follow the discussion on the nature of restitution for wrongs on the basis of the information acquired in the previous chapters.

Chapter 1

Chapter 1 explains what the terms 'restitution' and 'wrong' signify in the legal systems under examination. All three jurisdictions regard 'restitution' as meaning the giving up of a benefit, although they differ in matters of detail. Thus, it is debated in England whether the transfer of wealth from the defendant to the claimant should always be classified as 'restitution', or whether in cases of giving

---

[2] P Jaffey, *The Nature and Scope of Restitution* (Hart, Oxford 2000) 374-376.

up, as opposed to giving back, one ought to speak of 'disgorgement'. This relationship between 'giving up' and 'giving back' will offer the occasion for some interesting reflections on German law, which uses both terms. The concept of a civil wrong is quite challenging from a comparative perspective. 'Wrong' finds no direct equivalent in civil law. The traditional English view regards a civil wrong as a breach of a duty owed to persons generally. Civil law works with the more limited concept of 'delict', or 'illicit behaviour', which refers to unlawful violations of general legal relations between persons. Neither definition can apply to breach of contract. To provide a common ground for comparison, 'wrong' has been taken as meaning 'breach of duty'. In this fashion, it has been possible to accommodate the differences between common law and civil law. This definition allows also the inclusion, in the analysis of restitution for wrongs, of breach of contract, which English law now seems to accept as a wrong.

Chapter 2

The aim of the second chapter is to provide background information to the ensuing investigation of restitutionary damages. Some aspects of the law of damages and the law of unjust enrichment might hinder a development of restitution for wrongs. The chapter offers only an overview; a detailed analysis would move the focus away from the damages at issue. It emerges that all three legal systems share the pre-eminence of a compensatory model. Non-compensatory damages are regarded with suspicion, if not rejected outright. The tendency to regard the contentious issues of exemplary damages as concerning all non-compensatory damages does not help the case of restitutionary damages. The fact that exemplary damages cannot be linked to an objective measure, and therefore are potentially more open to abuse, might justify the judicial and academic unease. Yet, the same argument cannot apply to restitution for wrongs, in which the measure of restitution is objectively determined by the benefit of the defendant.

Chapters 3, 4 and 5

These chapters build the core of the legal comparison. I shall ascertain whether the obstacles identified in chapter 2 are insurmountable, or whether there are elements which support the introduction, or indicate the presence, of restitutionary damages. Drawing from a study of the Law Commission,[3] four topics will be considered. Chapter 3 deals with proprietary and intellectual property wrongs, chapter 4 with breach of contract, and chapter 5 examines the residual category

---

[3] Law Commission, *Aggravated, Exemplary and Restitutionary Damages* (Law Com No 247, 1997).

of 'other wrongs' and contains some reflections on the comparison of the three jurisdictions. The broadness of the subject precludes an exhaustive study of all, and even most of, the restitutionary situations for wrongs. The taxonomy of the Law Commission is extremely useful in identifying some selected areas of the law which emphasise key elements for the understanding of restitutionary damages.

An evaluation of merit of the various avenues pursued in each legal system is not one of the tasks of my research. I confine my investigation to an understanding of the reasons behind the legal developments in each system. In civil law, the expansion of restitution for wrongs, if this institution is recognised at all, has been hampered by the presence of a claim in unjust enrichment. In particular, German law has developed a new model of restitution beside the traditional model imported from Roman law. This claim, known as *Nichtleistungskondiktion*, does not require a direct transfer of wealth between the parties to the action, thus displaying some similarities with the mechanism of restitution for wrongs. Italian law, while sticking to a more traditional claim which lists a performance between the parties among its requirements, has also codified a general enrichment claim. The latter allows restitution when the enrichment would be regarded as 'unjust' and might comprise cases of wrongful enrichment. Chapters 3, 4 and 5 demonstrate that there are reasons outside the law of damages for the different fortunes of restitution for wrongs and restitution for unjust enrichment in civil law. Both German law and Italian law are characterised by a sophisticated law of unjust enrichment, which they largely derive from Roman law. It is difficult for the courts to leapfrog into what is perceived as *terra incognita*. This might explain the wider development of restitutionary damages in English law than in German and Italian law. However, German lawyers, unlike their Italian counterparts, express a certain interest[4] in the recent English developments.

Chapter 6

The historical investigation in chapter 6 substantiates the thesis according to which there is no structural incompatibility between non-compensatory damages, which include restitution for wrongs, and the law of damages. The analysis indicates that even in the Roman law of damages there are traces of what might be regarded as restitution for wrongs. More generally, Roman law shows that the law of damages can be built upon a non-compensatory pillar without losing coherence with the system. This finding applies to English law as well. Although the Common law was not characterised by the phenomenon of the so-called Reception of Roman Law, the law of obligations, a Roman structure upon which the law of damages rests, is still part of English law.[5]

---

[4] Eg J Köndgen, 'Gewinnabschöpfung als Sanktion unerlaubten Tuns' (2000) 64 *Rabels Zeitschrift* 661-695.

[5] See DJ Ibbetson, *A Historical Introduction to the Law of Obligations* (Oxford, OUP 1999) 1.

This chapter challenges the view according to which compensation has traditionally been the main aim of the law of damages. The Roman civil law of damages was characterised by the pre-eminence of punishment. Compensation became the major response only at a later point owing to some historical events. The role of restitutionary damages is more uncertain. There are indications that some actions might have led to restitution. Yet, it is arguable that they are true examples of restitution for wrongs. They were directed towards the heir of the wrongdoer and their subject matter was limited to the enrichment of the heir. I argue that such claims should be better regarded as compensatory, for the heir simply took the place of the wrongdoer. Besides these actions, an opinion delivered by Julian offers a stronger clue on a particular Roman claim for breach of contract. This important passage of the Digest, which has puzzled generations of Romanists, might acquire novel significance if is read as an instance of restitutionary damages. Thus, chapter 6 provides information to understand where restitution for wrongs comes from, and how it fits within the law of damages.

The study of Roman law underlines how restitutionary and exemplary damages diverge. Having been developed as responses active in different contexts, their only point of contact is their belonging to the group of non-compensatory responses. The historical development of restitution and punishment for wrongs indicates that there was absolutely no interaction between them. This outcome reinforces the view that any a fortiori argument, which justifies restitution wherever punishment is awarded, is dubious.

Chapter 7

The comparative analysis will have revealed that there are no structural obstacles to the introduction of restitution for wrongs into the three jurisdictions. Yet, there are other reasons for the minor role played by restitutionary damages. The understanding of the evolution of the Roman law of damages is central to explaining their limited significance. A further reason lies in moral philosophy. No theory of restitution for wrongs can ignore the Aristotelian account of justice. Chapter 7 deals with Aristotle's main concepts, focusing on corrective justice. In my opinion, this model of justice can account for restitution for wrongs. But in this chapter I shall not discuss my views or indeed the modern attempts to prove that restitutionary damages can be accommodated within corrective justice. This will be done in chapter 8. Here, I shall introduce the idea of corrective justice and examine its evolutionary pattern from Aristotle until Grotius. While the influence of Aristotelian philosophy on the law of damages is widely recognised, its relationship with restitution for wrongs is controversial. I shall follow the development of Aristotelian philosophy focusing on the Early and the Late Scholasticism. In particular, I shall show that when St Thomas referred to 'restitution', he often meant 'compensation *in natura*'. Later, Soto, de Vitoria, and other *scholastici*, linked Aristotelico-Thomistic concepts with legal analysis, thus providing Grotius with a conceptual basis for his work. The Late Scholastics took on the meaning of restitution as 'giving back to the victim that of which the victim has been deprived', which is very close to the function of compensation.

The analysis of Aristotelian justice sheds light on two points. First, it illustrates the profound influence of that account on modern constructions of the law of wrongs, providing an explanation for the pre-eminence of compensation. Secondly, it demonstrates that, from a legal perspective, the model of corrective justice espoused by Grotius, and subsequently by modern legal systems, concentrates on compensation.

Chapter 8

The eighth chapter considers the interaction between Aristotelico-Thomistic philosophy and modern normative approaches. Three schools of thought will be introduced: the German 'social' theory of damages, moral instrumental theories, and moral formalist theories.

There is a strong identification in Germany between law of damages and law of compensation. Josef Esser observes that, as society is not involved in the relationship which links agent at fault and victim, corrective justice alone establishes the rules of compensation. However, when the agent is not at fault, it is distributive justice which justifies an award of damages, for it deals with the just apportionment of goods within society. This view has been widely influential in German law. Esser gives distributive justice a prominent place near corrective justice. Yet, it will be shown that his account does not provide any support to the theory of restitution for wrongs.

The investigation of moral instrumental theories, primarily Jules Coleman's thoughts on corrective justice and its scope within the law of damages, supports my view that modern theories based on corrective justice encounter difficulties in accommodating restitution for wrongs because they tend to be loss-centred. Although he considers restitution for wrongs only *en passant*, Coleman's analysis contributes strongly to the understanding of the damages at issue.

Ernest Weinrib endeavours to demonstrate that Coleman's position is wrong. He argues that a single model of justice can account for the whole of the law of damages, including restitutionary damages. If his intuition were right, the theory of restitution for wrongs would have found a solid basis and corrective justice would be able to explain restitution for wrongs. However, rather than putting a case for corrective justice, his analysis seems to achieve the opposite result. Instead of unifying tort law, Weinrib's construction excludes all those institutions which do not fit his idea of tort law. This leaves Weinrib with a dilemma: either concluding that restitutionary damages cover an area which is much smaller of what legal analysis and judicial decisions potentially recognise to it or using a fiction to enlarge this area at the expense of the internal coherence of his theory.

Weinrib opts for the second avenue. Furthermore, Weinrib allows a restitutionary award only when a proprietary or quasi-proprietary interest has been affected. But when this is the case, the victim is claiming on the basis of his own loss, not of the wrongdoer's gain. The victim says to the agent: 'you have used my thing and have appropriated a benefit which should be mine. I want it back.' Therefore, the gain of the agent contributes to the quantification of the award, which however is based upon the loss of the victim. This is a measure of compensation, albeit less traditional, not of restitution.

My own account of restitution for wrongs starts from Aristotelian theory, which in my view, unlike the later Scholastic developments, is not loss-centred. I argue that it is possible to explain the damages at issue as corrective justice provided that 'pain' or 'loss' are not construed as meaning patrimonial disadvantage. As the wrong separates the agent and the victim as doer and sufferer of an injustice, the victim is the only person who can claim the wrongdoer's benefit. By awarding restitution for wrongs, the court allocates the gain to the most deserving party.

Chapter 9

After having confronted restitution for wrongs with moral philosophy in chapter 7, and with normative theories in chapter 8, in chapter 9 I shall consider some of the main descriptive explanations of positive law. If my previous analysis is correct, every descriptive approach to restitution for wrongs has to surmount at least two obstacles. First, it cannot rest on most of the work previously done by legal theorists, for no account has been able to capture the subject. Secondly, as the judiciary has not yet developed a firm theoretical structure, it is difficult to put together the different pieces into a coherent whole. This second point is best shown by the description of positive law advanced by Peter Birks. Birks provides three 'tests' to individuate restitutionary damages. However, since the tests are based upon legal authorities some of which do not deal specifically with restitution for wrongs, Birks' attempt to force them into a different model produces a prescriptive theory dressed as a description of positive law. A similar problem affects Jackman's approach. The author adheres closely to the judicial view, but in so doing he cannot explain some situations in which restitutionary damages would be helpful to achieve justice. Jackman himself admits his inability to formulate a systematic account of the law of restitution for wrongs.

In his recent work, Edelman tackles the analysis from a different perspective and circumvents the difficulties mentioned. He distinguishes two measures of damages. One measure, termed 'restitutionary', is quantified by the benefit which the agent wrongfully obtained by the victim. The other measure, labelled 'disgorgement', identifies the pure enrichment of the wrongdoer, independent of any connection to the victim. The problem with this approach is that Edelman's 'restitutionary' award is compensation measured by the gain of the wrongdoer, not a case of restitution for wrongs. If such damages constitute 'a monetary award which reverses a transfer of value',[6] the wrongdoer gives back to the victim what belongs to the latter, which means that the victim claims a loss and the award is compensatory. Edelman's approach is flawed by the same taxonomical mistake which affects Weinrib's analysis of restitution for wrongs.

The second half of chapter 9 will be dedicated to expound the structure of restitution for wrongs on the basis of the information gathered in the previous chapters. It is sometimes said that, when compensation and restitution coincide, by compensating the victim the demands of restitutionary justice will be satisfied as well. This statement hides a misconception. If you wrongfully take my bicycle worth £100, my loss and your gain formally coincide. But I cannot claim £100 as restitutionary damages. This sum of money is linked to my loss, not to your gain. The latter could be higher or lower than your loss, and still it would not affect my claim for £100. Furthermore, my benefit will vanish as soon as you have returned my bicycle to me. On the contrary, restitutionary damages do not disappear owing to the compensatory performance. Thus, if you sell the story of my life to a newspaper in breach of a contract between you and me, and this causes a loss of £100 to me and a benefit of £100 to you, my compensatory claim of £100 will not deprive you of your benefit of £100, which is independent of my loss. To take your £100 benefit away from you, I shall have to claim restitution of your £100 gain and compensation of my £100 loss. £100 which I claim by way of compensation is linked to my loss; your £100 gain is linked to the wrong which connects you and me, but not to my loss. The restitutionary claim is justified by your connection with the wrong and by your wrongful benefit. My position is irrelevant: I might have suffered a loss or not, be upset or not, and in all cases I would be able to claim restitution.

Although loss in the sense of compensation and benefit in the sense of restitution are independent of each other, still the structures which govern the awards are mirroring images of each other. Compensation aims to return the victim to the position in which the victim was before the wrongful event; restitution aims to restore the conditions in which the agent was before the wrongful event. Consequently, any compensation-yielding wrong is potentially restitution-yielding too. If this conclusion is correct, then it is not a matter of legal principle but a matter of policy whether restitution for wrongs should be introduced into a system.

Chapter 10

Chapter 10 contains the final observations. The results of the research will be presented according to the different perspective under which they have been analysed: comparative, historical, theoretical.

---

[6] Edelman, *Gain-Based Damages* (Oxford, Hart 2002) 66.

1

Terminology and Introduction to the Concept of Restitution for Wrongs

I First Things First

THIS STUDY EXAMINES both comparative and theoretical issues in restitution for wrongs. The analysis of the legal systems under comparison in the first part provides the data for the theoretical account in the second part. The first chapter is dedicated to a brief examination of a few terminological issues by way of introduction to the material discussed in the following chapters. The legal comparison requires first the ascertainment of the meaning of 'restitution for wrongs' in English, German and Italian law. The expression will be deconstructed into its original components, 'restitution' and 'wrong', to see whether there is or there can be a common understanding of their significance in the three legal systems. In particular, the absence of the concept of a wrong in German and Italian law requires some adaptation. But this is not an insurmountable obstacle: the concept can be accommodated within the taxonomy of the German and Italian law of obligations.

In the final part of this chapter, I shall examine some issues which are relevant to all three jurisdiction considered, albeit to different degrees. The concept of restitution for wrongs is of limited avail if it is not located on the map of the law of obligations. In this context, I shall distinguish restitution for wrongs from compensation for wrongs and from the law of unjust enrichment. I shall then use the comparative analysis of the concept of a wrong to conclude that this term is compatible with the structure of the law of obligations in civil law systems. Finally, I shall consider the concepts of 'law of torts' and 'law of delict', which for the purposes of this study will be treated as referring to the same area of law.

II Restitution

All three jurisdictions use the term 'restitution' in a similar sense. The Latin root *restituere/restitutio* is generally, albeit not exclusively, linked to the law of unjust enrichment. In England and Italy this term denotes at least the duty upon the defendant to transfer his enrichment to the claimant. In Germany, the expression of German etymology '*Herausgabe*' is technically more precise than '*Restitution*', which has a more general connotation. Restitution is the response which consists in causing one person to give up to another a benefit received at his expense or its value in money.[1] The claimant could be the person from whom the enrichment of the defendant derives directly, as in case of a mistaken payment. On the other hand, 'giving up' leaves open also the possibility that the claimant does not just claim 'back' the object of his own performance, but that he claims a benefit accruing to the defendant which, according to some predetermined criterion, ought to go to the claimant. In this last case, no direct connection between the parties is required, for the defendant could derive his enrichment from a source other than the claimant.

A   English Law

Two main issues must be addressed. The first issue is purely terminological. It is disputed in English law whether 'restitution' encompasses either or both expressions 'giving up' and 'giving back'. The second issue is related to categorisation. There seems to be a large degree of uncertainty as regards the relationship of restitution for wrongs with the law of unjust enrichment.

'Right to restitution' will be used here to define the right to obtain a gain made by the other party to a contract, by the party who has been enriched without legal ground, by the wrongdoer, or by other persons in particularly qualified situations independently of the claimant's loss. The term 'restitution for wrongs' means an award, normally of money, calculated so as to effect surrender of gains accruing to the wrongdoer from his wrong. These definitions are controversial, as will become apparent in the following section.

i   Restitution and Disgorgement

In the literature, there has been a long and still ongoing discussion on the legal responses which should be connected to the concept of restitution. Lionel Smith has suggested[2] that 'restitution' should be used only in the sense of 'giving back', hence in the cases in which there is the direct relationship between the parties which is embodied by the expression 'at the expense of' (the claimant). In his view, the right term to describe a 'giving up' situation, where the claimant does not claim back what he performed, but rather claims the benefit which the defendant obtained from the wrong, ought to be 'disgorgement'. If, for instance, butler D publishes a book describing his employer's life in breach of his employment contract, according to this view employer C would not be able to

---

[1] Birks, *Restitution* 13.
[2] LD Smith, 'The province of the Law of Restitution' (1992) 71 *Canadian Bar Review* 672-699, 694-699.

bring a claim for restitution for wrongs to strip D of ill-gotten gains, but would be successful in an action for disgorgement of D's profits.

It seems to me that a wider meaning of 'restitution', which includes the cases beyond 'giving back', is more appropriate for various reasons. Etymologically, the term '*restitutio*' was used by the Romans to indicate both 'giving up' and 'giving back'.[3] Civil law systems have kept this meaning. Thus, there are an historical and a comparative argument which militate in favour of a common term for all situations in which the wrongdoer should transfer his benefit to the victim. If history and comparison were not persuasive enough, there also is a strong ground for English law to keep the terminological unity. It seems inappropriate to introduce a new term in a field of the law in which definitions have not yet been settled. In a phase in which the law of restitution[4] is rapidly creating its own vocabulary, there is a risk that the strict link between the two concepts be forgotten. If this happened, the further step might be the creation of separate responses – with different requirements – which would lead to a complete severance of 'restitution' and 'disgorgement': a merely terminological difference would trigger a classificatory mistake according to which 'law of disgorgement' and 'law of restitution' would refer to different legal phenomena.[5] Whatever the word used, both depict, at common law, the situation in which a benefit has been wrongly obtained by the wrongdoer and should be transferred to the victim of the wrong.

Signals of a movement towards the creation of two separate remedies are already visible in the literature, where disgorgement alone is sometimes defined as 'stripping the defendant of ill-gotten gains'.[6] But the most serious attack to the development of a unitary model of restitution for wrongs comes from James Edelman. This author has recently advanced a proposal which accommodates both 'restitution' and 'disgorgement' within restitution for wrongs.[7] There are two models of gain-based damages, he urges, with differing functions. One award is aimed at the reversal of a transfer of value. This response is 'restitutionary'.

---

[3] P Birks, 'Equity in the Modern Law: an Exercise in Taxonomy' (1996) *University of Western Australia Law Review* 1-99, 28 n 57. With reference to the Roman *condictiones* see, in general, R Zimmermann, *The Law of Obligations* (Clarendon, Oxford 1996) 838-857; D Liebs, 'The History of the Roman *Condictio* up to Justinian' in N MacCormick and P Birks (eds), *The Legal Mind Essays for Tony Honoré* (OUP, Oxford 1986) 163-184.

[4] This is a category of the law of legal responses which comprises both unjust enrichment and restitution for wrongs.

[5] M McInnes, 'Disgorgement for Wrongs: An Experiment in Alignment' [2000] *Restitution Law Review* 516-546, 521, favours the opposite solution, ie the adoption of a different terminology, for the same reason – to avoid confusion – which is advanced here. For similar reasons, EA Farnsworth, 'Your Loss or My Gain? The Dilemma of the Disgorgement Principle in Breach of Contract' (1985) 94 *Yale Law Journal* 1339-1393, 1342, prefers 'restitution' for unjust enrichment and 'disgorgement' for wrongs. Still, at the present stage of evolution of this field of the law, the risk of confusion seems enhanced, not diminished, by the use of a larger spectrum of terms.

[6] Thus S Worthington, 'Reconsidering Disgorgement for Wrongs' (1999) 62 *MLR* 218-240. The author takes over this definition from the Law Commission Report No 247: *Aggravated, Exemplary and Restitutionary Damages* (Law Com No 247, 1997) Part II para 1.5. But the Law Commission does not seem to see a concrete difference between disgorgement and restitution.

[7] *Edelman, passim* esp 66-79.

Through the other award – 'disgorgement' – the wrongdoer is deprived of ill-gotten gains. Edelman's construction provides a useful tool to describe some of the mechanisms at work in the system. Yet, this approach would lead to unsatisfactory results if it were applied to justify a legal theory of restitution for wrongs.[8] A proper case for the inappositeness and artificiality of a distinction between 'restitution' and 'disgorgement' will be made when the theoretical basis of restitution for wrong is examined. At this stage, I would only like to point out that this is a central issue with important consequences for the understanding of the structure of restitution for wrongs. At present, 'disgorgement' has not yet succeeded in replacing 'restitution'.[9] They live side by side, with 'restitution' conserving its double meaning and 'disgorgement' having only the meaning of 'giving up'[10] as opposed to 'giving back'.

The courts for their part formerly showed extreme caution when using restitutionary language. This is likely to be due to an historical accident: the way of application of the old forms of action. Instead of innovating through the introduction of new writs, the courts preferred to enlarge the existing ones.[11] The language of unjust enrichment was avoided as superfluous, because the existing actions were deemed to cover also situations of non-tortious misplacements of wealth. In the second half of the 20th century, notably after a famous opinion by Lord Wright,[12] this caution has lost part of its grip. Ever since the *Lipkin Gorman* case,[13] the positive evolution of the law of unjust enrichment could not avoid influencing the judicial attitude towards restitution for wrongs.[14]

Although judicial approval has not affected the definition according to which restitution means 'giving up an enrichment received at the expense of the claimant', the different function and structure of restitution and compensation have not always been understood by English courts, which sometimes experience difficulties in drawing a neat divide between the two terms.[15] Nevertheless, the new judicial position towards the law of unjust enrichment has brought an important change in the approach to restitution for wrongs. In fact, the judges have asked themselves why they should not also use the expression 'restitution' in a tortious context when it is appropriate to do so.[16] Even a recent change in this

---

[8]   See a more detailed analysis of Edelman's theory at ch 9, VI.

[9]   Jaffey's statement according to which '[d]isgorgement is not a term of the art in the law' is, at least since Lord Steyn's speech in *Attorney-General v Blake* [2001] 1 AC 268 (HL), no longer correct. *Cf* P Jaffey, *The Nature and the Scope of Restitution* (Hart Publishing, Oxford 2000) 363.

[10]   Among others D Friedmann, 'Restitution for Wrongs: the Basis of Liability' in WR Cornish R Nolan and J O'Sullivan (eds) *Restitution Past, Present and Future, Essays in Honour of Gareth Jones* (Hart Publishing, Oxford, 1998) 133-154; N Andrews, 'Civil Disgorgement of Gains: the Temptation to Do Justice' *ibid* 155-162.

[11]   *Cf* JH Baker, 'The History of Quasi-Contract in English Law' *ibid* 37-56.

[12]   *Fibrosa Spolka Akcyjna v Fairbairn Lawson Combe Barbour Ltd* [1943] AC 32 (HL) 61.

[13]   *Lipkin Gorman v Karpnale Ltd* [1991] 2 AC 548 (HL).

[14]   *A-G v Blake* (n 9).

[15]   *Cf* the different opinions of Denning and Romer LJJ in *Strand Electric & Engineering Co Ltd v Brisford Entertainments Ltd* [1952] 2 QB 246 (CA) esp 255 and 256. See ch 3, n 46 and text thereof.

[16]   In his dictum in *Ministry of Defence v Ashman* (1993) 66 P & CR 195 (CA) 201, Hoffmann LJ said: 'I do not see why we should not call a spade a spade'.

judicial trend is unlikely to affect the centrality of restitution. Lord Nicholls in *Blake* famously rejected the expression 'restitutionary damages' as 'an unhappy expression'[17] preferring to it an 'account of profits'. Harvey McGregor[18] remarks that there is only a partial overlapping between an account of profits and restitution for wrongs, from which it must follow that the expression still plays an essential role in the identification of a restitutionary award for wrongs.

ii   Quadrationism versus Multicausalism

The 'law of restitution' and the 'law of unjust enrichment'[19] are not synonyms. They do not even belong to comparable categories.[20] 'Unjust enrichment' is a legal event. The law attaches to this event a given response. The response is, necessarily, restitution. The same response can be awarded also for other events, such as contract and tort. Unlike unjust enrichment, contract and tort comprise multiple, heterogeneous responses, whereby compensation, restitution and punishment are the most common.[21] 'Restitution for unjust enrichment' and 'restitution for wrongs' have their roots in different areas of the law of obligations and consequently the requirements of their causes of action are dissimilar. The first expression refers to the only response which his triggered by the event 'unjust enrichment', the second expression concerns restitution as one of the various responses which can be triggered by the event 'wrong'. In other words, restitution for wrongs is a wrong-based response to an enriching event whereas restitution for unjust enrichment is a non-wrong-based response to an enriching event. Still, the two responses share a similar mechanism of restitution and therefore they are both part of the 'law of restitution'.[22] For example, if I mistakenly pay my debt twice to you, I cannot recover the overpayment with a claim for restitution for wrongs, for you have committed no wrong. A claim for restitution for unjust enrichment, on the other hand, can help me to redress my financial disadvantage.

This civil law distinction creates some difficulties to English scholars, who do not have the classificatory background of civil law. The academic dispute is now polarised between two different views. The view which – *mutatis mutandis* – is in line with the civil law approach is known as multicausalism. 'The multicausalists maintain that restitution … does not always respond to unjust enrichment but

---

[17]   *Blake* (n 9) 284.

[18]   H McGregor *on Damages* (17th edn) (London, Sweet & Maxwell 2003) para 12-006.

[19]   The expression 'law of unjust enrichment' is quite generic. It would be more appropriate to distinguish between 'unjust' and 'unjustified' enrichment. But such distinction does not seem to be appreciated by English lawyers. For reasons of convenience, I shall use the expression 'law of unjust enrichment' as comprising also the law of unjustified enrichment. For a detailed analysis of this partition, see F Giglio, 'A Systematic Approach to 'Unjust' and 'Unjustified' Enrichment' (2003) 23 *OJLS* 455-482.

[20]   Birks, *Restitution* 16-22. Professor Birks' last exposition of this 'event-based classification' can be read in *Unjust Enrichment* (2nd edn) (Oxford, OUP 2005) 21-28.

[21]   *Cf* Birks (n 3) 17-20.

[22]   Birks re-examined the relationship between restitution as a response to the event 'unjust enrichment' and restitution as a response to the perpetration of a wrong in 'Unjust Enrichment and Wrongful Enrichment' (2001) 79 *Texas Law Review* 1767-1794.

may be triggered by one of a number of distinct causative events'.[23] Restitution can be caused by an unjust enrichment, but also by the perpetration of a wrong or by an original acquisition which leaves the previous owner empty handed. Multicausalism traces its roots to the Roman partition of the law of obligations which is accepted in modern English law.[24] As David Ibbetson remarked, '[t]he Common law of obligations grew out of the intermingling of native ideas and sophisticated Roman learning'.[25]

Those who reject the Roman law approach maintain that the 'law of restitution' and the 'law of unjust enrichment' are interchangeable expressions with identical meaning.[26] The two institutions are seen as two sides of the same quadrate, which explains why the supporters of this view are called 'quadrationists'. Their arguments have been summed up by Andrew Burrows in a powerful essay.[27] Burrows opens his analysis with a premise: in the last 20 years, much has been done by the judiciary; '[t]here is a danger that much of this ground will be lost if that picture is shattered'.[28] The author has four objections to 'the new approach' of the multicausalists.

The first objection concerns the risks involved in the departure from 'the natural use of the language, and language commonly adopted by the courts'.[29] The courts would identify the claim for restitution with the claim in unjust enrichment; hence, one should be very careful before abandoning this terminology. This objection is not based on legal argument. Either the 'traditional approach' is correct, and then no amendment is required, or it is not correct, and then it is a scholarly duty to provide solutions to rectify the mistake. The sooner the mistake is amended, the easier it is to apply the correct categories without having to modify consolidated structures. Examining judicial dicta, Burrows appears to ask, 'Does this choice of language by the judiciary not reveal that, in awarding restitution for wrongs, one is reversing unjust enrichment?' This question does not compel an affirmative answer. The use of inappropriate terminology cannot justify a mistaken approach. Burrows has later reinforced

---

[23] *Ibid* 1770.
[24] It suffices to mention the *Fibrosa* case (n 12) 61. Referring to cases of 'unjust benefit', Lord Wright said: 'Such remedies in English law are generically different from remedies in contract or tort, and are now recognized to fall within a third category of the common law which has been called quasi-contract or restitution'. This dictum, which provided an important basis for the construction of unjust enrichment as an autonomous category, accepts the Roman perspective on the law of obligations as developed by Gaius D 44.7.1.pr.
[25] DJ Ibbetson, *A Historical Introduction to the Law of Obligations* (Oxford, OUP 1999) 1.
[26] Yet, not all those who question the event-based classification query the importance of Roman law as well. Thus, G Samuel, 'English Private Law: Old and New Thinking in the Taxonomy Debate' (2004) 24 *OJLS* 335-362, 360-361, is very critical of Birks' taxonomy, but does not doubt the importance of Roman law: 'Nothing in this article should be taken as suggesting that the contributions of the Romans ... should be considered no longer worthy of serious study ... What is to be regretted are single-minded and intellectually authoritarian projects that are backward-looking.' On the other hand, it appears that no quadrationist refers to, or accepts, Roman law taxonomy.
[27] A Burrows, 'Quadrating Restitution and Unjust Enrichment: A Matter of Principle?' (2000) 8 *Restitution Law Review* 257-269.
[28] *Ibid* 258.
[29] *Ibid* 261.

this point stating that 'restitution for a wrong can be equally well classified as part of the law concerning the wrong or as part of the law of restitution'.[30] In his view, a claim in unjust enrichment is available every time in which a 'giving back' claim for wrongs – what Edelman calls a claim for 'restitutionary damages'[31] – can be awarded. Yet, even if it were accepted for the sake of argument that more than one claims might be available to the victim, this should not be a bar to the introduction of new actions. At any rate, the two claims concern remedies which use different measures of quantification, so that no overlapping is possible. In chapter nine, I shall argue that restitution for wrongs cannot target any gain directly linked to the victim's loss, which is normally the case in unjust enrichment.[32]

Burrows's second objection rests on the existence of a 'closer affinity' between restitution for wrongs and restitution for unjust enrichment than between restitution for wrongs and compensation for wrongs. This assumption depends on the set of criteria selected. Just as valid an argument could assert that there is an even closer affinity between restitution for wrongs and punishment for wrongs. Indeed, it has been often stated that a restitutionary response for wrongs should be awarded a fortiori whenever a punitive response could be awarded.[33] This supposed affinity between punishment and restitution in the law of wrongs is argued by Lord Diplock in the same dictum[34] which Burrows quotes in support of his own view. As regards Burrows' objection, restitution for wrongs and restitution for unjust enrichment indeed share some common elements. Yet, this should not surprise, given that they both belong to that area of the law which deals with restitution.

A further objection concerns the role of the defence of change of position, which is linked to restitution for wrongs and restitution for unjust enrichment, but not to compensation for wrongs.[35] A first difficulty with this objection emerges from its author's admission that 'it is unclear whether change of position can ever apply to restitution for wrongs'.[36] At any rate, even if it applied to restitution for wrongs, the presence of this common factor seems too feeble an element to justify an identity of the two institutions.

---

[30]   A Burrows, *The Law of Restitution* (2nd edn) (London, Butterworths 2002) 459.
[31]   *Edelman* 66.
[32]   See ch 9, text to n 49.
[33]   See ch 9, XI.
[34]   *Broome v Cassell* [1972] AC 1027, 1130. Lord Diplock, referring to exemplary damages, and not to restitution for wrongs, remarked that one of the functions of such damages might 'be a blunt instrument to prevent unjust enrichment'. Yet, he thought that exemplary damages go over and above that function. Previously, 1129, Lord Diplock had observed that an award of exemplary damages in the case in which a tort was committed in the belief of material advantages 'would seem to be analogous to the civil law concept of enrichessement indue subject to a similar limitation that the act resulting in enrichment must be tortious'. That his Lordship applied the wrong category is evident from his words: there is no example of '*enrichessement indue*', both in French and German law, which requires the perpetration of a wrong to activate the claim.
[35]   Burrows (n 27) 264.
[36]   *Ibid* 266.

Burrows's final objection has fundamental character. The 'new approach' would abandon the principled approach which had qualified the 'law of restitution' so far. For Burrows, the law of restitution is based upon the principle of unjust enrichment, whereas the multicausalists would adopt an event-based or a response-based categorisation. Both in England and in the United States, the multicausalists 'saw themselves as identifying a new subject based on principle … that was different from the two other principles of the law of obligations'.[37] Again, this objection is not founded on strictly legal argument. The internal coherence of the law is a legal argument. And the event-based classification of the multicausalists rests on the Roman categorisation of the law of obligations. If this coherence is sacrificed in favour of policy considerations, the latter must be so cogent as to justify the sacrifice.

Burrows ends his analysis with a question to all multicausalists: what are the practical advantages of the 'new approach', given that the 'traditional approach' has been so successful? One could turn the argument and observe that unjust enrichment and the concept of restitution have been so successful *despite* the incorrect classification because they filled an important gap in English law. There hardly seems to be the need to illustrate the advantages of a correct taxonomy.[38] If a natural scientist asserts that, say, horses belong to the same genus 'fish' as trout, that scientist will not be able to understand horses, trout, and fishes.

Geoffrey Samuel disagrees with my last statement. In his view, 'positivism and rule models cannot in themselves provide an adequate basis for legal knowledge.'[39] Considering the event-based classification and taxonomy, he writes:

> There is of course epistemological trickery here in that the association of causative events in legal science with causative events in natural science is misleading to say the least. Causative events in the natural sciences … can be tested by correspondence with a physically existing object … In legal science the object does not exist externally to the science … There is no compelling reason that demands that rights *in rem* must be distinguished from rights *in personam* while there are very compelling practical reasons why one should distinguish between viruses and bacteria.[40]

In fact, taxonomy in legal science and taxonomy in natural science aim to achieve the same result: a coherent classification of phenomena, which might well be external or even internal to the science itself. One could object to Samuel that a distinction between viruses and bacteria is not compelling at all: it is just *one* possible form of classification among many – all equally good and purposeful. The point is that this classification is coherent with its premises and allows us the understanding of a branch of nature. Similarly, event-based legal taxonomy is coherent with its premises and allows us the understanding of an area of law.

---

[37] *Ibid* 267.

[38] E McKendrick, 'Taxonomy: Does It Matter?' in D Johnston and R Zimmermann (eds) *Unjust Enrichment, Key Issues in Comparative Perspective* (Cambridge, CUP 2002) 627-657, 657, observes that '[t]axonomy is a vital part of the quest to eliminate anomalies and inconsistencies in the law and to ensure that like cases are treated alike'.

[39] Samuel, above (n 26) 343.

[40] *Ibid* 340.

That considerations not strictly based upon legal principle might intervene and modify the rule as it is applied by the courts or the legislator is not a sufficient reason to reject the legal classification.

B German Law

There is no reference to 'restitution' in the context of wrongful claims in the statutes or in the judicial decisions. To understand the technical meaning of the term at issue in German private law it is necessary to refer to the highly refined *ungerechtfertigte Bereicherung*, that is – literally translated – 'unjustified enrichment'. It will be shown later in the analysis that, unlike what most English authors purport, there is little overlapping between restitution for unjust enrichment and restitution for wrongs, for these claims aim at different goals. Still, as they are often considered together, it is useful to examine briefly the codal classification of the unjust enrichment claims. The German civil code, BGB, employs two different sets of terms to define the rights and duties of the parties. The first set is used with reference to the defendant; the second with reference to the claimant.

According to para 812 (1) BGB the defendant must *herausgeben* anything he received at the expense of the claimant. The first sentence of the provision states:

> A person who, through an act performed by another, or in any other manner, acquires something at the expense of the latter without any legal ground, is bound to return it to him.[41]

The noun which goes with the verbal form of the duty is *Herausgabe*. The terms *Herausgabe/herausgeben* recur in paras 812, 816 and 817 BGB. The verb *herausgeben* expresses the restitutionary duty placed upon the enriched defendant. It means 'to give up'. The German term of Latin origin '*Restitution*' does not belong to the terminology of the code. It occurs in the legal language, which associates the term *Restitutionsanspruch*, that is claim for restitution, with the codal *Herausgabeanspruch*. Outside the law of unjustified enrichment and also the law of delict, in which it describes the duty to give the claimant the very thing which has been wrongfully obtained, the term '*Restitution*' finds other applications which are irrelevant for the matter at issue.[42]

Corresponding to the duty of the defendant to give up his enrichment there is a correlative right of the claimant to seek restitution. To express the action of 'claiming back' anything which has been delivered *ohne rechtlichen Grund*, that is 'without any legal ground', as stated in para 812 (1) BGB, the statutory terminology refers to *zurückfordern/Rückforderung*. The terms, which denote the verb and the noun respectively, recur in paras 813, 814, and 815 BGB.

The two sets of terms do not cover, literally taken, the same area of application: the defendant has to give 'up', whereas the claimant can only claim 'back'. The

---

[41] SL Goren (tr) *The German Civil Code* (revd edn) (Littleton, Colorado, Rothman 1994).

[42] For more details and other meanings of *Restitution* see C Creifelds, *Rechtswörterbuch* (14th edn) (München, Beck 1997).

terminology suggests that from the viewpoint of the recipient it is not relevant whether the benefit which is claimed comes directly from the claimant or from another person. It is only essential that somebody has a stronger title upon the 'something' ('*Etwas*', para 812 (1) BGB) received than the recipient has, so that the latter must release the benefit. On the other hand, the claimant may merely 'claim back'. This verb implies that only a direct transfer from the claimant to the defendant gives rise to the action, excluding at the same time the possibility of claiming a benefit which is not a direct consequence of the claimant's act. Hence, the *littera legis* seems to indicate that the obstacle to be surmounted to allow restitution of profits made at the expense of, but not directly by, the claimant lies exclusively on the side of the claimant. Therefore, if the claimant were granted a restitutionary right, the defendant would not be able to plead in opposition the lack of a direct performance by the claimant to the defendant himself.

The etymological argument is useful to clarify the meaning of the German equivalent of the English term 'restitution'. It also provides a valuable insight in the *mens legislatoris*. Yet, it is in itself too weak to found a theory of restitution for unjustified enrichment. And this discord between the positions of the parties would not constitute a problem in practice. A *zurückfordern*, or 'claiming back', is never required by the code for the so-called three-party relationship, *Dreiecksver-hältnis*, in which the claimant is granted a restitutionary claim against a defend-ant who has not been directly benefited by the claimant himself. Accordingly, the letter of the law never defines the right of the claimant as a *Rückforderung* where there is no direct performance among the parties.

The giving up formula of the term '*herausgeben*' is likely to have been adopted by the draftsmen with the aim of extending the radius of the Roman restitution-ary claim, that is the *condictio*, which was based upon a direct performance between the parties,[43] to cover the situations in which the defendant did not receive the benefit through a direct performance by the claimant. Those cases are collected by German scholars and courts – but not by the code – under the label *Nichtleistungskondiktionen*, which means 'claims not based upon a performance' (by the claimant).[44] When there is no performance connecting the transfer from the impoverished *solvens* to the enriched *accipiens* it is difficult to justify a duty of the defendant to give back. A duty to give up would avoid the problem.

The results deriving from the judicial construction of a duty to give up, which theoretically paves the way for the claim for restitution against third parties, most feared in Germany, are subject to considerable criticism in the literature[45] and have raised problems before the courts. Judges have not yet found a formula which can explain once and for all between which parties a restitutionary claim arises where the subject-matter involves three or more persons.[46] Yet, Werner

---

[43]   See the literature at n 3.

[44]   MünchKomm/Lieb, '§ 813' para 222.

[45]   *Reuter and Martinek* 22, define para 812 (1) BGB, which comprises the so-called *Nichtleistung-skondiktionen*, as being the result of an 'unhappy formulation of the law'.

[46]   Normally, a claim against the party is granted, which was in some sort of contractual relation to the claimant which, if valid, could have justified the transfer of wealth, (1989) BGHZ 105 365. Yet

Flume[47] has shown that most of the judicial difficulties originate in the above-mentioned fear of excessively enlarging the scope of the claim, rather than in the identification of the formula itself.

In my opinion, the interpretative uncertainties arising from the law of unjustified enrichment are explicable from an historical perspective. The fear of the unpredictable consequences of a too-wide enrichment claim, which might allow the claimant to force 'remote' parties to give up their benefit, stems from the suspicion with which German lawyers have always looked at general legal clauses. The wider the clause, the more difficult it becomes to grant a uniform application of the law. An example of such general clauses is given by the so-called *Versionsklage*. This is a modern version of an equitable restitutionary claim applied in Roman law, known as *actio de in rem verso*,[48] through which the impoverished claimed restitution of that part of a transfer of wealth which the enriched had 'turned to his advantage'. In contrast to the performance-based claim of Roman origin, the *condictio*, this action does not require a lack of legal cause. Initially, it could be applied only to three-party situations. In due course, it was extended to cover even two-party situations and soon it became a very successful, practical alternative to the *Leistungskondiktion*, which is the modern version of the old *condictio*.

The *Versionsklage* was familiar to German courts. To bar any further extension of its application radius, the draftsmen decided to create a new kind of *condictio* which, on the one hand, could have made possible in specific circumstances a claim against a third party, but which, on the other hand, would have made difficult a claim against other parties beyond the third. The reason for this choice is primarily to be found in the different principles which support the claims. The new *Nichtleistungskondiktionen*, unlike the *Versionsklage*, were anchored to the requirement of an absence of cause, that is to a legal principle with dogmatic relevance, and not to a general concept of injustice as the Roman *actio de in rem verso*.[49] Hence, the German model is characterised by two causes of action depending on the existence or lack of a direct performance between the parties. Even though any express reference to three-party relations was avoided in para 812 (1) BGB, it emerges from the letter of the provision and from judicial interpretation that the *Nichtleistungskondiktion*, or non-performance-based *Kondiktion*, is a sort of residual category which collects all cases not falling under the heading '*Leistungskondiktion*', or performance-based *Kondiktion*. As a direct

---

sometimes the restitutionary action involves third parties which do not derive their enrichment from a performance of the claimant, (1982) BGHZ 81 395.

[47]　W Flume, 'Der Bereicherungsausgleich in Mehrpersonenverhältnissen' (1999) *AcP* 199 1-37.

[48]　On this claim in general see G MacCormack, 'The early History of the "Actio de in Rem Verso" (Alfenus to Labeo)' in F Pastori et al (eds), *Studi in onore di Arnaldo Biscardi* (Milano, Giuffrè 1982) vol 2 319-339.

[49]　However, even the German code cannot avoid re-introducing the *Versionsklage* in some special cases. Thus, para 816 (1) BGB allows an action towards the third party which was enriched – but *with* a legal cause – by a gratuitous transfer of wealth which was not authorised by the true owner.

transfer of wealth normally takes place on the basis of a performance, the *Nichtleistungskondiktionen* cover principally three-party situations.

C   Italian Law

The major difficulty is to narrow down a precise, contextual definition among the many which can be attached to the word 'restitution'. Adolfo di Majo has stated that *restituire*, which is the verbal form of the term restitution, means principally restoring the factual and legal conditions which characterised the situation of the claimant before a specific mutation in that situation occurred.[50] This statement, which is part of a passage on restitutionary responses, cannot comprise restitutionary awards for wrongs. Indeed, restitution for wrongs aims to expropriate a benefit of the wrongdoer which would have never reached the claimant had the wrong not being committed so that a simple restoration of the *status quo ante* would not achieve the desired outcome. Furthermore, even restitution of the gains derived from alienation by the defendant of the thing claimed back, which is allowed by Art 2038 (1) cc, seems to fall outside the boundaries of such statement. di Majo's formula, therefore, is inappropriate to describe the process of giving up a benefit as required by some cases of restitution for unjust enrichment in the *Codice civile* and of restitution for wrongs. Comparative law supports the doubts regarding the definition of restitution as restoration. In England, Peter Birks underlined properly the different technical meanings of the term 'restitution':

> [t]here can be restitution of a thing or a person to an earlier condition and restitution of a thing to a person. These two usages shade into one another but it is important to be aware of the difference.[51]

As has been observed also for German law, in Italian law there is no reference in the statutes or in judicial decisions to restitution for wrongs. The model of restitution relevant for the present study is to be found in the civil code under the heading 'undue payment', Arts 2033 to 2040 cc. 'Undue' corresponds to the Italian *indebito*, which on its part stems from the Latin *indebitum*. This was a performance which was never owed to the defendant and which the latter has no right to keep.[52] The code examines the situation of the parties and connects two different terms to the right of the one and the duty of the other.[53] On the one hand, Arts 2033-2036 cc are dedicated to the restitutionary right of the claimant. The claimant's basic position is stated in the first sentence of Art 2033 cc: 'Whoever has made a payment which was not owing is entitled the return of what he has paid.'[54] The claimant has unduly paid and has a right to *ripetere*. The noun for

---

[50]   A di Majo, *La tutela civile dei diritti* (2nd edn) (Milano, Giuffrè 1993) 295.
[51]   Birks, *Restitution* 10.
[52]   *Zimmermann* 834.
[53]   Only P Rescigno, 'Ripetizione dell'indebito' in *Novissimo Digesto italiano* (Torino, UTET 1968) vol 15 1223-1237, 1224, seems to take notice of the two sets of terms used by the civil code.
[54]   M Beltramo G Longo and JH Merryman (trs), *The Italian Civil Code* (New York, Oceana 1969).

this claim is *ripetizione. Rem repetere*[55] was the expression with which the Romans described the aim of the *condictio*, that is their main restitutionary claim. According to its etymology,[56] *ripetere* underlines a direct relation between the parties, which relates to a 'claiming back'. In fact, 'undue payment' refers exclusively to the case of a performance of the impoverished to the enriched. Thus, cases of three-party relations, or, more generally, cases in which the benefit of the defendant does not derive directly from the claimant, are outside the scope of the institution. The meaning of the set '*ripetizione/ripetere*' is therefore consistent with the function of undue payment. On the other hand, the duty of the defendant is linked to the terms *restituire/restituzione* in Arts 2037 and 2038 cc. The letter of these provisions indicates that those terms cover both the meaning of giving up and giving back. Art 2037 (1) cc requires the defendant to give back the thing to the claimant. However, if the thing has been alienated by the defendant, then, according to Art 2038 (1) cc, he must give up the profit to the claimant.

The code integrates the claim for 'undue payment' with the general enrichment claim of Art 2041 cc, which is a subsidiary restitutionary claim akin to the Roman *actio de in rem verso*. Its requisites and subject-matter are different from the 'undue payment'. The action does mention the term 'restitution', although only in the context of the rare case[57] in which the thing still exists at the time of the claim. Art 2041 (2) cc states: 'If the enrichment consists of a specified thing, the person who received it is bound to return it in kind if it is still in existence at the time of the demand'.[58] Here the duty to *restituire* has clearly the wider meaning of giving up. By far the most important provision is Art 2041 (1) cc, which is subject to the requirement that the thing itself cannot be given up any longer. This provision substitutes the duty to effect restitution with a duty to make good the loss within specific parameters which do not normally coincide with full compensation:

> A person who has enriched himself without a cause at the expense of another shall, to the extent of the enrichment, indemnify the other for his correlative financial loss.[59]

Apart the exception of Art 2038 cc, which is not a true exception, as the provision covertly rules a case of *actio de in rem verso*, three-party situations are not covered by the title on 'undue payment'. Yet, they are not ignored. Unlike German law, there is no mixed model of *Nichtleistungskondiktion* which comprises even three-party situations. A claim against a third party is possible only by means of the general enrichment claim of Art 2041 cc. One of the reasons for the little attention which has been paid to the law of unjustified enrichment in Italy is the

---

[55] A Pernice, *Labeo* (2nd edn) (Halle, Niemeyer 1900) vol 2 abt 2.1 93.

[56] *Retro petere, repetere datum, solutum. Cf* Academia Scientiarum Borussica. *Vocabularium Iurisprudentiae Romanae* (Berlin, 1939).

[57] The small relevance of Art 2041 (2) cc is confirmed by the almost absolute lack of judicial decisions on it.

[58] M Beltramo et al (n 54).

[59] *Ibid.*

fact that restitutionary claims based upon it have a remedial character. A void contract, for mistake or whatever ground, does not give rise immediately to a restitutionary action. It must be brought before the court which will declare the nullity and thus enable restitution. The latter does not originate in the void contract itself, but in the judicial decision. Consequently, the attention of scholars has been concentrated mostly on contract law, the law of unjustified enrichment being relatively neglected.

III Wrong

With reference to the English separation of torts from equitable wrongs, Birks observed that the division between common law and equity should not obscure important unities.[60] The attempt to free the concept of a wrong from what is becoming an increasingly less comfortable historical constriction has stimulated studies in the English law of restitution which clarify what lies behind this expression. As in the German and Italian legal orders 'wrong' is not a term of the art, a legal comparison can take place only if the English concept of a wrong proved to be compatible with the structures of German and Italian law. A comparative analysis of restitution for wrongs, therefore, presupposes an assessment of the level of compatibility of the concept of a wrong within the jurisdictions under examination. In the following analysis, I conclude that it is possible to compare the three legal systems using a common definition of wrong despite the fact that 'wrong' is not a civil law concept.

A   English Law

In the 1930s, Percy Henry Winfield[61] depicted tortious liability as arising from the breach of duty primarily fixed by law. Such duty, he explained, is towards persons generally and its breach is redressible by an action for unliquidated damages. Winfield argued that the so-called equitable wrongs are examples of breach of duty. Furthermore, he observed, both torts and equitable wrongs are violations of rights in rem. Winfield seemed to toy with the idea that torts and equitable wrongs belong to the same category. Eventually, he rebutted this conclusion: to admit the existence of 'equitable torts' would be to go too far,[62] for an action for breach of trust is not an action for unliquidated damages but an

---

[60] Birks, *Restitution* 39.
[61] PH Winfield, *The Province of the Law of Tort* (Cambridge, CUP 1931) 32.
[62] *Ibid* 112.

action for compensation.[63] Yet Winfield had to acknowledge that equitable wrongs are separated by torts principally by an 'historical gulf which lies between them and the Common Law'.[64]

It is now generally accepted[65] that the main reason to classify torts and equitable wrongs as different legal responses is the divide between common law and equity, which has mostly historical significance. This notwithstanding, some academic circles are still quite reluctant to abandon the approach based upon two different and separate legal categories.[66] Judicial authority has confirmed that it still plays a significant role in the law of damages, where 'it is still necessary to take account of the distinction between common law and equity',[67] because 'the origins of both common law and equitable rules are always relevant to their scope, although we should endeavour now to identify the underlying common principles'.[68] Discussing a particular measure of compensation, Peter Smith J in *World Wide Fund for Nature v World Wrestling Federation Entertainment* uses stronger tones to reject the divide between law and equity:

> Part of the difficulties in my judgment arises from the refusal of lawyers to shed the differences between law and equity which were intended to be eliminated by the Judicature Act 1873. What a court should be concerned with is providing effective and balanced remedies to solve disputes and less with concepts that used to be called equitable relief or common law relief.[69]

Legal comparison requires a clear-cut definition of a civil wrong. For the purposes of this study, a wrong is 'a breach of legal duty owed to a claimant'.[70] Every act or omission made in breach of duty can theoretically elicit a restitution-ary response, independently of the question whether the duty is legal or equita-ble. This approach is in line with English law, for the judiciary recognises that the principles underlying an award of damages are the same at law and in equity.[71]

According to Burrows, a 'sure test' to decide whether a particular form of conduct can be classified as a wrong in the sense of breach of primary duty is that compensation must be an available remedial measure if the loss is caused to the claimant by that conduct.[72] Edelman adopts a similar approach: a 'conclusive indicator' of the presence of a wrong is whether exemplary or compensatory

---

[63] For a convincing rebuttal of the idea that equity does not deal with unliquidated damages, see *Edelman* 26-29.

[64] Winfield (n 61) 231.

[65] For instance RFV Heuston and RA Buckley, *Salmond and Heuston on the Law of Torts* (21st edn) (London, Sweet & Maxwell 1996) 12: '[t]he reason for this exclusion is historical only'.

[66] Winfield (n 61) 231. Thus, for instance, no text on torts deals with equitable wrongs and *vice versa. cf* the definition of torts given in *Salmond and Heuston on the Law of Torts ibid* 13.

[67] *Swindle v Harrison* [1997] 4 All ER 705 (CA) 714 (Evans LJ).

[68] *Ibid.*

[69] *WWF v WWF* [2006] EWHC 184 (Ch) para 132.

[70] Thus P Birks, 'The Concept of a Civil Wrong' in DG Owen (ed), *Philosophical Foundations of Tort Law* (Oxford, Clarendon 1997) 31-51, 33.

[71] *Swindle* (n 67) (Hobhouse LJ).

[72] Burrows (n 27) 457-458.

damages are available.[73] Yet, he accepts that there are instances of events which are wrongs, but for which no damages are obtainable, such as innocent breach of copyright. And the 'conclusive indicator' would not work in a few events, which could be conclusively classified as wrongs. He mentions in this context the equitable action for unconscionably inducing entry into a transaction.

These approaches present at least one difficulty. They are so purely descriptive that they do not contribute to any definition of the category of civil wrong. They do not provide any guidance as regards the criteria which should determine whether a particular event is a wrong, for the reasoning is conducted a posteriori. Thus, Edelman's test is but a *petitio principii*. In his view, a 'civil wrong is a cause of action to which the law responds with a remedy because it is a breach of duty'.[74] Yet, as the cause of action triggers damages because it is a wrong, one cannot infer from this description when an event is a wrong, that is which requirements identify a wrong. The circularity of this argument is all the more highlighted by Edelman's recognition that there are examples of similar actions which sometimes do and sometimes do not trigger damages. Such cases are explained somehow obscurely as causes of actions which are 'of their nature' wrongs.[75]

There is little doubt that restitution in a wrongful context has long been accepted in English law. However, this model of restitution leads normally to a giving up of something which has been tortiously obtained by the wrongdoer from the claimant or, at any rate, something which comes to the defendant through a 'chain of transfer' – German lawyers call it '*Bereicherungskette*' – which starts from the claimant. If C gives a book to his friend F for him to read and return, but F offers it to D as a present, C can sue D in conversion. In this case, the court will have no difficulties in acknowledging specific restitution in favour of C.[76] The fact that specific restitution is not a right of the claimant, being but a remedy in the discretion of the courts, does not affect its existence and application in tort law. After the recent judicial recognition of restitution for wrongs in the context of breach of contract in the *Blake* case,[77] the real question is not whether restitution in a wrongful context is possible *in abstracto*, but whether restitution in the sense of giving up a benefit due to the defendant's own conduct should be an instrument at the disposal of the claimant even in the case of a gain-based award which does not come directly from the claimant. The Law Commission describes the process as 'strip[ping] away some or all of the gains made by a defendant from a civil wrong'.[78] Hence, rather than the question of the existence of a category of restitution for wrongs, it seems that the main issue to be addressed ought to unravel the structure of a mechanism according to which some wrongs give rise to restitution, and some others do not.

---

[73]   *Edelman* 42.
[74]   *Ibid* 62.
[75]   *Ibid* 52.
[76]   *Greenwood v Bennett* [1973] QB 195 (CA); see also *Fleming* 60-82, esp 81-82.
[77]   *Blake* (n 9).
[78]   Law Com No 247, 1997, Part II para 1.5 above (n 6).

B   German Law

The analysis of the compatibility of the common law concept of a wrong with German law must start from the law of delict, 'delict' being equivalent to tort.[79] Most wrongs are likely to fall within this field of the law, which in the BGB is labelled '*unerlaubte Handlungen*', or non-permitted actions. Equity plays in German law a much smaller role than in English law.[80] Indeed, the idea of a conceptual difference between various wrongs does not belong to German law; nor is it part of any other civil law system, because the historical conditions for the English divide between torts and equitable wrongs do not characterise Roman-rooted jurisdictions.[81] As will be seen, it is debated in German literature whether the law of delict consists of homogeneous categories or whether its categories are so heterogeneous as to question its unity. This discussion, however, does not affect the statutory classification of the law of delict, nor is it related to a distinction between law and equity. In fact, events which would be classified as wrongs in English law are not categorised according to whether they are within or outside the BGB.

A '*Handlung*' is controllable conduct, whether act or omission, which is steered by one's will and, as such, can be imputed to a human being.[82] Conduct consists of a series of events. Some of these events send external signals which play a fundamental role because they show that the agent is fundamentally responsible for his own activities. Thus, everybody is liable for one's own conscious acts, even for the ones which are not specifically wanted. If, moving my arms awkwardly in a china shop, I damage some items, I cannot avoid my responsibility by saying that I did not want what happened. In fact, my movements in the shop were controllable; they were steered by my will. On the other hand, if I am unconscious, under the influence of medicines,[83] or if I do not have control over my body, as in cases of *vis absoluta*, my volition is impaired. Therefore I cannot be held responsible for my actions.[84]

Not every conduct – even if controllable – triggers a delictual response. The *Handlung* must be of a specific kind: it must be '*unerlaubt*', that is not allowed. To give the conduct this particular colour, according to para 823 (1) BGB there must be a concurrence of an objective and a subjective element. The objective element is the unlawfulness. Its meaning varies. Among the general delictual categories of the BGB, it ranges from violation of protected rights (para 823 (1)), to violation of statutes which seek to protect specific categories of persons (para 823 (2)), to

---

[79]   *Cf* Birks (n 70) 39. See IV B in this chapter.

[80]   That the affirmation that equity does not exist in civil law countries is imprecise is proved, among others, by para 829 BGB, which allows the courts to grant compensation in special cases where – 'at law' – there would be no delictual cause of action. However, it is correct to say that civil law and common law have two different ideas of what equity is.

[81]   On the possible function of the concept of wrong in civilian systems see IV A in this chapter.

[82]   This is a standard formula. *Cf* P Schlechtriem, *Schuldrecht Besonderer Teil* (6th edn) (Tübingen, Mohr 2003) para 824.

[83]   (1987) BGHZ 98 135.

[84]   *Larenz and Canaris* 361.

actions performed *contra bonos mores*[85] (para 826). Beyond those three general categories, some delictual causes of action, both in the code and in other statutes, may require a different, more specific definition of unlawfulness. The subjective element requires fault-based conduct on the part of the wrongdoer, that is *Schuld*. This fault-principle, *Verschuldensprinzip*, knows many exceptions, but it can be taken as one of the pillars of the German law of delict. The Federal Court (BGH) has stated that the nature of *unerlaubte Handlung* consists of the unlawful violation of general legal relations between persons, which must be respected by everybody because they form the basis of society.[86]

According to an influential view,[87] strict liability lies beyond the scope of the law of delict. Damage is imputed to the 'wrongdoer' not because his conduct violates a legal standard, but because the loss arising from it falls within his sphere of risk[88] and the agent is in the better position to bear the negative consequences engendered by his own conduct. From this perspective, it could be argued that strict liability is located beyond the realm of wrong-based liability, for the conduct which causes a loss to the claimant is considered to be in itself lawful. The discussion on strict liability therefore is conducted in terms of risk, rather than in terms of unlawfulness (*Rechtswidrigkeit*).[89] This view is not convincing. The legal principle of strict liability which follows from this theory is: when one's conduct causes a loss, the richer party must pay. Even though the evaluation of the richer party is made a priori, such postulate, if it were correct, would be incompatible with the general principles of the law of delict. Studies of comparative tort law have shown that a too rigid partition of delict between fault-based and strict liability leads to an inaccurate evaluation of this field of law.[90] In civil law, fault is not dependent on a subjective assessment of the intention of the wrongdoer. In fact, all major legal systems have developed an objective definition[91] of fault which allows the courts to decide, on the basis of objective criteria, whether specific conduct must be held to be characterised by fault or not. From this objective perspective, the volition of the defendant is substantially irrelevant.[92] On this premise, it cannot be said that strict liability differs from

---

[85]   This is normally translated with a reference to public policy.

[86]   (1961) BGHZ 34 375, 380.

[87]   Staudinger/Hager, 'Vorbem zu §§ 823 ff' para 31.

[88]   On the role of the risk and the difference between fault-based and strict liability see T Honoré, 'Responsibility and Luck' (1988) 104 *LQR* 530-553, esp 541-542 and 547-553: '[t]o bear the risk of bad luck is inseparable from being a choosing person' (553).

[89]   The prevalent view both in the judiciary and in the literature denies that unlawful conduct is a requirement of strict liability altogether. *Cf* (1988) BGHZ 105 65, 68; and *Larenz and Canaris* para 84 I 3 a.

[90]   *von Bar* para 68, depicts clearly this approach with reference to children's liability in French tort law.

[91]   See for the common law Honoré (n 88) 531-537: 'the objective standard of competence'.

[92]   This is particularly evident in French law, in which the existence of an – objective – *faute* tends to obscure all other elements of the cause of action, so that the wrongdoer is responsible just for the fact of finding himself in a specific situation which is deemed to be *fautive*. *Cf von Bar* paras 66-67. Interestingly, the Belgian codification, which is based upon delictual rules very similar to the French *Code civil*, has rebutted a thus strict definition of *faute* with reference to the so-called *gardien*-liability; *von Bar* para 114.

fault-based liability in the role assumed by the unlawfulness, for, in the end, both use an objective definition of liability. Thus, the difference assumed by the prevailing doctrine is spurious.[93]

This point seems to have been taken by the German judiciary in a case discussed before a Düsseldorf court:[94] housewife D turned her two-year-old washing machine on and left the apartment for a quarter of an hour. During her absence, the machine broke down and water flowed into the apartment underneath damaging the furniture. The court held D liable in delict. In leaving the apartment, albeit for a short time, D fell short of the standard of care required in society. To leave a washing machine in operation without supervision exposes the property of others to danger. Thus, a conscientious and thoughtful housewife who has a washing machine in an upstairs apartment ought to take steps to guard against this risk. The court added that it was well aware that, *in concreto*, no housewife could be expected to stay by the washing machine for the whole time in which the washing programme is running. Thus, according to the court, this virtually amounts to imposing strict liability: no conscientious housewife would stay by a running washing machine all time. Yet, if an accident occurs, the housewife knows that she would be liable for the resulting damage.[95]

If the majority view is rejected, according to which strict liability does not fall within the law of delict, then the unity of the law of delict is preserved. On this basis, the term 'wrong' would embrace events based upon a breach of duty including both fault-based and strict liability. There is no need to devise the category 'wrong' so as to exclude cases of strict liability. In German law, fault does not seem to be an obstacle to the adoption of the term 'wrong' as breach of duty which encompasses torts, equitable wrongs, breach of contract, and delict.

C   Italian Law

In 1942, the Italian civil code redefined the law of delict in Arts 2043-2059, which are dedicated to the *fatti illeciti*, or acts which do not conform with the law.[96] The new statute made redundant a theory[97] supported under the old code which divided this area of the law into delicts and quasi-delicts, the former being characterised by wilful conduct, the latter by negligence of the wrongdoer. Art 2043 cc makes clear that modern delict law is based on one general category:

> Any fraudulent, malicious, or negligent act which causes an unjust damage to another obliges the person who has committed the act to pay damages.

---

[93]   Legal theory supports this conclusion: '[a]ll liability in torts is fundamentally strict liability in the sense that it is imposed whether or not the agent is to blame for her conduct'. Thus Coleman, *Risks* 221.

[94]   Oberlandesgericht Düsseldorf [1975] *Neue Juristische Wochenschrift* 159.

[95]   *Cf* the opening sentence of Honoré's article (n 88) 530: '[B]eing responsible in law and in ordinary life is not the same thing as being at fault or to blame'.

[96]   P Trimarchi, 'Illecito (Diritto privato)' in *Enciclopedia del Diritto* (Milano, Giuffrè 1970) vol 20 90-112, 90; Tribunale Verona 13 December 1988 [1989] *Foro italiano* I 3234.

[97]   G Pacchioni, *Elementi di diritto civile* (3rd edn) (Torino, UTET 1926) 348.

An influential view[98] has observed that a *fatto* is a series of events. *Fatto* and its consequences are not notions which can be determined a priori, for the human mind decides what a *fatto* is by selecting some of the events which are part of a causative chain. A few important remarks are linked to this widely accepted definition. First, the concept of a *fatto* has been conceived traditionally as narrowly tied to human actions. Secondly, it comprises not only human actions, but also their outcome, so that the human action is a necessary, but not sufficient element of the chain of events. A third relevant point is that *fatto* is a concept created by the human mind, and as such it can be filled with all sorts of qualifications. The draftsmen gave a particular colour to the concept of a *fatto* by adding the adjective *illecito*. According to classic interpretation, only human conduct can be qualified as *illecito*, not natural events which are independent of human intervention. The requirement of human conduct is said to differentiate *illiceità*, or non-conformity with the law, from *antigiuridicità*, or unlawfulness, although the borderline between the two seems to be uncertain. In fact, unlaw-fulness is stretched to include all situations, even those without human interven-tion. Apparently, unlawfulness is supposed to have a wider and vaguer meaning than non-conformity. It is not always clear which content is connected to the idea of unlawfulness. Renato Scognamiglio[99] observes the oddity of the law's deriving legal effects from a situation which is classified as unlawful. Be that as it may, the notion of unlawfulness is rebutted in favour of the one of non-conformity.

Echoes of the German discussion on the relationship between strict and fault-based liability in the law of delict are reflected in the Italian literature. Thus, the notion of *illiceità* is confined by some solely to fault-based liability, because strict liability would not require it, being built upon the notion of risk.[100] Against this view it is observed that *illiceità* is based upon the notion of fault, whereas the idea of risk is completely independent of it. The two terms belong to different categories and therefore the one does not necessarily exclude the other.[101] This latter opinion has recently taken into consideration the fact that *illiceità* is used throughout the civil code in so different contexts that a general description would be completely useless. One should rather isolate the scope of *illiceità* in the context of the law of delict and give this word a meaning which is in harmony with its function in this field of the law. It seems time to depart from the old notion of *illiceità* as an element strictly linked to human conduct. According to this more recent approach, *illiceità* depicts a responsibility judgment which connects an event with an 'unjust damage', that is the *danno ingiusto* described in

---

[98] G Gorla, 'Sulla cosiddetta causalità giuridica: "fatto dannoso e conseguenze"' *Rivista di diritto commerciale* 1951 I 405-421, 410.

[99] R Scognamiglio, 'Illecito (Diritto vigente)' in *Novissimo Digesto Italiano* (Torino, UTET 1962) vol 8 164-173, 165.

[100] Trimarchi (n 96) 91-92.

[101] *Cf* M Franzoni, 'Dei fatti illeciti Art 2043 – 2059' in A Scialoja and G Branca (eds), *Commentario del Codice Civile* (2nd edn) (Bologna-Roma, Zanichelli 1993) 77-83.

Art 2043 cc The older literature[102] interpreted the idea of injustice in the sense of 'illegality', that is *contra ius*: that loss gave rise to damages, which violated the general principle of *neminem laedere* intended as the sum of legal duties which are imposed upon persons. This interpretation was later abandoned in favour of a definition of unjust damage as arising from a conduct which was not authorised by a norm, that is *non iure*.[103] Those two doctrines have been taken over by the courts, which coalesced them in the idea of loss *contra ius et non iure*.[104] The definition describes a loss which touches the legal sphere of a third person in the absence of causes of justification. Such theory ought to eliminate every difference between *illiceità* and unlawfulness. This would be a welcome improvement which contributes to clarifying the law.

A *fatto illecito* is a wrong. Using the wide meaning with which especially the more recent theories construe the notion of *illiceità* it becomes possible to overcome the difficulties which the divide between fault-based and strict liability has raised in German law. Even Italian law, therefore, seems compatible with a definition of wrong which focuses upon the breach of duty, the latter being represented by the *illiceità* as a connection between conduct and damage. Whether the damage must be qualified in terms of economic loss concretely sustained by the claimant, or whether there is some room for a theoretical construction in terms of giving up the benefit, will be matter of further analysis in the next chapters.

IV   Setting the Terminological Premises

In this chapter, I have introduced the terminology on which legal comparison will be founded. The analysis was opened with a question. It was asked whether the three jurisdictions share a common understanding of the concepts of 'restitution' and 'wrong'. As the answer to this question has been in the affirmative, there is no fundamental obstacle to a comparative analysis of 'restitution for wrongs'. Whereas the concept, if not the term, of 'restitution' is compatible with the law of all three jurisdictions, the meaning of 'wrong' has required some interpretation to be accommodated within German and Italian law. The following points are not specific to one legal system; they are generic observations shared by all systems compared.

---

[102]   S Pugliatti, 'Alterum non laedere' in *Enciclopedia del Diritto* (Milano, Giuffrè 1958) vol 2 93-108.

[103]   P Schlesinger, 'L'ingiustizia del danno nell'illecito civile' (1960) *Jus* 336-347.

[104]   Cassazione, 11th November 1978 No 4538 [1978] Repertorio Foro italiano Danni civili No 67.

A   Wrongs

In English law, a wrong is a breach of a duty.[105] For their part, civil lawyers see delicts as unlawful violations of general legal relations between persons.[106] These notions are therefore considered from a different angle: duties breached by the wrongdoer in the common law, violated rights of the victim in the civil law. The different perspectives do not have a great impact on the topic under examination because both refer to wrongful behaviour, categorised as a hazard for society. Yet, common lawyers tend to admit that breach of contract is a wrong.[107] On this, Graham Virgo has observed that

> Although breach of contract cannot be considered to be of the same magnitude of wrongfulness as committing a tort or crime or even a breach of fiduciary duty, it is wrongful as has been recognised for the purposes of economic duress.[108]

This quote illustrates the level of caution displayed by English lawyers while linking breach of contract with the category 'wrongs'. Yet, Virgo's distinction between different grades of wrongfulness is confusing: breach of contract can be a wrong or not a wrong, but it cannot be 'less' a wrong than other wrongs. In civil law, on the other hand, breach of contract falls within contract law. Lacking the concept of 'wrong', civil lawyers do not ask themselves whether breach of contract is linked to delict law by some overarching theory.

The evolution of English legal thought shows that the definition of 'wrong' has moved towards giving more weight to the element of the breach of a duty. If 'wrong' is defined as a breach of duty without any further qualification, torts, equitable wrongs and breach of contract are all embraced by it, for they find their origin in a breach of a duty, be it a duty owed to society or to the other contracting party. On the other hand, from the absence of a category of 'wrongs' intended as breach of duty in civil law it follows that the question of the relevance of a breach of contract for the law of wrongs is alien to both civilian systems under comparison. Hence, at this point the avenues of common law and civil law diverge. The English concept of a wrong does not seem to be 'translatable' into German and Italian concepts. Any comparison needs uniform definitions to allow research on a common ground in all systems under examination. The identification of a common ground is obtained here by setting the following premise: independently of the jurisdiction considered, the analysis will be based upon a definition of a wrong as a breach of duty. In this context, it will be investigated whether there is room for recognition of a response which deprives the wrongdoer of the benefit accruing to him as a consequence of a breach of duty on his part.

---

[105]   Birks (n 69).

[106]   (1961) BGHZ 34 375, 380.

[107]   *Cf Surrey CC v Bredero Homes Ltd* [1993] 1 WLR 1361 (CA) 1371 (Steyn LJ): '[g]iven the fact of the breach of contract the only question is whether restitution is an appropriate remedy for this wrong'.

[108]   G Virgo, *The Principles of the Law of Restitution* (2nd edn) (Oxford, OUP 2006) 493.

This description of wrong enables the examination of restitution for wrongs as a consequence of breach of contract in Germany and Italy. One downside of this approach, however, is the risk of falling over the same obstacles which authors like Burrows and Edelman have tried to surmount: it does not explain when an event is a wrong. Yet, from a comparative perspective the question of the meaning of 'wrong' does not necessarily need an accurate answer. For the purposes of the investigation, it is sufficient to refer to the three legal systems: what is regarded as an actionable breach of duty will be treated as a wrong in all jurisdictions considered. In this context, 'tort', 'equitable wrongs', 'delict' and 'breach of contract' are distinct categories which belong to the same *genus* 'wrongs'.

B Law of Tort and Law of Delict

'Tort' and 'delict' might indicate similar categories, which perform a comparable function in their own legal systems. However, the two institutions do not cover the same area of the law of wrongs. The different label goes beyond a merely terminological differentiation. A definition of the English tort and of the civilian delict would require a satisfactory analysis of their respective nature. 'But this', as was remarked, 'is a difficult business'.[109] At any rate, such analysis is not necessary in the present context as long as it is clear that 'tort' and 'delict' refer to different legal families: the former to the English common law, the latter to the civilian systems. The origins of tort and delict have to be traced to different sources. The law of torts is an original and peculiar feature of the common law, whereas the civilian systems of civil delict developed from Roman law, notably from the *lex Aquilia*.[110] Some characteristics of the Roman law of delict will be pointed out in chapter five. As far as the relationship between English law and civilian systems are concerned, modern scholars tend to admit that, all things considered, particularly on account of judicial activity they are nowadays 'not so dissimilar'.[111]

Thus, the convention will be adopted that 'tort' is used with reference to English law and 'delict' is the correspondent term in civilian systems. This is a simple recognition of the different origins of the two institutions, not a statement on their intrinsic difference.

C Compensation and Restitution for Wrongs

A major obstacle to the understanding of the damages at issue is the incorrect assessment of the relationship between restitution and compensation as responses of the law of wrongs. As will emerge in chapter three, there is a substantial group of cases which are treated as restitutionary whereas the legal

---

[109] WW Buckland, AD McNair and FH Lawson, *Roman Law and Common Law – A Comparison in Outline* (2nd edn) (Cambridge, CUP 1952) 338.
[110] *Ibid* 338-351.
[111] B Markesinis, '*The Not so Dissimilar Tort and Delict*' (1977) 93 *LQR* 78-123.

response realises a compensatory goal. Compensation seeks to nullify the loss of the claimant. This result can be achieved through different avenues which all share the characteristic that the transfer of wealth from the wrongdoer to the victim is justified by the victim's loss: where there is no compensable loss, there is no compensatory transfer of wealth. On the other hand, a restitutionary transfer can take place even in the absence of a compensable loss, for the aim of restitution for wrongs is to take away from the wrongdoer a benefit accruing to him as a consequence of the perpetration of the wrong. It is the defendant's gain, not the claimant's loss, which provides the perspective to decide whether to award the response. Compensation and restitution realise different results, but the mechanism in operation is the same for both responses: after compensation, the victim should be in a position of indifference between the pre-wrong and the post-compensation situation. After restitution, the wrongdoer should be in a position of indifference as regards his pre-wrong and post-restitution situation.

D   Restitution for Wrongs and Restitution for Unjust Enrichment

The relationship between restitution for wrongs and restitution for unjust enrichment has been illustrated in the analysis of the concept of restitution. Peter Birks observed that there can be restitution within unjust enrichment – and in fact this form of restitution is in his view the only legal response for unjust enrichment – but also restitution outside unjust enrichment.[112] Among the different restitutionary responses which are outside unjust enrichment, there is also restitution as a response to wrongful behaviour. So far, I have discussed situations related to this response. But an example of restitution for unjust enrichment might help to highlight the difference between the two legal institutions.

The most direct and clear instance of a situation involving restitution for unjust enrichment is likely to be mistaken payment: in the erroneous belief to owe you £100, I pay you this sum of money. In reality, I owed you only £50. If you have never solicited any payment higher than my debt to you, no tortious claim is possible, given that you have committed no wrong. This takes restitution for wrongs out of the picture. Contract law is just as useless, for I have not paid on the basis of a contractual obligation. The only avenue for me to recover my payment is to bring a claim in unjust enrichment. The case of the mistaken payment shows clearly why restitution for wrongs and restitution for unjust enrichment do not coincide. They are related to different areas of the law of obligations, which are the law of wrongs and the law of unjust enrichment respectively. They have different requirements: restitution for unjust enrichment does not need a wrong. They even achieve different aims, because the claimant in unjust enrichment founds his action upon the fact that wealth which should belong to the claimant has been unjustly transferred to the enriched – by the

---

[112]   P Birks, *Unjust Enrichment* (2nd edn) (Oxford, OUP 2005) 11.

impoverished himself or a third party. In other words, the claimant in unjust enrichment bases his action upon the violation of a right which has caused him a loss, whereas an award of restitution for wrongs transfers to the claimant the defendant's benefit independently of any loss sustained by the claimant. This last point explains why I reject restitution for wrongs in cases of violation of property rights. Its theoretical underpinning will be discussed at length in chapter nine.[113]

---

[113] See ch 9, VI and VII.

2

Restitution in the Context of the Law of Obligations

I Legal Analysis

THIS CHAPTER PLACES restitution for wrongs in the appropriate context of the law of obligations. In all three legal systems, the legal response triggered by the perpetration of a wrong is normally compensation. Yet the leonine role played by compensation does not necessarily imply that other responses to wrongful behaviour are unknown or incompatible with the structure of the law of obligations. The comparative investigation in this and in the following chapters rests on an 'event-based classification': a taxonomy introduced into English law by Peter Birks,[1] the original model of which can be traced to Roman law. It presupposes a fixed relationship between legal events and legal responses: any legally relevant event triggers a reaction on the part of the legal order in the form of a legal response. I shall deal mainly with the event 'wrong'. There are unequivocal indications from authoritative sources that the relationship between 'wrong' as an event and 'compensation' as a response is not exclusive. With reference to English law, the judiciary admits – within limits – awards of exemplary damages.[2] It follows that compensation is not the only valid response for wrongs. The spectrum of responses has been recently modified by judicial intervention when the House of Lords in *Attorney-General v Blake*[3] added restitution to the list of legal responses to a wrong – again, within limits. Yet, this short chapter is not dedicated to a direct analysis of restitution for wrongs, but rather to provide background information in support of the comparative investigation of restitutionary damages which takes place in the next chapters. The focus of the examination is deliberately narrow. I shall assess the overarching significance of compensation at the expense of other responses to wrongs and, to a minor extent, the role of non-wrongful responses. The picture which emerges from this comparative overview is remarkably constant. Compensatory reasoning

---

[1] P Birks, *Unjust Enrichment* (2nd edn) (Oxford, OUP 2005) 21-28. Birks adapted the Roman model to reflect the peculiarities of English law.

[2] *Rookes v Barnard* [1964] AC 1129 (HL).

[3] *A-G v Blake* [2001] 1 AC 268 (HL).

undoubtedly exerts a predominant influence in the law of damages of all three jurisdictions. Furthermore, especially in civil law systems non-wrongful responses have a direct impact upon the expansion of restitution for wrongs, which contributes to explain a central finding of the comparative investigation: that restitution for wrongs as such is widely unknown in German and Italian law, although arguably at least in German law instances of restitutionary damages can be identified.

A   English Law

After the judicial recognition of restitution for wrongs in *Attorney-General v Blake*, the focus of the research has moved to the individuation of those areas in which this legal response should be applied. In the *Blake* case, the House of Lords suggested that a lenient approach would not be appropriate.[4] The judicial introduction of restitution for unjust enrichment into the legal system is seen by many as a point of reference for, or indeed in some cases a preferable avenue to, restitution for wrongs.[5] This reinforces the impression that restitutionary damages should be awarded with parsimony – mainly to fill gaps in the system when the victim would be left in a position of disadvantage. However, there is no indication that restitution for wrongs is incompatible with the tenets of the law of obligations or that the field of application of restitution for wrongs is already occupied by identical legal responses.[6]

I shall first assess the relationship between restitution and compensation in the law of damages; then I shall briefly move on to waiver of tort, only to refer its analysis to chapter three. Finally, I shall distinguish restitution for wrongs from restitution for unjust enrichment.

i   The Compensatory Principle

Mining works conducted by the defendant coal company damage a house built upon the mine. Neither the owner of the house nor the coal company knows that the coal under the house belongs to the owner of the house. At first, despite the damage, the owner does not object to the underground work. Yet, when he becomes aware of his legal rights, he claims for damages. On these facts, the House of Lords established the following rule:

> [W]here any injury is to be compensated by damages, in settling the sum of money to be given for reparation of damages you should as nearly as possible get at the sum of money which will put the party who has been injured, or has suffered, in the same

---

[4]   *Blake* (n 3) 285 (Lord Nicholls).

[5]   See the analysis of the 'quadrationist' theory in ch 1, II A ii.

[6]   One of the main conclusions of my research is that there are very few legal institutions which truly run parallel to restitution for wrongs. Restitution for unjust enrichment, for instance, concerns a different detriment of the claimant.

position as he would have been in if he had not sustained the wrong for which he is now getting his compensation or reparation.[7]

The identification of the application ambit of this judicial rule constitutes a seminal passage for the understanding of the law of obligations. If with this statement Lord Blackburn sought the development of a general rule for the whole field of the tortious law of damages, the consequence would be a drastic reduction in the significance of non-compensatory awards. The dictum would not rule out restitutionary damages completely, but it would strongly delimit their role, leaving particularly to statutes the task of introducing them in appropriate circumstances. This seems to be the direction taken by part of the judiciary[8] after the *Livingstone* case. Yet, this is not the only fashion in which the judicial rule in *Livingstone* can be construed. The dictum can be read also as a general rule of compensatory damages. It would formulate a principle to which the courts must stick when awarding compensation, as opposed to a non-compensatory award. On this construction, the rule would not affect the reasoning of the judges in establishing the appropriateness of non-compensatory responses. Hence, the role of the judicial formula depends on its validity as 'the' tortious rule, or as merely 'a' rule confined to compensatory damages.

James Edelman has shown that the Law Lords in the *Livingstone* case did not rule out non-compensatory damages.[9] This more lenient judicial approach supports the idea of a formula limited to the law of compensation. Compensatory damages are undoubtedly the main response of the law of damages and every decision taken on compensatory issues is likely to have repercussions upon this whole field of law. However, there is no ground for thinking that in English law compensatory damages cover the whole range of responses to wrongful behaviour. Any theory purporting an exclusive role of compensation amongst the law of legal responses would clash with judicial authority which expressly admits punishment[10] and restitution[11]. Besides, any thesis centred upon the exclusivity of compensation risks to fall into the trap of a circular argument: damages can only compensate the victim of a wrong because they are compensatory. The influence of such arguments upon judicial reasoning is evident in cases such as *Cassell v Broome*,[12] where Lord Hailsham[13] quoted a definition of damages which used to open Harvey McGregor's seminal work on damages until the sixteenth edition: '[d]amages are the pecuniary compensation, obtainable by success in an action, for a wrong which is either a tort or a breach of contract.'[14] His Lordship

---

[7]   *Livingstone v The Rawyards Coal Co* (1880) 5 AC 25 (HL) 39 (Lord Blackburn).
[8]   *Stoke-on-Trent CC v W & J Wass Ltd* [1988] 3 All ER 394 (CA) 397-398 (Nourse LJ).
[9]   J Edelman, 'Gain-Based Damages and Compensation', in A Burrows and Lord Rodger, *Mapping the Law* (Oxford, OUP 2006), 141-160, 144.
[10]   *Rookes v Barnard* (n 2).
[11]   *Blake* (n 3).
[12]   *Cassell & Co Ltd v Broome* [1972] AC 1027 (HL).
[13]   *Ibid* 1070.
[14]   *McGregor on Damages* (16th edn) (London, Sweet & Maxwell 1997) para 1.

gave no explanation to justify this narrow formula, which confines non-compensatory awards to the role of mere exceptions. Even in McGregor's work it was unclear why the category 'damages' should be confined to compensation.[15] In fact, the narrowness of a definition of damages which includes only compensation was recognised by McGregor himself[16] even before he changed his line of thought in the 17th edition of his work.[17] Such want of flexibility was probably seen as a small sacrifice by comparison with the advantages deriving from certainty in the law. Yet, Lord Wilberforce in *Cassell v Broome* stressed that it 'cannot lightly be taken for granted, even as a matter of theory, that the purpose of the law of tort is compensation'.[18] Indeed, especially as a matter of theory, such equivalence does not seem to be supported by cogent reasoning.

The Law Commission Report No 247 is testimony to the difficulties which emerge in legal analysis even in the cases in which there is no a priori rejection of non-compensatory solutions. In the Report, exemplary damages, as well as restitutionary and aggravated damages, are collected under the label of 'exceptional' damages.[19] However, the Report contains no explanation for their exceptional status. The proposition that '[d]amages are normally concerned to compensate the victim of a wrong'[20] is no justification, for it does not give any morsel of information to clarify the relationship between 'normal' compensation and 'anomalous' other remedies.

On the one hand, the courts have often reaffirmed that all questions of damages

> are to compensate the plaintiff for his loss or injury by putting him as nearly as possible in the same position as he would have been had he not suffered the wrong.[21]

This approach tends to establish a coincidence between loss and damages, according to which the values of damage and of compensation should be as close as possible if other factors such as rules on remoteness or contributory negligence do not intervene. On the other hand, decisions such as *Rookes v Barnard*[22] brand damages other than compensatory damages as anomalies[23] which should be confined to a very strict field of application or, ideally in the case of exemplary damages, completely excluded from the law of damages.

---

[15]   But see Edelman's reflections on the development of the concept of damages, (n 9) 142-143.

[16]   *McGregor (n 14)* para 5.

[17]   In the 17th edition, para 1-001, McGregor writes: 'The impossible search for a clear-cut, comprehensive definition is ... abandoned ... [T]he definition from earlier editions ... is taken but it is qualified to indicate that it applies generally but not invariably'.

[18]   *Cassell* (n 12) 1114 (Lord Wilberforce).

[19]   Law Commission, *Aggravated, Exemplary and Restitutionary Damages* (Law Com No 247, 1997) Part I para 1.4.

[20]   *Ibid* Part I para 1.1.

[21]   *Tito v Waddell (No 2)* [1977] Ch 106 332 (Megarry V-C); *Swindle v Harrison* [1997] 4 All ER 705 (CA) 713-714 (Evans LJ)

[22]   *Rookes v Barnard* (n 2) (esp Lord Devlin).

[23]   *Cassell* (n 12) 1086 (Lord Reid): 'I thought and still think that that is highly anomalous', 'that' being 'a pure and undeserved windfall at the expense of the defendant'.

This particular point emerged clearly in *Stoke-on-Trent CC v W & J Wass Ltd.*[24] In that case, the court held that restitutionary damages could be part of the system, but only if some other court introduced them in the legal order.[25] The recent judicial recognition of restitutionary damages for breach of contract in the *Blake* case[26] indicates that the courts have changed their view on the role of this head of damages – at least in one particular instance. The strict interpretation followed in *Blake* suggests that restitutionary damages should be treated as an exception. Yet this time the definition of their exceptional status is based upon legal analysis, as shall be seen.[27]

ii   Waiver of Tort

A further obstacle to restitution for wrongs in the context of the law of damages is related to a debate on the so-called waiver of tort. There is some disagreement on the evaluation of the relationship between compensation and restitution as legal responses and between tort and unjust enrichment as legal events. It is not always clear[28] how the two pairs mentioned interact. The traditional view tended to exclude restitution – for wrongs, but also for unjust enrichment – whenever compensation is an avenue open to the claimant. A more modern approach[29] distinguishes among different situations and looks for the legal principle which justifies the award of the claim or of the remedy.

This particular issue is not debated in German and in Italian law, which have a more structured law of obligations. Of itself, it does not cause excessive harm, given that a correct answer to the interaction between the different responses follows from a classification which is coherent with the law of obligations and therefore is not a terminological issue. Yet, in a general context of mistrust towards the topic in question, it has assumed considerable importance. The explanation for the difference with the civil law systems is likely to lie in the more consistent theoretical approach of civil law and in the historical evolution of the English law of obligations. Owing to its relevance within proprietary wrongs, especially conversion, this institution will be examined in detail in chapter three.[30]

iii   Unjust Enrichment

Another hindrance on the path to recognition, which is implicitly shared by all three jurisdictions, concerns the supposed uselessness of restitution for wrongs in legal systems which already have a law of unjust enrichment. Thus, Andrew

---

[24]   *Stoke-on-Trent* (n 8).
[25]   P Birks, 'Civil Wrongs: A New World' in *Butterworth Lectures 1990-1991* (London, Butterworths 1992) 55-112, 58, stigmatised this reasoning as 'the *Wass* illusion'.
[26]   *A-G v Blake* (n 3).
[27]   See the analysis in ch 4, text to n 23.
[28]   See *United Australia v Barclays Bank* [1941] AC 1 (especially V-C Simon LC and Lord Atkin).
[29]   Birks, *Restitution* 314-318.
[30]   Ch three, II A i.

Burrows observes that – given that restitutionary damages are analogous to unjust enrichment – it is doubtful whether 'the wrong adds anything to the justification for restitution'.[31] This statement is questionable. Legal responses which share all their requisites and nevertheless are independent from one another represent an anomaly in the law and are normally justifiable only on historical grounds. This is not the case for restitution for wrongs and restitution for unjust enrichment, the requirements of which are not identical. They differ at least in the element of wrongfulness, which is central to their classification. The need to prove the wrong, the limitation period, and the consequences of the claims as regards the quantum of the award do not necessarily coincide – making available extra weapons to the parties to the legal dispute. What is even more significant is the object of the two claims. I shall argue in chapter nine that the benefit which the wrongdoer must give up is in most cases different from the benefit which is returned to the impoverished in a claim for unjust enrichment. The latter is a claim normally based upon a transfer from the claimant to the defendant or a diversion of a transfer of wealth which should have gone to the claimant and instead went to the defendant. Here, the claimant seeks to recover what should belong to him and the defendant's enrichment is founded upon the claimant's impoverishment. The victim claims because of this impoverishment, and the claim is compensatory, not restitutionary, in nature. I shall make the case of the compensatory nature of this remedial model, which appears in the law of damages as well, in my analysis of 'pseudo-restitutionary damages'.[32]

B   German Law

Some principles of the German law of damages might appear to deny to restitutionary responses for wrongs access to the legal system. Yet it will be shown that such principles have no impact upon restitution for wrongs, for their proper aim is limited to the determination of the application ambit of compensation. A further point which necessarily impinges into any discussion on restitution in a wrongful context is related to a non-wrongful structure of restitution for unjustified enrichment, known as *Nichtleistungskondiktion*, a non-performance-based claim which is peculiar to the German legal system. As intimated in the analysis of English law, it will be demonstrated that, even in German law, unjustified enrichment deals with issues which are different from restitution for wrongs and therefore it is not in itself an obstacle to restitutionary damages. It becomes so because of the risk of muddling up the two legal figures. Further-more, the existence of this structure in unjustified enrichment might convey the – incorrect – impression that, in its presence, the development of a restitutionary model for wrongs becomes a less pressing issue. This particular non-wrongful response will be introduced here but investigated in the next chapter.[33]

---

[31] A Burrows, *The Law of Restitution* (2nd edn) (London, Butterworths 2002) 246.
[32] Ch eight, IV C iii.
[33] Ch three, II B.

i The Law of Damages

In determining how to make good a loss, German law is oriented towards compensation, not deterrence or punishment.[34] The foundation of the law of damages has been built upon a doctrine which dates back to a master of the civil law of the19th century, Friedrich Mommsen. It was his idea that the *id quod interest* of the victim of a delict, that is his *Interesse*, could be quantified in the formula according to which damages correspond to the difference between the assets of the victim after the damaging event and the hypothetical situation of those assets at the time of the claim if the event had not taken place.[35]

The *Interesse* doctrine has permeated the law of damages completely.[36] It is neither possible nor methodologically correct to ignore it when referring to the German law of damages. The strong position acquired by the *Interesse* doctrine might indeed appear to constitute a hurdle to the introduction of restitution for wrongs. The preponderance of compensation tends to obscure every other delictual response. Mommsen's formula has survived almost intact in para 249 BGB, which applies to all *Schadensersatzschulden*, that is all duties to compensation, which arise from contract, delict or directly from the law.[37] Its first sentence states:

> A person who is obliged to make compensation shall restore the situation which would have existed if the circumstances rendering him liable to make compensation had not occurred.[38]

Para 249 BGB is read as giving rise to two legal principles which complement each other. The first one is called 'principle of compensation', or *Ausgleichsprinzip*, and states that the attention of the law must be paid to the victim, not to the wrongdoer.[39] The former should obtain full compensation for every loss which originates from the damaging event. Incidentally, it must be observed that this principle could be affected by some limiting factors, such as causation and remoteness of damage, which intervene at an early point to bar an excessive enlargement of the quantification of the damage. The principle of compensation finds its boundaries in the so-called *Bereicherungsverbot*, or prohibition of enrichment (at the defendant's expense). According to this second principle, the victim should not be put in a better position than the one in which the victim was before the damage occurred. The *Bereicherungsverbot* is inferred directly from the letter of para 249 1st sentence BGB. If the victim stood in a better situation, this would imply that the wrongdoer has not simply restored the

---

[34] For instance see K Larenz, *Lehrbuch des Schuldrechts Band 1 Allgemeiner Teil* (14th edn) (München, Beck 1987) 424.

[35] F Mommsen, *Beiträge zum Obligationsrecht II: Zur Lehre von dem Interesse* (Braunschweig, Schwetschke 1855) 3.

[36] *Cf* the *travaux préparatoires* of the First Commission in Mugdan (ed), *Die gesamten Materialien zum Bürgerlichen Gesetzbuch für das deutsche Reich* (Berlin, 1899; repr Aalen, Scientia 1979) 11.

[37] H Lange, *Schadensersatz* (2nd edn) (Tübingen, Mohr 1990) vol I 1.

[38] SL Goren (tr), *The German Civil Code* (revd edn) (Littleton, Colorado 1994).

[39] Lange (n 37) 9.

situation as required by para 249 BGB, but has gone much further. An enrichment of the victim would alter the outcome of the mechanisms activated by the damaging event, not restoring but increasing the victim's assets. It is remarked that the *Bereicherungsverbot* is not really an autonomous principle because it is a mere logical consequence of the *Ausgleichsprinzip*.[40] Nevertheless, the courts underline strongly its importance as if it had almost an autonomous life. In fact, they define it as an element of *ordre public* within the law of damages.[41]

The two principles together provide a clear picture of the state of the law of damages and are relevant to the topic at issue. In particular, the *Bereicherungsverbot* invites some reflections on the relationship between restitution and compensation in the context of the delictual responses. If the prohibition of enrichment could be read as having autonomous life outside compensation, it would constitute a serious menace to any attempt to construe restitution for wrongs as a valid remedy. Yet this is not the case. The *Bereicherungsverbot* cannot be extracted from its own limited context and developed into a general delictual rule because its function is restricted to compensation. The prohibition of enrichment is mentioned exclusively in the context of *Schadensersatzrecht*, that is the law of compensation, and both the prohibition of enrichment and the principle of compensation rest upon para 249 BGB, which deals exclusively with compensation. Never is it suggested that such principles should be extended to other heads of damages – for good reasons: it would be quite difficult to construe para 249 BGB as containing a general principle for the law of damages, given its clear and direct reference to one particular legal response. The strictly compensatory scope within which the prohibition of enrichment applies is confirmed by its close connection with the *Ausgleichsprinzip*: the former is but another way to indicate, from the victim's viewpoint, the compensatory duty placed upon the wrongdoer. As will be seen in the following investigation, cases such as the violation of personality rights, in which damages have a non-compensatory function, highlight the compensation-related role of the *Bereicherungsverbot*.[42] In such cases, the victim might end up better off than he would be had the damage never happened.

Mommsen's doctrine on the evaluation of the difference between the real state of the victim's assets and a hypothetical situation, which is known as the *Differenzhypothese*, or hypothesis of difference, has been object of criticism. It is remarked that it takes the whole of the victim's assets as the measure for quantifying the loss, and not only the part of those assets which is concretely affected by the wrong.[43] Such criticism has no bearing on the theory of restitution for wrongs. Indeed, it is often repeated that, independently of the role of the *Differenzhypothese*, the general function of paras 249 ff. BGB lies in the individuation of an adequate substitute for the loss suffered by the victim. The substitute

---

[40]   MünchKomm/Oetker, '§ 249' para 18.
[41]   (1993) BGHZ 118 312, 338.
[42]   (1996) BGHZ 128 1 (*Caroline von Monaco* case). See ch 5, I B iii b and c.
[43]   MünchKomm/Oetker, '§ 249' para 19.

should lead as near as possible to a hypothetical state of 'freedom from damage',[44] but nothing more. Even those[45] who disagree with the *Differenzhypothese* do not formulate any alternative to the compensatory principle.

The discussion in German law is mainly[46] centred upon two different models of damages. The model which is deemed to suit best the function of the law of delict is based upon compensation and finds express approval in the code at para 249 BGB. The other model seeks to punish the wrongdoer. The means by which this objective is reached is exemplary damages. As for such damages, a chorus of voices unites to deny not only their existence, but also their theoretical compatibility with the German delictual model. The arguments[47] used against exemplary damages do not differ much from those which commonly circulate among English lawyers:[48] punishment is alien to private law and falls exclusively within criminal law. Only the latter provides the protection necessary to avoid a disproportionate punishment of the defendant. Moreover, the introduction of exemplary damages is considered a step back from the more developed model which keeps criminal and private law separated. However, it is recognised that a function of prevention, if not really of punishment, is at least a welcome side effect[49] of the law of damages, for the thought of the expensive consequences deriving from the perpetration of a wrong can work as a deterrent against wrongful conduct.

To compel the wrongdoer to give up the benefit obtained through the wrong is not understood to be an issue of the law of delict. Whereas compensation *in natura*, that is by way of restitution of what has been wrongfully taken, is admitted judicially, restitution of the profits independently of the loss of the victim never arises in normal delictual situations. This notwithstanding, as will be pointed out in the next chapters, there are some cases in which restitution as a consequence of a wrong is allowed; but such cases are held to be limited exceptions.

ii   Non-Wrongful Responses

The interaction of the law of delict with the law of unjustified enrichment provides a significant reason for the alienation of restitution from the German law of delict. In line with the Roman legal tradition, German law has developed

---

[44] Staudinger/Schiemann, 'Vorbem zu §§ 249 ff' para 3.

[45] See MünchKomm/Oetker, '§ 249' para 19.

[46] In the last few years, some authors have shown some interest for restitution in a delictual context; but it is too early to speak of an interest of the same level of that which surrounds compensation and punishment. See eg J Köndgen, 'Gewinnabschöpfung als Sanktion unerlaubten Tuns' (2000) 64 *Rabels Zeitschrift* 661-695. The judiciary has never explicitly taken restitution for wrongs into consideration.

[47] *Cf* Lange (n 37) 8.

[48] Eg A Burrows, 'Reforming Exemplary Damages: Expansion or Abolition?' in P Birks (ed), *Wrongs and remedies in the Twenty-First Century* (Oxford, Clarendon 1996) 153-173, 159-163.

[49] Thus K Larenz (n 34) 423. Incidentally, it can be observed that a punitive and educational function of delict law was plainly recognised in the civil code of the German Democratic Republic, the ZGB. See R Motsch, 'Schadensersatz als Erziehungsmittel' [1984] *Juristische Zeitung* 211-221.

an impressive apparatus to cope with the situations in which the enrichment of the recipient – be it wrongful or not – is not justified by a legal ground. The existence of this restitutionary device has an indirect, but powerful, impact upon the widespread German thesis that restitution is outside the realm of the law of delict: the latter pursues only compensation, restitution being an issue for the law of unjustified enrichment. German authors are not particularly worried by the fact that unjust enrichment cannot be of help in all circumstances. They do not realise that restitution for wrongs overlaps with restitution for unjust, as opposed to unjustified,[50] enrichment only in some marginal cases, because restitution for unjust enrichment and restitution for wrongs normally target a different gain of the defendant, or rather quantify this gain in different fashion. This lack of understanding should not surprise. The concept of restitution for wrongs does not belong to the German legal tradition and therefore there is very little research on restitutionary damages, let alone their relation with other legal responses such as restitution for unjust enrichment. In chapter three,[51] where the relationship between unjust enrichment and delict will be analysed more in detail, it will be shown why a response in unjust enrichment is normally unable to make up for restitution for wrongs. At the present stage, it is enough to point out that there are different reasons for the apparent absence of a restitutionary structure for wrongs qua wrongs. It is still to be seen whether such structure is really missing and whether the introduction of a restitutionary response would improve the flexibility of German law.

C   Italian Law

The attraction exerted upon Italian lawyers by theoretical issues has led to a proliferation of studies on the law of delict. One would expect that a legal system open to theoretical influences such as the Italian system ought to be flexible enough to accommodate restitution for wrongs. Yet, Italian law does not seem to take notice of this legal response.

The investigation will follow the same analytical pattern as the one adopted for German law. First, I shall examine the structure of the law of damages, looking for any signal of incompatibility with restitution for wrongs. Then, I shall turn to the non-wrongful responses. Among them, the only claim relevant to the topic at issue is the general enrichment claim. This is a restitutionary, highly original structure which, although it might appear to have some similarities with restitution for wrongs, addresses a different issue: the injustice of the defendant's enrichment per se, that is whether or not the behaviour which secured the benefit was wrongful. Owing to its strict link with the principle of justice, this claim can

---

[50]   The two terms qualify different aspects of the law of *ungerechtfertigte Bereicherung*. 'Unjustified' enrichment presupposes the lack of a legal ground for the transfer of wealth, whereas an 'unjust' enrichment claim can be successful even if there is such legal ground. See F Giglio, 'A Systematic Approach to "Unjust" and "Unjustified" Enrichment' (2003) 23 *OJLS* 455-482.

[51]   *Cf* the analysis of the *Flugreisefall*; ch 3, n 57 and text thereof.

be awarded even when the defendant's benefit is obtained without violating any legal rule. From this perspective, the claim shares some similarities with the English idea of equity.

i   The Law of Damages

The methods for the quantification of damages in delict and contract were partially unified under the present code. Art 2056 cc, which determines the measure of damages in delict law, refers to the law of contract for the practicalities. It states that 'compensation must be determined according to articles 1223, 1226, and 1227.' Art 1223 cc contains the basic rule for the evaluation of the measure of damages: Compensation of the damage

> arising from non-performance or delay shall include the loss sustained by the creditor and the lost profits insofar as they are a direct and immediate consequence of the non-performance or delay.[52]

The reference to causation is of no interest for the present analysis. The provision mentions only non-performance and delay but the letter of Art 2056 cc makes clear that it comprises also delictual situations.

The basic rule on damages describes a compensatory model. The heading of Art 1223 cc reads 'compensation of the loss', thus suggesting that the courts must direct the award at making good a loss suffered by the claimant. In line with the tradition of the French *Code civil*, Art 1223 cc lists two elements which must be considered by the judges: *damnum emergens* and *lucrum cessans*, that is the loss sustained and the lost profits, for instance the loss of earnings. Both the delictual and the contractual damage are hence primarily seen as a negative, financially quantifiable effect, which touches upon the victim's assets and person.[53] As regards the delictual damage, Pier Giuseppe Monateri[54] has pointed out how this model seeks essentially a correspondence between the victim's loss and the compensatory duty upon the wrongdoer. This correspondence does not have to be absolute identity, because other factors such as remoteness or contributory negligence can intervene and curb the award of damages, which consequentially will not cover the entire loss. Even a theoretical identity seems only possible when the interest affected by the wrong concerns a pecuniary loss which can be proved easily and can be made good entirely by a compensatory award. In this latter case only, restoration can put the victim in a state of indifference as regards a choice between the situation altered by the damaging event and the hypothetical situation without the alteration at the moment of the claim.[55] In all other cases, which constitute the vast majority, the courts can only minimise the gap between the loss suffered and the ensuing compensation.

---

[52]   M Beltramo, G Longo and JH Merryman (trs), *The Italian Civil Code* (New York, Oceana 1969).
[53]   CM Bianca, 'Dell'inadempimento delle obbligazioni Art 1218-1229' in A Scialoja and G Branca (eds), *Commentario del Codice civile* (2nd ed) (Bologna-Roma, Zanichelli 1979) 249.
[54]   Monateri, *Responsabilità* 314.
[55]   *Ibid* 318.

Such analysis still belongs to scholarly reflections. Judicial authority prefers a much more pragmatic approach. Italian courts[56] refer expressly to the German *Differenztheorie* as the proper instrument to evaluate damages. Liability rules become the protective shield of the victim's assets because through them the victim is put in the same position in which the victim would be had the damaging event never taken place.[57] On the other hand, the academic authors do not seem convinced that an assessment of the damages in terms of the *Differenztheorie* is completely appropriate to civil liability. Adolfo di Majo for instance remarks that this German doctrine cannot explain the whole complexity of compensation. It can only constitute a basis on which damages can be measured, because it is of no use to damages which cannot be quantified straightfor-wardly.[58] The so-called affection-interest provides a good example of these difficulties with quantification. It is the monetary award over and above the objective value of the thing due to the very special significance which the thing has for its owner.

The *Differenztheorie* and, more generally, any approach to the law of damages which is centred upon compensation, question the level of compatibility between the Italian system of responses and restitution for wrongs. The difficulty lies in the tendency of the theories on compensation to cloud every other response which is non-compensatory. Often, a circular argument seems to prevail in such theories, which state that non-compensatory responses have no room in the law of compensation because the latter admits only compensation. Yet nothing is said as regards the relation between the law of damages in general, which does not include only compensation, and non-compensatory damages. Italian law has no equivalent to the prohibition of enrichment of the German law of delict. Thus, the fact that compensation and restitution are independent responses within the law of 'wrongs', or more properly delict and contract, should be a powerful argument to contrast a possible rejection of restitution for wrongs on the basis of circular compensatory reasoning. This notwithstanding, the force of traditional views on compensation is still widely prevalent.

On the other hand, if one considers all the responses available within the law of obligations, one can find non-wrongful structures which might convey the impression that results similar to those of restitutionary damages can be achieved – at least partly. Similarly to German law, the presence of such structures helps explaining why the need for a restitutionary response for wrongs is not as compelling in Italy as it is in jurisdictions where the law of unjust enrichment is less developed. The next section is dedicated to such structures.

---

[56] For instance Cassazione, 18 July 1989 No 3352 [1990] *Foro Italiano* I 933.
[57] Cassazione, 3rd October 1987 No 7389 [1987] Repertorio Foro italiano Danni civili No 85.
[58] A di Majo, *La tutela civile dei diritti* (2nd edn) (Milano, Giuffrè 1993) 186-187.

ii Non-Wrongful Responses

Art 2041 (1) cc contains the only cause of action properly based upon the injustice of the enrichment. It states:

> A person who has enriched himself without cause at the expense of another shall, to the extent of the enrichment, indemnify the other for his correlative financial loss.[59]

This is the general enrichment action, which the Italian draftsmen were probably the first to codify. The requirements of the cause of action are:[60] (1) an enrichment by the defendant; (2) an impoverishment by the claimant; (3) a causative relation between the two; and (4) an element of injustice in the transfer of wealth. The great limit of this action is the subsidiarity imposed by Art 2042 cc: if any other claim is available to the victim, he cannot seek restitution through Art 2041 cc. As wrongfulness is not one of the requirements, the avenue chosen when bringing the general enrichment claim is unjust enrichment, not delict. This difference bears practical consequences, such as the different limitation period and the role played by negligent or wilful behaviour.

The rationale of this claim is that nobody should benefit unjustly at the expense of another. It seems an idea which would fit restitution for wrongs too. Still, the two responses rest on different legal structures. The general enrichment claim presupposes that the victim suffered a patrimonial loss (*diminuzione patrimoniale*) and that the defendant has been unjustly enriched. A claim for restitutionary damages on the contrary is directed towards the benefit obtained by the wrongdoer regardless of any financial decrease in the victim's assets. It would be therefore incorrect to conclude that, in the presence of a general enrichment claim, restitution for wrongs becomes redundant. A discussion on the relationship between the general enrichment claim and restitutionary damages has not yet been conducted in Italian law; but this pattern of confusing restitution for unjust enrichment and restitution for wrongs has already appeared in English law[61] and in German law[62] whenever there has been a discussion on the opportunity of restitutionary damages, so that it would hardly be surprising if a similar argument were advanced in Italy too. One major negative contribution of the general enrichment claim in relation to restitutionary damages, therefore, consists of the fact that it transmits the false impression that a change in the law in favour of restitution for wrongs does not present any character of urgency given that many wrongful situations can be redressed with the existing legal tools. It will be shown in the next chapter and particularly in the theoretical analysis of chapter eight that any explanation based upon this thesis misunderstands the nature of the two legal figures.

---

[59] Beltramo et al (n 52).
[60] See P Cendon, *Commentario al Codice civile* (Torino, Utet 1991) Art 2041 para 2.
[61] See n 31.
[62] See n 47.

II   Some Remarks

Neither the English nor the German or the Italian law of damages seems to contain substantial impediments to the introduction of restitution for wrongs. The idea of a natural predominance of the compensatory model is the main argument in all the jurisdictions under comparison which is advanced or could be advanced – albeit to a different degree – to oppose restitutionary awards for wrongs. It plays a major role in English law and it is used by German courts to reject awards which are non-compensatory. It is more than likely that the same argument would occur in Italian law if restitutionary damages became an issue. It runs as follows: the law of damages deals exclusively with compensation, as tortious, delictual and contractual rules only seek to make good a loss, that is a negative patrimonial modification in the victim's legal sphere which affects property, assets or the person. Thus, the law of damages would have no room for restitution for wrongs. Yet this reasoning hides a *petitio principii*. It is said that the rules on compensation do not give the claimant the right to oblige the defendant to give up his enrichment and on this basis it is inferred that restitution is not allowed.

There are two difficulties with this line of thought. The first is the inappositeness of a thesis founded on the brocard: *ubi lex voluit, dixit* – 'where the law wants something, it says so explicitly'. According to this principle, restitution cannot be granted because the law does not refer expressly to this response. Such reasoning is, however, inconsistent with a system of law in action such as the common law and with a system based upon general claims such as Italian law. Furthermore, in civil law there are many examples of legal institutions which are judicially shaped *praeter legem*, that is beyond what statutes regulate.[63] Every application of the Latin maxim would clash with the evidence of such institutions. The second and main difficulty stems from the circularity of the thesis. The criticism mentioned does not hold against restitution for wrongs that the statutes do not contemplate restitution, but that the provisions on compensation do not regulate any further response. This is interpreted as an implied rejection of restitution by the legal system. However, this line of reasoning overlooks that it would be up to norms on restitution, and not on compensation, to perform such regulatory function. Therefore, it is indispensable to abandon the compensatory approach to comprehend the real role of restitution for wrongs within the law of responses. Only the law of restitution, as opposed to the law of compensation, can provide the correct framework for the investigation. There might well be arguments against an introduction of restitutionary awards. Yet those arguments ought to be based upon non-compensatory reasoning.

---

[63]   Eg according to para 817 BGB, a restitutionary claim is barred if 'acceptance of the performance' was *contra bonos mores*, ie against public policy. The judiciary has extended this provision to cover all performances *contra bonos mores*, not only cases of acceptance of such performances. See MünchKomm/Lieb, '§ 817' para 8.

On the other hand, the fact that most legal systems recognise restitutionary claims for unjust enrichment, which are qualified by various degrees of generality and are situated outside the law of wrongs, is not a sufficient reason to conclude that restitution for wrongs is compatible with the tenets of the respective laws of obligations. Restitution for wrongs and restitution for unjust enrichment can occasionally overlap. Yet, as will emerge in the theoretical analysis, their – rare – overlapping is purely accidental. It is due mainly to the similarities in some aspects of the respective causes of action. A further fallacy is linked to any theory which would argue that admitting broad enrichment actions and refusing restitutionary awards for wrongs should be regarded as a contradiction, as both claims share the same function of compelling the wrongdoer to give up his benefit. Again, in the theoretical analysis I shall demonstrate that, unlike restitution for wrongs, most unjust enrichment actions rest upon compensatory reasoning, so that no a fortiori argument can link restitution for wrongs and restitution for unjust enrichment.

3

Comparative Analysis: Proprietary and Intellectual Property Wrongs

I Organisation of the Analysis

THE FIRST TWO introductory chapters have dealt with terminological issues and have placed restitution for wrongs on the map of the law of obligations. In this chapter, the focus is narrowed down to a comparative analysis of restitution for wrongs in a stricter sense. As there is no authoritative recognition of restitutionary damages in German and Italian law, English law provides the model which will be used to trace those German and Italian institutions which in England would be listed under the heading 'restitution for wrongs' and to find out which legal constructions – if there are any – supply to the lack of restitutionary damages in civilian systems. The results of the comparison of the law in action furnish useful information for the theoretical analysis of restitution for wrongs which will be pursued in the second part of this study.

The search for restitutionary awards for wrongs in the jurisdictions under comparison is set in the context of the law of obligations, rather than only within the law of wrongs. The enlargement of the scope of analysis is particularly useful with regard to civil law systems, where non-wrongful institutions such as unjust enrichment have had a wider impact upon the shaping of the law of damages than in English law. The classificatory model adopted here owes much to the work of the Law Commission. The approach of the Commission seems appropriate for two main reasons: on the one hand, its classification suits all three systems under consideration. On the other hand, English law presents the most developed model of restitution for wrongs, a topic which in Germany and Italy has never gone beyond purely academic disputes.

My vision of restitution for wrongs, which I shall premise by way of introduction, will emerge in the comparative analysis. An initial qualification of my understanding of restitutionary damages is all the more important because my view is often at odds with the received view in the literature. A detailed presentation of my account will take place in chapters eight and nine.[1] Here, I shall draw only its general lines. I distinguish real instances of restitution for wrongs from non-restitutionary awards which present superficial similarities with this legal response and are commonly – but mistakenly – held as instances of restitution for wrongs.

A   Compensatory Damages which Resemble Restitutionary Damages

Particularly after the publication of James Edelman's seminal work on gain-based damages, many influential voices have referred with increasing frequency to certain compensatory awards which measure the victim's loss on the basis of the wrongdoer's gain as 'restitutionary damages'. I have termed such awards 'pseudo-restitutionary damages'. This expression is just descriptive; it is useful to highlight that these damages are not restitutionary. It should be clear from the outset that there is no separate category of damages which are pseudo-restitutionary: 'pseudo-restitution' means 'proper compensation'. Against a widely diffused view,[2] I argue that a wrong which violates a proprietary or quasi-proprietary interest triggers normally a non-restitutionary response which does indeed compel the wrongdoer to transfer his benefit to the victim. Yet the transfer takes place in a compensatory framework.

I give you a precious book of mine. I intend it to be a loan of use. I do not want to deprive myself of the book. Yet, you are so fond of my book that you decide to keep it although you are aware that you should give it back to me at some point. I found my claim to compel you to return the book on my loss, not on your gain. With this action, I am not interested in depriving you of any benefit; I just want my book back. Let us change the scenario a little. Now, you are ready to give the book back to me, but before doing so you forget it one night on the table in your garden and the day after you find out that the book has been seriously damaged by the rain. Both situations justify a claim based upon my property right over the book. Yet, many commentators would distinguish the first scenario, which in their view might trigger restitution for wrongs, from the second scenario, which can be remedied only by a compensatory award. In my interpretation of restitution for wrongs, I question the correctness of this distinction. In both scenarios you have taken my property away from me and I want back my property or an appropriate substitute. Ernst Weinrib explains this outcome clarifying that 'the potential for gain is an incident of the right that the wrongdoer violated'.[3] In other words, the potential for gain was part of my right and you deprived me of it. I bring an action for compensation of my loss.

---

[1]   Ch eight IV C iii, and ch 9 VII, VIII and X.
[2]   For instance Weinrib, *Restitutionary Damages*; Edelman, *passim.*
[3]   Weinrib (n 2) 37.

B   Proper Restitutionary Damages

When the claim based upon the wrong is completely independent of the claimant's loss, the award which targets the defendant's gain is properly restitutionary. For example, you find out that I am looking for a new house in the area where you live and you show me a nice house with a beautiful garden. I purchase the house and then discover that I paid far too much for it. You told me that it was a bargain; but in reality you did not disclose to me that you had previously agreed with the seller that you would receive a certain sum of money if I buy the house relying on your advice, so that you inflated the price counting on my trust in you. In this case, the judiciary would correctly award restitutionary damages.[4] You did not violate a proprietary interest of mine so that I cannot claim anything back from you. My claim will rather address your wrongful benefit with the aim of depriving you of something which you do not deserve. You must give your benefit up and I am the beneficiary of your duty. The basis of the claim is purely your wrongful benefit. Whether I have suffered a patrimonial loss is from this perspective largely irrelevant.

C   Scheme of the Comparative Analysis

The ensuing examination of restitution for wrongs is broken down into the following categories: proprietary wrongs (excluding intellectual property wrongs), intellectual property wrongs, breach of contract, and other wrongs. This chapter investigates the first two categories; chapter four considers the third category; chapter five brings to a close the comparative survey of living legal systems with an exposition of 'other wrongs' and of the concluding observations. This categorisation takes little account of the historical divide between common law torts and equitable wrongs.[5] The category 'other wrongs' includes cases of wrongful violations of rights which do not fall into the more detailed headings. This method avoids a proliferation of ad hoc categories for every single wrong which does not belong to the three previous classes. No attempt will be made to analyse all possible instances of restitution for wrongs. The investigation considers only a few interesting examples. Within each category, every jurisdiction will be introduced separately: first the English, then the German and finally the Italian.

---

[4]   *A-G v Blake* [2001] 1 AC 268 (HL); *Aysha Mohammed Murad and Layla Mohammed Murad v Hashim Ibrahim Khalil Al-Saraj and Westwood Business Inc* [2004] EWHC 1235.
[5]   See ch 1, n 69 and text thereof.

II Proprietary Wrongs

The analysis of this category offers a good opportunity to compare the different avenues followed by common law and civil law. English law does not yet have a fully developed law of unjust enrichment but has an elaborated law of wrongs, in some cases with explicit references to restitution for wrongs. In Germany and Italy, the law of unjust enrichment rests on the rich Roman tradition and tends to play a more active role than the law of delict in the restoration of the claimant's patrimonial position when the defendant has obtained something which belongs or should belong to the claimant. In this chapter, I come to the conclusion that the civil law approach is more in line with the theoretical premises of the law of obligation. As I have intimated in the previous section,[6] a violation of a proprietary right might trigger a claim in unjust enrichment on the basis of which the impoverished claims *back* what has been subtracted to him – an action with a compensatory aim. This characteristic of the action excludes that any restitutionary award for wrongs can be granted by the court: as damages can only be compensatory, no award of restitution for wrongs follows a violation of a property right. This is clear to civil law, less clear to common law, as the following analysis will show.

A   English Law

There are no indisputable examples of restitutionary damages following the violation of a property right. Yet, in some cases it might be questioned whether the nature of the award is really compensatory. Even German law, which is opposed to the introduction of non-compensatory damages, accepts that there are some 'exceptions' in which the usual compensatory model does not seem to apply. Yet, I shall argue that these 'exceptions' refer to matters of compensation in which the 'normal measure' of quantification is of no avail: the award is compensatory in all cases which we shall consider under the heading 'property wrongs', but the quantification of damages rests upon criteria which are less common than those normally applied by the courts.

i Conversion

In *United Australia v Barclays Bank*,[7] a cheque payable to the claimant was converted by a third party, which handed it in to its bank. The claimant first brought an action in contract against the third party, then discontinued this action and claimed against the defendant bank in tort for conversion. The bank argued in defence that the prior contractual claim barred the subsequent tortious claim in accordance with the so-called waiver of tort principle. The point was

---

[6] See I A.
[7] *United Australia Ltd v Barclays Bank Ltd* [1941] AC 1 (HL).

rejected by the House of Lords, which gave its own interpretation of the meaning of 'waiver of tort'. On the basis of *Lamine v Dorrell*,[8] the court drew a distinction between choosing one of two alternative remedies on the one hand and choosing one of two inconsistent rights on the other.[9] In the latter case, once one avenue is preferred, the opposite avenue is barred. In the case of alternative remedies, it is only if the claimant has recovered through one of the alternative claims that the successful claim operates as a bar to the other claim.[10] On this point, Lord Atkin seemed to regard the remedies as located in different areas of the law of obligations, that is contract and tort.[11] Viscount Simon LC, by contrast, appeared to narrow down the election within the law of damages.

According to Peter Jaffey, an evaluation in terms of restitution for wrongs

> makes no obvious sense of the idea of 'waiver', or of choosing between different causes of action, since disgorgement is a different response to the tort claim, not a different type of claim.[12]

Rather than as offering a choice between responses within the law of damages, Jaffey sees *United Australia* as authority for the 'better view … that the claim arising from the waiver of tort is a claim for restitution for a vitiated transfer'.[13] In his opinion, therefore, *United Australia* does not deal with an alternative within the law of damages at all, but with two different claims, one in tort and one in unjust enrichment. Peter Birks uses historical analysis to conclude that, in the reasoning of the House, the 'tort, in this case the tort of conversion, simply had two remedial strings'.[14] Yet, conversion allows the recovery of assets which belong to the claimants. As the victim claims these assets back, the tort of conversion can have two remedial strings only if 'remedy' is taken in a very loose sense as meaning a solution to a legal problem, because 'two remedial strings' cannot stand for 'two legal responses', given that both strings are compensatory in nature. Furthermore, as Jaffey suggests, the same set of facts can also activate a response in unjust enrichment, which will achieve similar results without the need for the claimant to prove wrongfulness.

My last sentence is apparently disproved by Viscount Simon LC, who said in *United Australia*:

---

[8] *Lamine v Dorrell* (1701) 2 Ld Raym 1216, 92 ER 303.

[9] *United Australia* (n 7) 29-30 (Lord Atkin).

[10] *Ibid* 12 (Viscount Simon LC).

[11] *Ibid* 28 (Lord Atkin): '[h]aving recovered in contract it is plain that the plaintiff cannot go on to recover in tort'.

[12] P Jaffey, *The Nature and Scope of Restitution* (Oxford, Hart 2000) 368.

[13] *Ibid* 367.

[14] P Birks, 'Restitution for Wrongs' in EJH Schrage (ed), *Unjust Enrichment – The Comparative Legal History of the Law of Restitution* (2nd edn) (Berlin, Duncker & Humblot 1999) 171-195, 186.

> The substance of the matter is that on certain facts [the claimant] is claiming redress in the form of compensation, ie, damages as for a tort, or *in the form of restitution of money to which he is entitled, but which the defendant has wrongfully received.*[15] (emphasis added)

This passage seems to indicate that his Lordship is offering an alternative between compensation and restitution for wrongs: (1) the defendant wrongfully receives a benefit; (2) the claimant is entitled to claim the benefit for himself; (3) the claimant does not claim compensation but a different measure, that is restitution. The reference to money wrongfully received, if taken literally, would exclude that the court is awarding a claim in unjust enrichment, for the latter does not require a wrong. But this more immediate reading of Viscount Simon's statement cannot be correct. A strong argument militates against restitution for wrongs in this context. The victim brings an action to recover something to which he is 'entitled': in other words, the money should belong to the victim, not to the wrongdoer, who has no title to it. The victim is claiming the defendant's benefit *back*, which implies that he is claiming on the basis of a patrimonial loss, not of the defendant's enrichment. The Lord Chancellor's statement acquires novel significance if the reference to the 'money wrongfully received' is interpreted as indicating that the wrongfulness of the transfer was due to its injustice, rather than – as the wording might suggest – to the commission of a wrong. If, as I argue, the expression 'wrongful transfer' was an imprecise fashion to refer to an 'unjust transfer', then his Lordship is simply stating that this situation could trigger either a tortious claim for compensation or a claim for restitution of an unjust enrichment. At the time of the decision, the law of unjust enrichment was much less developed than today and it is understandable that the courts did not always use the correct terminology. In my view, the Lord Chancellor was pointing out the existence of two different claims, one wrongful and the other independent of the wrong.

There are other arguments which support my view according to which the tort of conversion does not trigger a restitutionary response. According to Graham Virgo,

> the remedy for the commission of such a tort is restitutionary because the defendant must pay the value of the proceeds of sale to the claimant without any inquiry being undertaken as to what the market value of the goods was at the time of sale, which would be the measure of the claimant's loss'.

'In other words', the author concludes, 'the remedy for conversion can be assessed by reference to the defendant's gain rather than the claimant's loss'.[16] Yet, a legal response might contain a non-compensatory element without necessarily being restitutionary. For instance, in the quantification of exemplary damages the

---

[15]   *United Australia* (n 7) 19, emphasis added.

[16]   G Virgo, *The Principles of the Law of Restitution* (2nd edn) (Oxford, OUP 2006) 470. See also ch 6, n 34 and text thereof.

courts can also take into consideration the gain accruing to the wrongdoer.[17] By awarding restitution for wrongs, the court aims to strip the defendant of the gains made by a civil wrong.[18] If the 'restitutionary' measure in conversion necessarily – as opposed to coincidentally, such as in exemplary damages – obtains this outcome, then the law of torts contains, in the context of the remedies for conversion, at least one example of restitution for wrongs and my account of these damages is incorrect. This conclusion needs to be tested.

S 3 (2) of the Torts (Interference with Goods) Act 1977 provides two basic forms of relief for conversion: delivery of the goods and consequential damages, or damages only. Instead of ordering delivery, it is at the discretion of the court to offer 'the defendant the alternative of paying damages by reference to the value of the goods'. The judiciary insists that the value of the goods is given by their market price.[19] There is some discussion on the time relevant for assessment of the price, but this does not affect the nature of the measure. Restitution, if it can be identified at all, must be sought in the quantification of the damages over and above delivery or its equivalent in damages. From this perspective, *Hillesden Securities v Ryjak*[20] offers good opportunities of reflection. The lessee of a car was in financial difficulties and purported to sell it to the defendant. The claimant, who was the creditor, brought an action in conversion for delivery and damages. Parker J calculated the damages on the basis of 'the use and enjoyment' of the car on the part of the defendant. Hence, the claimant obtained the value of the car plus a sum which was assessed on the value of the defendant's gain. Virgo uses this decision as a confirmation that damages in conversion can be restitutionary.

In the recent years, the thesis of the restitutionary nature of damages for conversion has found increasingly more consensus both in the literature[21] and in the case law.[22] The difficulty with an unreserved acceptance of this view lies in the fact that the tort of conversion includes a function which in civil law systems is performed by various non-tortious legal structures: *vindicatio, condictio*, and *actio de in rem verso* are but the most common among them. Being a proprietary tort, conversion enlarges the area of the loss suffered by the claimant, who could justify a quantification of damages on the basis of the defendant's benefit as compensatory by linking them to the good converted. Consequently, the claimant

---

[17] *Cf* the 'second category' of exemplary damages depicted in *Rookes v Barnard* [1964] AC 1129 (HL) 1226-1227 (Lord Devlin): cases 'in which the defendant's conduct has been calculated by him to make a profit for himself which may well exceed the compensation payable to the plaintiff'. *Cf Edelman* 9-21. The House of Lords in *United Australia* made no reference to exemplary damages.

[18] Law Commission, *Aggravated, Exemplary and Restitutionary Damages* (Law Com No 247, 1997) Part III para 1.2.

[19] *IBL v Coussens* [1991] 2 All ER 133 (CA).

[20] *Hillesden Securities Ltd v Ryjak Ltd* [1983] 2 All ER 184.

[21] D Friedmann, 'Restitution for Wrongs: The Measure of Recovery' (2001) 79 *Texas Law Review* 1879-1925, 1892-1893, seems convinced that damages for conversion can be restitutionary. Yet, his analysis does not distinguish clearly between restitution for wrongs and restitution for unjust enrichment.

[22] *Kuwait Airways Corp v Iraqi Airways Co (Nos 4 and 5)* [2002] 2 AC 883 (HL) 1094 (Lord Nicholls speaking *obiter*).

asks the court to obtain what should belong to him and the action aims to restore the integrity of the violated proprietary right of the victim. 'Restoration' is a concept which qualifies the position of the claimant after the judicial award, indicating that the victim's loss has been nullified by the award. For this reason, conversion does not provide a valid argument in support of restitution for wrongs. From the perspective of the quantification of the loss, there is rather an argument for affirming that damages for conversion are based upon a method of quantification different from normal compensation, for they are assessed, as Virgo put it, 'by reference to the defendant's gain'. In *Hillesden Securities*, the court used the position of the wrongdoer to determine the *loss* of the claimant. This case offers an excellent example of what I termed 'pseudo-restitutionary damages', that is damages which on the surface might appear to be restitutionary, which even entail restitutionary language, but which if properly analysed reveal their compensatory nature. A detailed investigation of pseudo-restitutionary damages will take place in chapter eight;[23] but some relevant information will be already discussed with reference to intellectual property wrongs in the present chapter.

ii   Other Cases

The Law Commission described *Ministry of Defence v Ashman*[24] as '[o]ne of the clearest judicial acceptances of restitution as an appropriate remedy for a property tort'.[25] In that case, the defendants lived in an apartment which the claimant ministry rented out only to employees of the Royal Air Force with very favourable conditions. When the husband left the household, the claimant tried to evict the remaining members of the family, who, however, did not vacate the apartment until they had found alternative accommodation. The claimant sought to recover mesne profits for the period between the formal termination of their tenancy and their departure. The court held that the defendants were trespasser who wrongfully benefited from paying a rent which was far below what they would have paid for a similar apartment rented at normal prices. In this context, Hoffmann LJ used the term 'restitutionary remedy' as a technical expression for the first time:

> A person entitled to possession of land can make a claim against a person who has been in occupation without his consent on two alternative bases. The first is for the loss which he has suffered in consequence of the defendant's trespass. This is the normal measure of damages in the law of tort. The second is the value of the benefit which the occupier has received. This is a claim for restitution. The two bases of claim are

---

[23]   IV C iii.
[24]   *Ministry of Defence v Ashman* (1993) 66 P & CR 195 (CA). See also *Ministry of Defence v Thompson* [1993] 2 EGLR 107 (CA).
[25]   Law Commission (n 18) Part III para 1.12.

mutually exclusive and the plaintiff must elect before judgment which of them he wishes to pursue … In this case the Ministry of Defence elected for the restitutionary remedy.[26]

The Ministry claimed only on the basis of the second measure. The Court of Appeal granted the claim in full without raising the point that the claimant was not seeking compensation according to the 'general rule', or that no evidence of the loss was given. Yet, Hoffmann LJ's approach was not followed by the other members of the court, who preferred a compensatory interpretation. Lloyd LJ's summarised his basic reservation to a restitutionary reading of the award thus:

As to mesne profits they are, as I understand it, simply damages for trespass recoverable against a tenant who holds over after the lawful termination of the tenancy.[27]

Hence, the Court of Appeal agreed that the claimant deserved to obtain what the defendants had saved by not paying the higher rent. The judgments diverged on the qualification of the award, not on its quantification. They identified two avenues to redress the claimant's loss: the 'normal measure of damages' and another, alternative measure, which Hoffmann LJ called 'disgorgement'. The key to understand this second measure rests in its alternative relationship with the normal measure. If the two measures really realised different aims, here compensation and restitution respectively, there would be little reason to consider them to be mutually exclusive. The Ministry of Defence claimed on the basis of the violation of its property right. The court restored the integrity of the violated right through an award which can be quantified using different, and necessarily alternative, compensatory measures.

In this context of quantification of the measure of compensation, a set of decisions which starts from *Wrotham Park*[28] has tried to solve the problem of the real nature of these damages awarded on the basis of a less usual measure by resorting to a fiction. The defendant had built houses in breach of a covenant. The claimant could no longer enforce the covenant, because the houses had already been built and, in the opinion of the court, it would have been a waste of valuable resources if the court had ordered their demolition. The starting point was given by Lord Blackburn's dictum in the *Livingstone* case,[29] which was adapted thus:

[T]he general rule would be to measure damages by reference to that sum which would place the plaintiffs in the same position as if the covenant had not been broken.[30]

As demolition was refused, damages were awarded. The problem lay in the determination of the quantum. Brightman J decided to stick to the 'general rule'

---

[26] *Ashman* (n 24) 200-201.
[27] *Ibid* 202.
[28] *Wrotham Park Estate Co Ltd v Parkside Homes Ltd* [1974] 1 WLR 798. See also *Jaggard v Sawyer* [1995] 1 WLR 269; *Gafford v Graham* [1999] 77 P & CR 73; *Severn Trent Water Ltd v Barnes* (CA) [2004] EWCA 570; *Horsford v Bird* [2006] UKPC 3 (PC).
[29] *Livingstone v The Rawyards Coal Co* (1880) 5 AC 25 (HL). See ch 2, n 7.
[30] *Wrotham Park* (n 28) 815 (Brightman J).

of the *Livingstone* case: if the claimants had granted a relaxation of the covenant, then would have received 'such a sum of money as might reasonably have been demanded by the plaintiffs from [the defendant] as a quid pro quo for relaxing the covenant'.[31]

The approach in *Wrotham Park* was not radically different from the one adopted by Lloyd LJ in the *Ashman* case, even if the compensatory award was justified in a more articulate fashion. Brightman J conceded that the claimants would have never given their consent to the relaxation of the covenant. Despite the use of a fiction, this construction is based upon proprietary analysis similar to what justifies – compensatory – damages for conversion. The court applied reasoning which rested upon what is generally known as the 'doctrine of the lost opportunity to bargain'.

Excursus: The Doctrine of the Lost Opportunity to Bargain

As it touches directly upon restitution for wrongs, it is necessary to devote some attention to this doctrine. In a seminal article, R Sharpe and S Waddams[32] argued that there are cases in which it might appear that the claimant does not suffer any loss. Yet in reality the violation of a legal right might cause a tangible loss, which can be quantified in the lost opportunity to bargain with the defendant. Thus, the measure of compensatory damages consists of the amount of money which the claimant would have obtained from the defendant had the former bargained with the latter.

As the claimant has not concretely bargained with the defendant, a lost opportunity is nothing but a chance which the claimant had at the time of the commission of the wrong to derive a future profit from his right. The character-istic feature of such damages for loss of a chance follows from the fact that the future benefit is possible, not certain, and can be quantified only through percentages. Accordingly, the courts[33] award only a percentage of the damage which the claimant would have suffered had the chance become reality. Yet, in cases such as *Wrotham Park* the situation appears to be different, since the claimant obtains in its entirety what he would have been able to get had the agreement gone through. Still, the award is based upon the loss of a chance, for Sharpe and Waddams restrict the application of their doctrine to the lost opportunity to bargain 'with the defendant'. As an agreement has never been reached between the parties to the claim, the claimant effectively loses the chance to obtain a profit from his right in the form requested by the wrongdoer. The complete loss of this chance calls for a 100 per cent recovery of the damage. The defendant's consent to payment is presumed just as the consent of the claimant to dispose of his right is presumed. This series of fictions obscures the characteristic

---

[31]   *Ibid* 815.

[32]   RJ Sharpe and SM Waddams, 'Damages for Lost Opportunity to Bargain' [1982] 2 *OJLS* 290-297.

[33]   *Chaplin v Hicks* [1911] 2 KB 786 (CA); *Allied Maples Group Ltd v Simmons & Simmons* [1995] 1 WLR 1602 (CA); *Gregg v Scott* [2005] 2 AC 176 (HL).

element of the damage for lost opportunity to bargain as a percentage of a merely possible damage, for the form of recovery might give the impression that it is not the loss of a 100 per cent chance which is recovered, but an entirely different loss. It is not surprising, therefore, that a recent decision has rejected a construction of the lost opportunity to bargain doctrine in terms of loss of a chance. In *Lane v O'Brien*,[34] Clarke J explained that any assessment of a loss of a chance involves the identification of a loss and then the identification of a chance for this loss to enter. In Clarke J's view, the lost opportunity to bargain doctrine does identify the loss, but it stops short of the second step, which requires the identification of the chance.[35] Yet, in reality the chance is an essential element of the quantification of the claimant's loss, which however through the mechanism described above is fictionally assumed to be a complete loss – that is a 100 per cent loss. Mitchell McInnes might have found a way to accommodate Clarke J's doubts. He circumvents the issue of the assessment of the loss as a chance by refining the doctrine of lost opportunity to bargain. In his view, the compensatory nature of the award is not automatically excluded by the lack of a patrimonial loss to the claimant, because compensation would go beyond reparation of a financial disadvantage. He argues that 'ownership entails a number of rights, including the right of *dominium* (*ie* the right to control access and use of a thing) … A loss of *dominium* is considered reparable through the payment of a price at which a reasonable purchaser would buy, and a reasonable vendor would sell, such a right.'[36]

Steyn LJ observed in *Surrey v Bredero Homes* that the 'argument that the *Wrotham Park* case can be justified on the basis of a loss of bargaining opportunity is a fiction'.[37] The fictional element of the doctrine, which most contributed to its success, has become the main reason for a mounting wave of academic criticism.[38] Edelman points to the risks linked to its application. In his view, this theory pushes the boundaries of compensation too far.[39] Andrew Burrows observes that

> it [is] artificial to pretend that the claimant would have ever [accepted to bargain with the defendant] … the damages are most naturally viewed as restitutionary.[40]

Yet, artificiality is an essential characteristic of the legal fiction and the latter is in itself a perfectly acceptable – and successfully applied – legal tool. As Peter Smith J said in *WWF v WWF*:

> The hypothetical bargain is to take place in the light of two artificial factors. First it regularly takes place when the seller would never actually have agreed to it … Equally it

---

[34]   *Lane v O'Brien Homes* [2004] EWHC 303.
[35]   *Ibid* para 22.
[36]   M McInnes, 'Gain, Loss and the User Principle' [2006] *Restitution Law Review* 76-92, 81.
[37]   *Surrey CC v Bredero Homes Ltd* [1993] 1 WLR 1361 (CA) 1369 (Steyn LJ).
[38]   Eg P Birks, 'Profits of Breach of Contract' (1993) 109 *LQR* 518-521; A Burrows, *The Law of Restitution* (2nd edn) (London, Butterworths 2002) 482-483.
[39]   *Edelman* 99.
[40]   Burrows (n 38) 483.

is not open to the notional buyer to refuse to agree the bargain. This is of course a *'bargain'* retrospectively imposed upon him … [A] good analogy in my view is the exercise that regularly takes place in the area of rent review where on the rent review date a notional lease is used as the basis for determining the rent. In those cases it is not possible to argue that no lease will take place or a lease would only take place in favour of the lessee who would thus be able to dictate the terms. Much the same seems to be the case here.[41]

Thus, the use of an artificial construction is no obstacle to the adoption of the doctrine of lost opportunity to bargain. But Burrows's criticism extends also to the artificiality of a legal interpretation of the doctrine in terms of compensation: in his view, restitution for wrongs would be a more 'natural' fashion to describe the award. But a description of the damages awarded in the cases such as *Wrotham Park* as restitutionary is incoherent with the structure of the law of obligations, for the victim brings an action to restore his violated property right to pristine condition, not to strip the defendant of ill-gotten gains.[42]

Still, the introduction of a fiction into the law of damages presents some risks, which have not been overlooked by the academic observers. For one, the claimant might obtain a sum which does not correspond to the market value; or the judges might impose a certain agreement to a claimant who would have never made any bargain at all.[43] Yet the courts are aware of these risks and ready to address any unfair outcome of a too strict application of the lost opportunity to bargain doctrine. Thus, in *Experience Hendrix v PPX Enterprises* Buckley J at first instance refused to apply the lost opportunity to bargain method because the 'evidence as a whole demonstrates that that would be a wholly fictional approach'.[44]

The normative value of the theory of lost opportunity to bargain will be considered in chapter eight.[45] Going back to proprietary wrongs, some cautious comments demonstrate that the courts realise that the quantification of the loss and the determination of the aim of the award is not always a straightforward matter. In *Strand Electric & Engineering*,[46] the claimant rented electrical gadgets to the defendant, who kept them after the contract had expired. As the claimant could not prove that he had suffered any loss, the court quantified the damage in the sum which the defendant would have had to pay had he hired the equipment for the entire period until the gadgets had been returned. The judges were uncomfortable with such quantification. Somervell LJ noted more than once that 'it is curious that there is no authority on the point'.[47] Nevertheless the majority stuck to a formulation of the measure of damages in accordance with the 'general rule' of the law of damages, that is compensation. Thus, it was pointed out that

---

[41]   *WWF v WWF* [2006] EWHC 184 (Ch) para 146 (Peter Smith J).
[42]   I shall provide ample justification for this statement in the theoretical part of this study in the analysis of pseudo-restitutionary damages.
[43]   *Edelman* 99-102.
[44]   *Experience Hendrix LLC v PPX Enterprises Inc* [2002] EWHC 1353 (QBD) para 50.
[45]   See ch 8, IV C ii and iii.
[46]   *Strand Electric & Engineering Co v Brisford Entertainments* [1952] 2 QB 246 (CA).
[47]   *Ibid* 250 (Somervell LJ).

only the loss of the claimant should be relevant for the quantification of the damage.[48] Yet, the majority left unanswered the question of how compensatory damages can make good a loss which could not be identified.[49]

This point was tackled by Denning LJ, who admitted that the claim 'resembles, therefore, an action for restitution rather than an action of tort'.[50] The significance of this statement was undermined by the observation that 'it is unnecessary to place it into any formal category'.[51] No reason was given for this conclusion, as the judge was probably well aware of the difficulties which any explicit mention of such category would have engendered. Denning LJ was right. The action was in tort, but it *resembled* an action in unjust enrichment – which is what probably Denning LJ meant by 'action for restitution'. The resemblance is due to the fact that the measure awarded was alternative to the normal measure of compensation. It was based upon the idea that the defendant made a wrongful profit using what belonged to the claimant, so that the claimant brought an action to claim back what was part of his right. This idea lies at the very core of the law of unjust enrichment and can be found in tort law when the courts award a measure of compensation for the violation of a proprietary interest.

B   German Law

There are no German cases in which the defendant has been compelled to give up a benefit originating from what in the English literature is called 'proprietary wrongs' through an action in delict.[52] German courts deal with such situations by applying the law of unjustified enrichment. An example will explain the interaction between these two areas of law.

C rents different models of cars. D hires a model 1 car from C for a period of one week for a holiday tour to Scotland. As he finds the surroundings most enjoyable, D extends his tour by one day and returns the vehicle after eight days. C requires the payment of the extra day, but D refuses. D's argument is that C has suffered no loss because he had several other model 1 cars which he did not rent on the day for which D extended his holiday.[53] As will be demonstrated, the judiciary does not allow for restitutionary relief for wrongs qua wrongs. The correct course of action is indicated in the first sentence of para 812 (1) BGB, which states: 'A person who through an act performed by another, or in any other manner, acquires something at the expense of the latter without any legal ground, is bound to return it to him.'[54]

---

[48]   *Ibid* 252 (Somervell LJ).
[49]   *Ibid* 256-257 (Romer LJ).
[50]   *Ibid* 255 (Denning LJ).
[51]   *Ibid.*
[52]   Whether this statement applies also to intellectual property wrongs will be considered later in this chapter.
[53]   My analysis is restricted to the violation of a proprietary interest. I shall examine the consequences of a breach of contract in the next chapter.
[54]   Translation by SL Goren, *The German Civil Code* (revd edn) (Littleton, Colorado 1994).

According to the majority view,[55] the 'act performed by another' triggers the so-called *Leistungskondiktion*, or performance-based claim, which is not relevant to an investigation of restitutionary damages. Much more interesting is the mention of a claim not based upon performance, that is a claim 'in any other manner', which German scholars call *Nichtleistungskondiktion*, or non-performance based claim. Beyond the requirement of the absence of a performance, the second element relevant for the *Nichtleistungskondiktion* is given by the term '*Etwas*', which is the 'something' whose acquisition by the defendant according to para 812 (1) BGB activates the restitutionary mechanism. This 'something' does not refer only to a pecuniary benefit which has been received by the defendant, such as money, or goods, or services:[56] The defendant is also enriched if he has saved expenses which he would otherwise have incurred, as shown by the following instance, known as the 'air travel case', or *Flugreisefall*.[57]

A minor succeeded in boarding a plane from Hamburg to New York without paying the fare. He was discovered only on arrival once it became clear that he did not have the necessary visa. Thus, the airline had to carry him back to Hamburg and subquently brought an action for the cost of the air return ticket. No delictual relief was sought – as the court itself pointed out with approval – because the claimant could not prove that it had suffered any relevant loss from the conduct of the defendant, for the aeroplane was not full and many seats were still available. Hence, no compensation could have been awarded because no damage was suffered. The claimant could only sue in unjustified enrichment, through a performance-based claim, to recover the value of the outbound flight, whereas restitution for the value of the return flight was granted under *negotiorum gestio*,[58] or necessitous intervention (paras 677-687 BGB). The judges affirmed that, even though an action in unjustified enrichment could be granted only when there was an increment in the defendant's patrimonial situation, this increment did not have to be positive, it being sufficient that the enriched had saved some necessary expenses.

Returning to the case of the car hired for eight days, the same reasoning can be applied to the claimant's proprietary action. The defendant has been enriched by not having paid to hire the car a further day. This enrichment is at the expense of the claimant, but not transferred through a performance by the claimant. Hence, C can recover from D what corresponds to the cost of hiring the car eight instead of seven days using a *Nichtleistungskondiktion* on the basis of para 812 (1) 2nd alternative BGB. Fearing an excessive expansion of the radius of application of the *Nichtleistungskondiktion*, judicial authority has developed many hindrances for the 'non-performance' impoverished who wants to claim in unjustified

---

[55]   *Cf* the seminal work by W Wilburg, *Die Lehre von der ungerechtfertigten Bereicherung nach österreichischem und deutschem Recht* (Graz, Leuschner und Lubensky 1934).

[56]   P Schlechtriem, *Schuldrecht Besonderer Teil* (6th edn) (Tübingen, Mohr 2003) para 724.

[57]   (1971) BGHZ 55 128. See the English translation in the internet: www.iuscomp.org/gla/index.html (15 June 2006).

[58]   This institution deals with cases in which someone is bound by acts done for his benefit by third parties even if he has not authorised these acts.

enrichment the gains made by third parties at his expense. Thus, even in some cases which theoretically would justify the action, the claim is barred on other grounds such as the non-codified principle of the subsidiarity of the *Nichtleis-tungskondiktion*.[59] As a result, the function of the *Nichtleistungskondiktion* has been utterly reduced in practice.[60]

The car-hire example offers the occasion for some reflection on the interaction between restitution for unjustified enrichment and restitutionary damages. In the context of the violation of property rights, the victim argues that his right has been affected, and thus his patrimonial value reduced, by the wrongful action of the defendant. The judicial response should address this situation by restoring the violated right to the pre-wrong situation. This can be done through a wrong-based claim or through an enrichment-based claim: both are triggered by a patrimonial loss of the victim. Thus, even a claim in unjustified enrichment can apply compensatory reasoning when the defendant has violated the proprietary interest of the claimant, that is an incident of his right to ownership. The *Flugreisefall* indicates that the German courts prefer to stick to a traditional measure of compensation – similar to the *Livingstone* formula in English law – leaving if possible any alternative quantification of the loss to the law of unjustified enrichment. In the *Flugreisefall*, the court held that no patrimonial loss had arisen to the claimant. Yet, some form of detriment must have been suffered by the claimant, which otherwise would have not been able to claim in unjustified enrichment.

My contention that restitution for unjustified[61] enrichment and restitution for wrongs do not normally overlap requires some support. Among all unjust enrichment claims, the *Nichtleistungskondiktion*, being independent of a transfer of wealth from the claimant to the defendant, provides the best conditions to illustrate my reasoning, as this example shows.[62] D is working as an estate agent for the housing society C. C would like to enlarge its business and requests D to purchase land on which C could build new houses. D is secretly in contact with the third party T and suggests that the latter purchases some land which D knows is up for sale. Once T has become the owner of the land, D will buy it at a much higher price on behalf of C. In return, D will receive from T a large bribe. When the plot is discovered, C claims the money paid to T and what D obtained as a bribe. A well-known judgment of the Privy Council[63] has held that this situation

---

[59] (1964) BGHZ 40 272, 278.

[60] Follow the debate on the *Nichtleistungskondiktion* in *Reuter and Martinek* 232-387.

[61] As already intimated, in my view 'unjust' and 'unjustified' enrichment claims have different structures. Yet, I shall use both terms as synonymous here, although I tend to use the second expression in the context of the German '*ungerechtfertigte Bereicherung*', which means literally 'unjustified enrichment'. See ch 1, n 19.

[62] This example is not related to proprietary wrongs. But it is useful to highlight the different roles played by the two legal institutions and to illustrate why only unjustified enrichment is helpful to the claimant in the proprietary context.

[63] *T Mahesan S/O Thambiah v Malaysia Government Officer's Co-op Housing Society* [1979] AC 374 (PC). This decision was confirmed as sound law in *Fyffes Group v Templeman* [2000] 2 Lloyd's Rep 643.

can give rise to a right of the victim to recover the bribe. The question is whether the same situation triggers a claim in unjustified enrichment under German law. The correct answer is arguably that it should not. From the outset, there had never been any valid obligation to pay the bribe. If D had not received the bribe, C would not have been entitled to it in his stead, with the effect that D never interrupted or diverted a transfer of wealth destined for the claimant. D's enrichment is, therefore, not at the claimant's expense. C has no possibility of securing the money obtained as bribe through the avenue of the *Nichtleistungs-skondiktion*. Reasoning *per absurdum*, even if all requirements of a non-performance-based claim in unjustified enrichment were met, in practice the claim would be barred by the concurrence of a performance-based claim, which the housing society C could bring against the party to which the impoverished has paid the money. It follows that in German private law restitution for wrongs has a different scope than the *Nichtleistungskondiktion*. Still, the latter offers some parameters to allow a prognosis on a possible reception of restitution for wrongs in German law. The judicial mistrust for the *Nichtleistungskondiktion* has already been highlighted. Given that the these non-performance claims are awarded only within strict boundaries, it is quite unlikely that the courts would be better disposed to accept a different institution which exposes the system to the same risks of widening the area of the subjects protected and of the awards obtainable in court. Thus, policy factors would probably play an important role in the rejection of any attempt to enlarge the categories just mentioned: where there is the danger of an excessive amount of claims, the judiciary tends to be very restrictive.

There is no indication that German law would apply restitution for wrongs to redress situations in which a proprietary wrong has been committed. The German approach is correct, given that the claimant brings an action to recover a loss related to his proprietary right. The proper avenues to restore the violated right to its integrity are either a compensatory claim in delict or a claim in unjustified enrichment. The comparison with Italian law comes here particularly useful, as the law of unjust enrichment has followed a partly different avenue.

C   Italian Law

Wrongful interference with property falls within the realm of unjust enrichment in Italian law. The normal cause of action for restitution has its roots in Art 2041 cc, which contains the general claim in unjust enrichment:

> Whoever has enriched himself without just cause at the expense of another shall, to the extent of the enrichment, indemnify the other for his correlative financial loss.[64]

The provision does not classify the interference as 'wrongful', but as 'unjust'. The adjective highlights the function of the action and the irrelevance of wrongful behaviour, which is an essential requirement for restitution for wrongs. The

---

[64]   M Beltramo G Longo and JH Merryman (trs), *The Italian Civil Code* (New York, Oceana 1969).

reference to injustice rather than wrongfulness, on the other hand, does not mean that the conduct itself becomes legal. In effect, conduct may be wrongful and give rise to delictual liability on the part of the wrongdoer. Yet, the unjust enrichment claim may be more convenient for particular reasons, for instance because the delictual claim is time-barred. Looking at the requisites of the action, it strikes that direct performance by the claimant to the defendant is not necessary. In fact, the provision in question does not depict a performance-based claim, as such a claim, which arises from an undue performance, is already provided by Art 2033 cc. The adjective 'general', which qualifies the claim in unjust enrichment, does not actually mean 'available under any circumstance'. Indeed, the subsequent Art 2042 cc explains that the action can be brought only subsidiarily, that is under the condition that no other claim can help the claimant.[65] 'General' stands for 'last resort available': if all else fails, and the court thinks it unjust to leave the claimant without redress, it can weigh the interests of the parties on an equitable basis and grant an action ex Art 2041 cc. This allows the claimant to be indemnified up to a level which lies between his own impoverishment and the enrichment of the defendant.[66]

For a better understanding of Italian law on this point, let us revert to the example which I introduced above to test the relationship between the German *Nichteistungskondiktion* and restitution for wrongs: the defendant hires a car from the claimant for a period of seven days but does not return it until the eighth day. D's argument in refusing to pay for the extra day is that the claimant has suffered no loss from his conduct. The analysis of German law has revealed that that jurisdiction uses a *condictio*-like structure to compel the payment of the eighth day's rent to the claimant. German law applies the following reasoning: 'there is no legal cause which sustains the transfer of wealth to the defendant. What is more, the wealth transferred ought to belong to the claimant'. On this basis, action is granted. The *Codice civile* builds the general enrichment claim upon a different principle, although both legal orders ultimately produce similar results. The statutory rules convey to the claimant this message: 'you must try to find your satisfaction through another claim and ought not to count on Art 2041 cc. Yet, if you really do not have anything else at your disposal, then you will be allowed an equitable response, because otherwise leaving the situation as it is would produce greater injustice'. It does not matter whether the legal cause for the transfer is valid or not. What is important is that without such response there would be an unjust enrichment of one party at the expense of the other.

Expanding on the example of the hired car, it is possible to draw some general conclusions on the measure of damages. Let us assume that the basic rule on compensation contained in Art 1223 cc[67] does not have any exceptions or

---

[65]   *Cf* B Nicholas, 'Unjust Enrichment and Subsidiarity' in F Santoro Passarelli and M Lupoi (eds), *Scintillae iuris: Studi in memoria di Gino Gorla* (Milano, Giuffrè 1994) vol III 2037-2045.

[66]   For further details, see ch 2, I C ii.

[67]   Art 2056 cc, which determines the measure of damages in the law of delict, refers to the law of contract, and especially to Art 1223 cc This norm provides that 'the measure of damages arising from

alternatives.[68] This assumption does not affect the correctness of the analysis; it only simplifies it. The claimant most likely would not use a delictual avenue because he would not be able to prove any compensable loss apart from trivial expenses. In theory, a delictual claim would be available to the victim. But, as in German law, in practice the courts would reject the claim, leaving the door open only to a claim in unjust enrichment. In particular, the victim would not be able to claim for restitution of an undue payment, as none of the parties has received any payment at all. This leads to the conclusion that, without the claim of Art 2041 cc, no other action would be available to the impoverished. This cannot be a fair result; the general enrichment claim must intervene. The requirements of the cause of action are met: D is enriched to the amount of one day's free car travel; C has not received his due for the hiring of the car. Furthermore, there is a causal link between the two events, for the car used by D belongs to C, who has an interest in renting it for money. Finally, it would be contrary to justice if D were able to avoid the payment of the extra day for which he had the car at his disposal merely on the basis of a technical argument. Thus, it is probable that the court would grant a claim in unjust enrichment to the impoverished.

Although the *Nichtleistungskondiktion* and the general enrichment claim have their roots in different legal principles, some of the considerations previously formulated on the former also apply to the latter. Once again, cases such as *Mahesan v Malaysia Government Officer*[69] demonstrate that restitution for wrongs has a different scope of application than a corresponding non-delictual claim such as the one set out in Art 2041 cc. Indeed, on the facts of the *Mahesan* case, no claim would have lain under unjust enrichment in Italian law. The general enrichment claim can hardly be used to seize the bribe obtained by the defendant. Although the defendant has been enriched, the payment of a bribe has not impoverished the claimant, for the sum paid to the defendant by the third party was never meant to reach the claimant. Thus, C cannot be granted any claim in restitution because D has not been enriched at his expense, and this holds true even if the transfer of money turns out to have been part of some plot which was detrimental to the claimant. Yet, it cannot be excluded that, in practice, the court might grant restitution on the basis of policy considerations. This is due to the particular function of the general enrichment claim, which has become an extremely flexible instrument to restore justice. In this respect, it is different from the *Nichtleistungskondiktion*. The German claim targets a mis-placement of wealth, that is it enables a transfer of wealth to the impoverished because the enriched has no legal ground to keep it. In contrast, the Italian

---

non-performance or delay shall include he loss sustained by the creditor and the lost profits insofar as they are a direct and immediate consequence of the non-performance or delay' (Beltramo et al (n 64). See ch 2, n 52 and text thereof.

[68]   In effect, Art 1223 cc does have an important exception in Art 1226 cc, which will be examined later on. This exception allows the courts to exert technical discretion in assessing damages which cannot be proved precisely.

[69]   *T Mahesan S/O Thambiah* (n 63).

general enrichment claim is not granted following the absence of a legal ground of the transfer. It mainly seeks to re-establish a certain balance according to equitable principles.

Beyond non-delictual claims, the fact that the basic rule of damages in contract and delict, that is Art 1223 cc, refers only to a compensatory model does not mean that any other model should be automatically rejected. The introduction of such an instrument as the general enrichment action, which can theoretically pave the way to a large amount of claims,[70] suggests a positive disposition of the law towards restitutionary claims in general, which are not viewed with real suspicion, but rather with cautious interest. Such caution emerges within the judiciary against excessively broad claims in restitution, as the decisions on the general enrichment claim demonstrate. The question is now whether there is any room and a real necessity to develop a restitutionary remedy even in the law of delict. The legal framework indicates that a positive answer should be preferred. Art 2041 cc allows a claim 'to the extent of the enrichment', but not beyond the claimant's 'correlative financial loss', that is the object of the action must lie between the enrichment of the defendant and the impoverishment of the claimant. Even if the term 'impoverishment' were stretched beyond the mere pecuniary loss, the assessment of the indemnity requires an evaluation of the situation of both parties, whereas restitution for wrongs ignores the victim and concentrates exclusively upon the wrongdoer. This difference between the two responses is accentuated by the fact that under 'impoverishment' judiciary and scholars understand a pecuniary loss of the victim: the position of the wrongdoer is in this context irrelevant.[71] Therefore, the introduction of a restitutionary award triggered by a wrongful behaviour would close a loophole rather than furnishing an alternative response.

As there seems to be enough room for restitution for wrongs within the Italian system, it has to be determined whether, in the present legal context, it is possible to introduce this legal response into the system without changing the governing legislation. Some analyses indicate that it should be feasible, even though their authors develop their views with reference to non-compensatory damages in general, rather than specifically for restitution for wrongs. These approaches use Art 1226 cc as their starting point. This provision states: 'If the loss cannot be determined precisely, the judge will quantify damages on an equitable basis'. Art 1226 cc is one of the three provisions expressly referred to by Art 2056 cc, which determines the measure of delictual damages. According to the traditional view,[72] the 'equity' mentioned by Art 1226 cc is nothing but the technical discretion of the courts. The judges, therefore, may exercise their discretion only once a loss has been proved, but it cannot be proved to its precise amount. This doctrine interprets Art 1226 cc as granting to the courts limited discretion when it is

---

[70] *Cf* Cassazione, 10 February 1993 No 1686 [1993] *Giustizia civile* I 1836.

[71] F Astone, *L'arricchimento senza causa* (Milano, Giuffrè 1999) 72.

[72] CM Bianca, 'Dell'inadempimento delle obbligazioni' in *Commentario del codice civile a cura di A Scialoja e G Branca* (2nd edn) (Bologna/Roma, Zanichelli 1979) 388-394.

particularly difficult to assess damages, but it does not question the instruments at the court's disposal, which remain the same as for every other head of damages. Recently this traditional approach has been challenged by a new interpretation of Art 1226 cc which construes the provision as allowing the judges to circumvent the 'general rule' of compensation and grant non-compensatory damages.[73] Even though this later view does not mention restitution, it does refer to the possibility that the courts also take the enrichment of the wrongdoer into consideration, thus paving the way to damages linked exclusively to that enrichment. Therefore, even if there is no plain recognition of restitution for wrongs yet, there is at least a delictual theory which furnishes arguments in support of such recognition. Indeed, there are signals from the judiciary[74] which show that a certain relationship between delict and enrichment has already been established, albeit not with reference to proprietary wrongs.

No matter how tempting it might appear to adhere to the more recent theory which proposes to use Art 1226 cc as an avenue to introduce non-compensatory damages, this explanation must be rejected because it takes little notice of the proper function of this norm. As has been pointed out by the traditional view, Art 1226 cc contains no indication of the response which ought to be granted by the courts. On the contrary, it presupposes that a decision on damages has already been taken. It is a two-tier mechanism: the judges first choose what they consider the appropriate legal response, for instance compensation or punishment. In a second step, they then have to decide how to assess damages in relation to the criteria chosen. Therefore, Art 1226 cc intervenes after the courts have decided which kind of damages they will allow. Moreover, it only comes into play if the victim cannot prove the exact amount of his loss. Should any difficulty arise, the judges will apply their technical discretion according to Art 1226 cc The conclusion must be that this provision does not provide any support to the theory of restitution for wrongs. It only supplies a higher degree of flexibility to the judges once they have decided which head of damages is relevant to a given case.

Within the general framework of delict and unjust enrichment, the question of the room which restitution for wrongs might potentially occupy in the structure of Italian law remains open. On the one hand, the presence of a general enrichment claim might entice the false conclusion that there is less need for it given that the system already provides non-delictual responses which cover a similar area. I have tried to show that such reasoning is incorrect, for restitution for wrongs touches upon a benefit which is beyond the reach of any claim in unjust enrichment. On the other hand, some academic writing[75] has suggested an enlargement of the law of damages to include non-compensatory claims. Even though this attempt does not seem to rest on a sufficiently solid basis, it

---

[73] Monateri, *Responsabilità* 337.
[74] Cassazione, 12 April 1995 No 4192 [1995] Foro italiano I 1716. This decision does not concern proprietary wrongs and will be examined under the category 'other wrongs'.
[75] Monateri, *Responsabilità* 337.

nevertheless proves that Italian lawyers are becoming more benign towards non-compensatory damages. If this new doctrinal vein is further explored, it seems possible that in a not-too-distant future the topic of restitution for wrongs will no longer be alien to the Italian courts. This is all the more true if one considers that in Italy scholars exert a considerable influence upon the judiciary. The category 'proprietary wrongs' does not and cannot contain instances of restitution for wrongs. However, it shows a tendency in favour of non-compensatory remedies which could pave the way to a restitutionary approach.

III   Intellectual Property Wrongs

The analysis of intellectual property wrongs is particularly useful to highlight the options available to a court in the quantification of compensatory damages, given that in this area the judiciary applies more than one method of assessment in all legal systems examined. Owing to the peculiarity of intellectual property rights, the victim of the wrong can seek the normal measure of compensation but also other measures which tackle the loss from different perspectives. These measures compel the wrongdoer to give back his benefit to the victim, but this does not mean that they have restitutionary nature. The victim has been deprived of a benefit which corresponds to the wrongdoer's gain: the level of the loss might be determined by the defendant's benefit, but the victim acts because the victim has suffered a loss, not because the wrongdoer has obtained a gain, as is confirmed by the restorative character of the claim. This is an essential difference between compensatory and restitutionary damages. On the basis of this difference, I conclude that the damages awarded as an alternative form of compensation are an instance of what I call 'pseudo-restitutionary damages': they might appear to be restitutionary, because they tackle the benefit of the wrongdoer. But this benefit is given *back* to the victim who brings a claim for compensation of his loss.

A   English Law

The legal response granted to the victim of an intellectual property wrong aims to compel the tortfeasor to give up the benefit which has been obtained through the perpetration of such a wrong whenever this measure of damages can benefit the victim more than the traditional measure of compensation of the loss.[76] The central role of the wrongdoer's gain in the determination of the measure of damages is undisputed. What I am going to question in this section is a definition of this mechanism as an instance of restitution for wrongs. The obligation which is imposed on the defendant is usually called an 'account of profits'. Andrew

---

[76]   On the proper measure of damages following the violation of an intellectual property right see *General Tire v Firestone* [1975] 1 WLR 819 (HL).

Burrows defines an account of profits as the remedy 'by which the defendant is required to draw up an account of, and then to pay the amount of, the net profits it has acquired by particular wrongful conduct.'[77] As will be shown, numerous statutory provisions entitle the victim of a violation of intellectual property rights to an account of profits. The account of profits is usually regarded as a right resulting from an infringement, and always as a right which is granted alternatively to damages. In the context of intellectual property wrongs, the loss of the claimant gives rise to damages; the benefit of the defendant triggers an account of profits. With regards to passing off, Slade J observed that

> [t]he purpose of ordering an account of profits in favour of a successful plaintiff in a passing off case is not to inflict punishment on the defendant. It is to prevent an unjust enrichment of the defendant by compelling him to surrender those profits.[78]

Despite the terminology used by the judge, this passage implies that the mechanism at work is compensatory, not restitutionary. The reference to unjust enrichment is particularly revealing. The law of unjust enrichment requires that the claimant has been unjustly deprived of 'something'[79] which has been obtained by the defendant, so that the former seeks to oblige the latter to return this something to him. In *My Kinda Town v Soll*, the claimant founded its claim on the misappropriation of the name of its chain of restaurants by the defendant. The defendant's benefit, therefore, followed from the misappropriation of the name – 'something' which belonged to the claimant. Through the action, the claimant reasserted its right. The defendant's benefit was attributable to the fact that some customers went to the defendant's restaurant believing they were going to the claimant's restaurant. The action compensated the claimant for the deprivation of an element included in its property right.

   The Law Commission recommends an abandonment of the label 'account of profits' in favour of the compendious term 'restitutionary damages'.[80] The general term is considered to be more useful than a more specific definition, as it would reduce confusion. Yet, its adoption is likely to achieve the opposite result, given that the 'account of profits' triggered by the violation of an intellectual property right is not an instance of restitution for wrongs.[81] As there are indeed cases in which a restitutionary award for wrongs – in the context of breach of contract –

---

[77]   Burrows (n 38) 384.
[78]   *My Kinda Town Ltd v Soll* [1982] 8 FSR 147, 156 (Slade J). The validity of the passage is not affected by the fact that, strictly speaking, passing off is a common law tort rather than a statutory intellectual property wrong; *cf Associated Newspapers v Insert Media Ltd* [1990] 1 WLR 900.
[79]   Para 812 BGB mentions as object of the claim in unjustified enrichment a '*Etwas*', that is a 'something'. This is a neutral description which enabled the draftsmen to circumvent a definition of what has been subtracted. *cf* ch 1, text after n 42.
[80]   Law Commission (n 18) recommendation 14.
[81]   Edelman's assumption that an account for profits awarded following the violation of an intellectual property right is a restitutionary response for wrongs is clearly incompatible with my approach. See *Edelman* 233-241. McInnes' intuition that the award triggered by the violation of property rights is compensatory would be consistent with my view. Yet, McInnes does not go as far as to extend his theory to intellectual property wrongs. See McInnes (n 36).

has been classified by the judiciary as an accounts of profits,[82] the term 'account of profits' in the judicial vocabulary does refer also but not only to restitutionary damages. As McInnes argues, '[t]here is a tendency to assume that an account must be directed toward some form of gain-based liability … Very often, however, an account is a prelude to compensatory relief.'[83] It is questionable whether it is useful to adopt a label which comprises both compensatory and restitutionary damages, especially given that, as McGregor remarks, an account of profits would not overlap completely with restitution for wrongs.[84]

The proposal of the Law Commission has not yet had any concrete impact on the statutes, where damages and accounts of profits are mentioned separately and therefore treated as conceptually different categories. S 61 (1) of the Patent Act 1977 lists, among the claims which can be raised within proceedings for infringement of patent, both damages in respect of the infringement and an account of the profits derived by the wrongdoers from the infringement. Again, s 96 (2) of the Copyright, Designs and Patents Act 1988 allows relief in an action for infringement of copyright, inter alia, by way of damages and of an account of profits. Moreover, in cases of infringement of design rights, damages and accounts of profits are also available. In this short list of statutory examples, s 14 (2) Trade Marks Act 1994 deserves mention. It allows a claim for damages and provides that 'accounts or otherwise [are] available … as [are] available in respect of the infringement of any other property right'. Sometimes, there are differences in the accessibility of both responses, but such differences are not relevant as regards the nature of those heads of damages. S 97 CDPA 1988, for instance, does not permit an award of damages when the defendant has acted in good faith.

An interesting question concerns the subject-matter of an account of profits. It seems to be undisputed that the defendant can be compelled to give up all of the benefits realised from the wrong which turn out to be a positive increment of his assets.[85] The question is whether an account of profits also includes the expenses saved through the commission of a wrong. The general position is stated by Millett J. in the *Potton* case: 'in principle I do not see why not'.[86] Indeed, there is no evident reason to bar a recovery of the 'unrealised profits' as well. A restriction to positive increments of the assets would be contrary to justice and common sense. Moreover, it would exclude from the scope of the action many situations which potentially engender enrichment in consequence of the defendant's behaviour. If restitution of the expenses saved lie outside the definition of enrichment, in numerous cases the victim of the wrong would be left without a remedy, and the same can be said for any claimant who has been impoverished by a non-wrongful enrichment of the defendant. Even if restitution for unjust enrichment and an account of profits in the context of intellectual property wrongs

---

[82] *Cf Blake* (n 4).

[83] M McInnes 'Account of Profits for Common Law Wrongs' in S Degeling and J Edelman, *Equity In Commercial Law* (Sydney, Thomson 2005) 407–8.

[84] *McGregor* para 12-006.

[85] *Ex multis, Rickless v United Artists Corp* [1988] QB 40 (CA).

[86] *Potton Ltd v Yorkclose Ltd* [1990] FSR 11, 15.

belong to two different categories and are characterised by different causes of action, from a comparative analysis of the two institutions emerges a concept of benefit which presents the same features: it must affect valuable assets and can be either positive or negative.[87]

Both judicial authority[88] and the statutes[89] tend not to admit compensatory damages alongside an account of profit. Stephen Watterson explains this situation with the need to avoid an excessive remedial cumulation. In his view, different remedies should be available only up to the minimum necessary to achieve their aims.[90] This limit is reached when 'one remedy, immediately directed at one aim, may indirectly realize the aims of the other.'[91] This approach is problematic. For one, it does not allow an a priori identification of the available awards, given that they can be identified only once it is decided which award is going to have the priority so that the other awards can be adjusted accordingly. A further, serious difficulty is related to the supposed overlapping of aims. In Watterson's view, a legal response can realise the aims of another legal response. This statement does not seem compatible with the structure of the law of obligations. According to the 'event-based classification', which describes the structure of the law of obligations, each legal response can realise one, and only one, aim. Responses with multiple aims would be useless because they do not allow a proper categorisation. Watterson seems to accept implicitly the relationship 'one response/one aim' when he states that further aims can be realised only indirectly. But the outcome is the same: following the lines of his reasoning, one would have to conclude that, say, compensatory damages would have compensation as their primary aim but might have also various other collateral aims. If this were the case, one single response would be enough to cover all aims, which again would hinder a categorisation and therefore a proper application of the response. Even Watterson's assertion that full compensation and full restitution 'may only be defensible in terms of an additional, punitive aim'[92] is questionable. Legal responses are not like colours. One cannot mix green and yellow to obtain blue. Two responses cannot be blended to create a new one. If full compensation is added to full restitution, the claimant will be able to recover his loss and to strip the defendant of his 'loss-independent' gain. To realise punishment, the award must be punitive.

---

[87]   A Burrows, *Remedies for Tort and Breach of Contract* (3rd edn) (Oxford, OUP 2004) 373.
[88]   *My Kinda Town* (n 77) 148. Among the older authorities see *Mawman v Tegg* (1826) 2 Russ 385; 38 ER 380.
[89]   *Cf* Patent Act 1977 s 61(2).
[90]   S Watterson, 'An Account of Profits or Damages? The History of Orthodoxy' in (2004) 24 *OJLS* 471-494, 473.
[91]   *Ibid.*
[92]   *Ibid* 486.

B   German Law

A company produces mechanical music players in which a rolling tape plays different songs. One of those songs happens to become a success, and its author, until that moment unknown to the audience, achieves great popularity. The problem is that the company has never asked the composer the authorisation which would have been necessary for the reproduction of his music. The author claims in delict for the infringement of his copyright. This is an outline of the facts in the *Ariston* case.[93] The then Supreme Court, the *Reichsgericht* (RG), established for the first time the judicial position on secondary rights triggered by intellectual property wrongs which is still considered to be good law. According to the court, the violation of such rights opens three avenues to the victim. First, the claimant can seek compensation for the patrimonial loss (*Schadensersatz*) which he has suffered from the wrong. Second, if the claimant thinks that it would be more convenient, he can claim for the amount of money which the defendant would reasonably have paid to acquire the rights to publication – a figure similar to the common law doctrine of the lost opportunity to bargain. Third, he can also compel the defendant to give up all of the benefits which originate in the usage of a protected good without authorisation. This last avenue is equivalent to the English account of profits. The *Ariston* case is interesting not only because it is the first decision on the point, but also because it was evident that the claimant had not suffered any disadvantage from the wrongdoing. On the contrary, the propagation of his music through the mechanical players gave him a fame which he probably would not have achieved otherwise.[94] The commission of the wrong had positively affected the wealth of the claimant. The *Differenzhypothese*, according to which the damage consists of the difference between the real situation in which the claimant stands and the situation in which he would have stood had the damaging events never taken place,[95] was of no help to the claimant,[96] for the wrong had not caused any damage which could have been made good by applying the formula of compensation contained in para 249 BGB.

Since the *Ariston* case the situation has hardly changed. The claimant who sues in delict law can still choose among three possibilities how to proceed against the wrongdoer in intellectual property cases.[97] Accordingly, the three-fold choice has been granted to the claimant in the case of infringement of patent,[98] design[99] or trade mark.[100] For copyright violations, para 97 (1) UrhG (Copyright Act)

---

[93] (1895) RGZ 35 63 (*Ariston* case).
[94] *Ibid* 69.
[95] On the *Differenzhypothese* see ch 2, n 35 and text thereof.
[96] HD Assmann, 'Schadensersatz in mehrfacher Höhe des Schadens' [1985] *Betriebs-Berater* 15-25, 17.
[97] *Ex multis* (1993) BGHZ 119 20; BGH [1993] *Neue Juristische Wochenschrift* 1989.
[98] (1980) BGHZ 77 17.
[99] (1977) BGHZ 68 90.
[100] (1966) BGHZ 44 372.

provides that the victim can claim for an account of profits instead of the standard measure of compensatory damages. Similar rules can be found in other statutes.[101] Although judicial intervention has shaped this field of law, there is little or no mention in judicial decisions of the nature of the award which is granted. The courts barely devote any attention to the legal analysis of the options open to the claimant beyond the more traditional measure of compensation because the judiciary treats both the fictional agreement and the account of profits simply as two normal methods of measuring damages.[102] The main explanation provided by the courts is that the peculiarity of the methods of quantification is a consequence of the peculiarity of intellectual property rights themselves. These rights can easily be violated and thus require particular instruments to integrate the compensatory rules.[103]

The aim realised by the remedies awarded on the rule developed in the *Ariston* case indicates that German law uses different measures of compensation, which are compatible as long as they concern different aspects of the same loss.[104] This is explicitly recognised by the judiciary, which points out that the victim has indeed a choice between various quantifications of the loss (*Schadensberechnung*), but the legal basis of the claim is the same in all cases.[105] It follows that the 'general rule' of para 249 BGB does not apply in all circumstances. One could define these situations as mere exceptions,[106] but in the face of such cases the 'general rule' seems to be a little less general. What is more, the scope of these so-called exceptions is rather wide. The vagueness which characterises the judicial analysis of the nature of the account of profits provides further information. Both the account of profits and the fictional agreement do not fit into any of the recognised categories of the law of damages. A very general description in terms of 'customary law', functional to the integration of the usual remedies, as the courts seem to prefer, does not explain the nature of such damages. The lack of any apparent interest on the part of the judiciary for a coherent legal explanation is a sign that the courts are not comfortable with such institutions. Although the judges introduce novel compensatory measures in practice, they prefer not to admit it explicitly in the face of a long tradition which sees the traditional measure of compensation fixed in para 249 BGB as the sole aim of damages.

A clear awareness of the judicial uncertainties can be spotted in the academic writings. Instead of trying to find a legal justification for the responses which use an alternative measure of compensation within the law of delict, scholars

---

[101]   See for instance para 14a I 2 GeschmMG (Design Act).
[102]   (1972) BGHZ 57 116, 118.
[103]   *Ibid* 119.
[104]   BGH [1980] *Neue Juristische Wochenschrift* 2522 (*Tolbutamid* case)
[105]   Thus, expressly, (1993) BGHZ 119, 20, 23 (*Tchibo/Rolex II* case). See also MünchKomm/ Oetker, '§ 252' para 56: '*ist . . . der Aussage des BGH zuzustimmen, dass es sich um verschiedene Liquidationsformen eines einheitlichen Schadensersatzanspruches und nicht um verschiedene Ansprüche mit unterschiedlichen Rechtsgrundlagen handelt.*'
[106]   Thus H Lange, *Schadensersatz* Vol I (2nd edn) (Tübingen, Mohr 1990) 9.

normally deny that the account of profits and the fictional agreement[107] belong to the law of damages.[108] They propose a different interpretation, in which they construe the account of profits as an example of *Nichtleistungskondiktion*, that is the enrichment claim triggered by a transfer of wealth not based upon a performance.[109] The judiciary has not followed this construction. From the perspective of my analysis, a definition of the award in terms of the law of unjustified enrichment reinforces, rather than rejects, the idea of a compensatory nature of the awards at issue: unjustified enrichment aims to reintegrate a violated right and from this viewpoint is akin to compensation.

A second line of scholarly attack is pursued by observing that the claims triggered by the infringements of intellectual property rights are *der Sache nach*, or as a matter of fact, nothing but examples of *negotiorum gestio*, or necessitous intervention. Such position is based upon a purported similarity with the cause of action in para 687 (2) BGB, which states:

> If a person treats the matter of another as his own, although knowing that he is not entitled to do so, the principal may enforce the claims based on §§ 677, 678, 681, 682. If he does enforce them, he is liable to the manager as provided for in § 684 sent 1.[110]

Paras 677, 678, 681, and 682 BGB describe the position of the manager in the *negotiorum gestio*. This analogical construction is coherent with the *littera legis* and offers a solution which is more solid than the vague explanation provided by the judiciary.[111] But, once again, the manager acts because he has suffered a patrimonial loss, and not because the defendant has been enriched. Thus, even necessitous intervention applies compensatory reasoning. Despite the divergences, the judicial and the academic views can be reconciled in so far as both affirm that the delictual avenue does not preclude the right to claim in unjustified enrichment whenever it is possible. The debate between the judiciary and scholars is still going on. The different perspectives share a certain discomfort when dealing with delictual rights arising from infringements of intellectual property rights. 'Exceptions', 'non-delictual claims' are some of the expressions used in this context.[112] This uncertainty follows from the fact that both judiciary and scholars alike accept as a starting point the doctrine according to which the 'general rule' in delict law is compensation as established by the *Differenzhypothese*. Compensation is regarded as 'the' function of the law of delict.[113] It appears that such definitions may be problematic not only for a development of restitution for wrongs, but also for a proper understanding of less common forms of compensation. In this sense, the investigation of intellectual property wrongs

---

[107] On the hypothetical license fees as a delictual measure of damages see BGH [1982] *Neue Juristische Wochenschrift* 1151 (*Schadensersatzlizenz im Wege der Lizenzanalogie*).

[108] MünchKomm/Oetker, '§ 252' para 55; Staudinger/Schiemann, '§ 249' para 201.

[109] See above, II B, in this chapter.

[110] SL Goren (tr) (n 54).

[111] MünchKomm/Oetker, '§ 252' para 55.

[112] Staudinger/Schiemann, '§ 249' para 201.

[113] See F Bydlinski, *System und Prinzipien des Privatrechts* (Wien, Springer 1996) 185-189.

furnishes a good example of the difficulties faced by non-traditional measures of damages in those delictual systems which are characterised by a strongly theoretical approach founded upon a strict preference for a compensatory response on the model of the *Differenzhypothese*. As the fictional agreement and the account of profits in the analysis of English law,[114] the German institutions offer a different measure of quantification of the loss; they are not forms alternative to compensation based upon the benefit accrued to the defendant. Those non-traditional measures of damages are able to creep in even in civilian systems, which prove to be flexible enough to integrate them into the pre-existing structure. It appears that no change of statutory rules will be required. Rather, it is the theoretical approach which needs to take due account of the existence of other measures of damages, including restitution for wrongs.

C   Italian Law

As far as intellectual property wrongs are concerned, the Italian legal system remains anchored mainly to a traditional compensatory model, although the so-called moral damages, which are non-pecuniary damages sometimes awarded in this context, may mitigate this rigid approach. No statutory regime intervenes to allow restitution of the benefit gained through the wrong; neither does judicial authority step in to fill the statutory loophole recognising the right of the victim to claim the enrichment of the wrongdoer *ex delicto*. The judiciary refuses even to admit that the breach of design rights is to be seen as triggering a loss *in re ipsa*, which would discharge the victim of the burden of proving the concrete existence of any damage.[115] Apparently, therefore, in the case of the violation of an intellectual property right the wrongdoer can partially escape liability, being able to keep the benefit obtained from the wrong. A legal system which is so favourable to the wrongdoer is hardly imaginable. Indeed, the impression of apparent friendliness of the law towards defendants in intellectual property cases is dispelled if the modus operandi of the legal system as a whole is observed. Other instruments step in to curb the benefit accruing to the defendant so that the victim is not fully deprived of protection.

   The use of the general enrichment claim of Art 2041 cc[116] in cases of unfair competition and violation of intellectual property rights is widely accepted.[117] Such claim allows a parallel with the German *Nichtleistungskondiktion*. As shown by the *Ariston* case, the German judiciary favours a delictual avenue, offering to the victim of an intellectual property wrong different measures to quantify the loss. German scholars are generally opposed to this judicial doctrine, favouring the adoption of the non-delictual *Nichtleistungskondiktion*. In Italy, the judiciary,

---

[114]   See previous section.
[115]   Cassazione, 21 October 1988 No 5716 [1989] Foro italiano I 764.
[116]   See above in this chapter, n 64 and text thereof.
[117]   *Cf* G Ghidini, *Della concorrenza sleale*, in P Schlesinger (ed), *Il codice civile – Commentario* (Milano, Giuffrè 1994) 430-431.

as will be seen shortly, supports a model akin to the English pattern of an account of profits, albeit through the less conventional avenue of non-pecuniary damages. On the other hand, academic analyses seem more attracted by a solution involving a stricter law of damages, more in line with the 'general rule', accompanied by a restitutionary claim in unjust enrichment. The weakness of this approach relates to the limited scope of application of the action ex Art 2041 cc: the victim may only claim restitution up to the amount of his own loss, so that the wrongdoer can retain the part of the benefit which exceeds the loss of the claimant. A more effective remedy, commonly used by the courts, is a response in terms of 'moral damages', which are a non-pecuniary head of damages. The content of these moral damages is stretched to cover the enrichment derived from the wrong. *In concreto*, moral damages will concern the part of the loss which cannot be made good through pecuniary damages up to the point at which the courts think that they have reached fair compensation according to the rules of technical discretion laid down by Art 1226 cc for the assessment of damages. The courts do not deny that moral damages have a compensatory function. Nevertheless, they admit that the quantification of damages must consider also the 'injurious intensity' of the wrong, of which the enrichment of the wrongdoer is expressly held out to be a good example.[118] Yet, moral damages are of limited avail as substitutes for non-compensatory responses. The main obstacle to this kind of approach is in Art 2059 cc, according to which '[n]on-pecuniary damages may be awarded only in the cases provided for by the law', which mainly involve criminal liability. Hence, where the wrongdoer has not committed any criminal offence, the victim cannot be awarded moral damages. Moreover, using moral damages to alter the measure of compensation is deceptive, because it could justify the impression that the courts are only allowing the traditional measure of compensation, whereas in reality they are quantifying the loss using a different criterion. Probably aware of these difficulties, the Cassation Court explored new territory in the 1980s. A seminal case[119] on the violation of copyright shows a judicial tendency to widen the scope of application of, and thus the role played by, Art 1226 cc In effect, a power/duty has been conferred upon the courts to evaluate the consequences of the wrong upon both parties. Through the conferment of this power, the judges have been given the possibility of including in their assessment of damages even the benefit which the wrongdoer has derived from the wrong. This new judicial doctrine also has been applied by some lower courts,[120] but still represents the exception rather than the rule. This is a clear attempt to enlarge the limits of the 'general rule' of compensation. Nonetheless, some elements militate against an assertion that this compensatory model has developed into a restitutionary claim. First, judicial reasoning is still mainly based upon the traditional compensatory principle. Even in the case of violation of intellectual property rights, where other legal systems accept a deviation from the

---

[118]   Appello Milano, 23 December 1986 [1987] Repertorio Foro italiano Danni civili No 185.
[119]   Cassazione, 24 October 1983 No 6251 [1983] Repertorio Foro italiano Danni civili No 140.
[120]   Eg Tribunale Milano, 20 June 1988 [1988] Diritto dell'Informazione e dell'Informatica 878.

'general rule', the Italian judiciary sticks to a narrow approach. It is up to the victim to seize the benefit obtained by the wrongdoer through the election of another restitutionary response, for instance by using the general enrichment claim of Art 2041 cc. A further relevant consideration concerns the role played by restitutionary thinking within the assessment of damages. The enrichment of the wrongdoer is not, in itself, a sufficient factor for granting a delictual claim. The judiciary requires a loss suffered by the victim in the sense of a diminution of his wealth. Once this loss is proved, it will be open to the courts to evaluate damages in a way which also takes into account the benefit gained by the defendant. However, this benefit is not targeted by an autonomous head of damages. Although the chosen way might be questionable, the result is correct: like German law, Italian law correctly identifies the issues raised by an intellectual property wrong as mainly compensatory. No attempt is made to create a restitutionary claim for wrongs because there is no need for it.

On the other hand, the rejection of a restitutionary model for wrongs does not mean that the system is still relying upon a purely compensatory model. The mixture of compensatory and punitive elements in the claim in delict which is triggered by the perpetration of intellectual property wrongs suggests that the response could be classified as exemplary damages. In fact, the victim often obtains more than his pecuniary loss, so that the *Differenzhypothese* seldom applies. The punitive purpose fits into the preventive function which the law of delict must exercise within the delicate field of intellectual property rights – which, as the German judiciary[121] has pointed out, are extremely easy to violate – where the potential benefits of such violations are huge, and the potential risks are low. It is therefore important to convey the message that the violation of such rights can trigger harsh consequences for the wrongdoer. This is done mainly through the application of moral damages. In this framework, these damages look like an empty box which can be conveniently filled by the judiciary. What can be excluded, however, is that the remedy awarded has any restitutionary value in the sense of restitution for wrongs. As in German law, the accessibility of the unjust enrichment claim flags the 'giving back' function of the response, which implies a quantification of the award on the basis of a loss.

---

[121] (1972) BGHZ 57 116, 119.

4

Comparative Analysis: Breach of Contract

O F THE FOUR categories in which the analysis of restitution for wrongs has been divided, 'breach of contract' presents the greatest challenge to the comparatist. The classification of breach of contract as a wrong is disputed in English law.[1] Even more problematic is the correct position of the topic at issue in civilian jurisdictions. Civil law does not use a concept of a wrong, and breach of contract cannot be put in the category of 'delict'. The definition of 'wrong' as a breach of duty, on which the investigation is based, becomes, therefore, particularly useful in the present context.

I English Law

The Law Commission has observed that 'there is no tradition of awarding restitution for breach of contract'.[2] Lord Steyn implicitly agreed with this statement in a landmark decision, the *Blake* case. There, his Lordship said that there is 'virtually no support for a general action for disgorgement of profits made by a contract breaker by reason of his breach'.[3] Yet, as the House of Lords remarked in the decision in point, this does not mean that restitution for wrongs cannot be an exceptional remedy, available at the court's discretion, whenever 'a just response to a breach of contract so requires'.[4]

Notwithstanding the great relevance of the ruling, the *Blake* case cannot be the starting point of the examination. This decision introduces only an exception, albeit an important one, to the general rule, which establishes that breach of contract does not trigger restitutionary awards, although some commentators[5]

---

[1] EA Farnsworth, 'Your Loss or My Gain? The Dilemma of the Disgorgement Principle in Breach of Contract' (1985) 94 *Yale Law Journal* 1339-1393, 1341-2.

[2] Law Commission: *Aggravated, Exemplary and Restitutionary Damages* (Law Com No 247, 1997) Part III para 1.37.

[3] *A-G v Blake* [2001] 1 AC 268 (HL) 291 (Lord Steyn).

[4] *Ibid* 284 (Lord Nicholls).

[5] Eg *Edelman*, 152.

point out the wide magnitude of the new rule introduced by the House of Lords. The analysis of judicial decisions, in particular in the phase prior to recognition, shows that the relationship between restitution for wrongs and breach of contract is controversial.

Surrey v Bredero Homes[6] offers an example of the difficulties encountered by the judiciary in its efforts to give clear legal shape to restitutionary damages as a response to breach of contract. The court rejected the award of restitutionary damages for breach of contract and 'reinforce[d] the orthodox English doctrine that damages for breach of contract are based on loss to the plaintiff'.[7] The claimant sold a parcel of land to the defendant. The transaction was subject to a covenant by the defendant, whereby the land was to be developed in accordance with the planning permission issued by the claimant. Ignoring the covenant, the defendant built on the land a number of houses which was in excess of the planning permission. The claimant brought an action for restitution of the gains accruing to the defendant from the breach of the covenant. The claim was rejected by the Court of Appeal. According to the court:

> [T]he starting point … is that the remedy at common law for breach of contract is an award of damages, and damages at common law are intended to compensate the victim for his loss, not to transfer to the victim if he has suffered no loss the benefit which the wrongdoer has gained by his breach of contract.[8]

The court did not see any good reason to depart from this rule. It was not denied that there were cases in which the claimant could recover in respect of the defendant's gain. Yet, those cases were all concentrated in the law of torts and '[t]he liability in the present case is solely in contract and not in tort'.[9] A justification given for the exclusion of restitutionary damages was that damages for breach of contract were assessed according to the compensatory rule in *Hadley v Baxendale*[10] so that there was no room for non-compensatory remedies. This last point is not convincing. The court did not explain why this line of thought applies only to contract law and not to tort law as well, given that both contract and tort show a similar profile as regards compensation, as demostrated by the compensatory rule which, according to the famous dictum of Lord Blackburn in *Livingstone*,[11] determines the measure 'where an injury is to be compensated by damages'. Hence, apparently, what is regarded as an obstacle in breach of contract is not perceived as such in tort.

In *Bredero*, the court did not rule out that a remedy for breach of contract could protect the aggrieved party's restitutionary interest. However, the cases in which such an interest might be taken into consideration were limited to the use made by the defendant of the claimant's property, where the term 'property' was

---

[6] *Surrey CC v Bredero Homes Ltd* [1993] 1 WLR 1361 (CA).
[7] P Birks, 'Profits of Breach of Contract' (1993) 109 *LQR* 518-521, 518.
[8] *Bredero* (n 6) 1364 (Dillon LJ).
[9] *Ibid* 1365 (Dillon LJ).
[10] *Hadley v Baxendale* (1854) 9 Ex 341; 156 ER 145.
[11] *Livingstone v The Rawyards Coal Co* (1880) 5 AC 25 (HL) 39 (Lord Blackburn).

interpreted in a wide sense.[12] This conclusion clashes with my account of restitution for wrongs, according to which a claim based upon the violation of a proprietary right cannot give rise to restitutionary damages, for the aim of the judicial award is to restore the integrity of the violated right placing the victim as far as possible in the same position in which the victim was before the wrongful event took place.[13] Thus, the court allows a restitutionary response for wrongs in situations in which the loss suffered requires a compensatory response and denies restitution in those cases in which it would be purposeful, for the wrongdoer has obtained a benefit independently of the victim's loss. The weakness of this reasoning was highlighted in the *Blake* case a few years later.

The Court of Appeal in *Bredero* rejected restitution for wrongs on the basis of a further consideration: restitution for breach of contract would collide with the need for certainty which characterises particularly sensible areas such as commercial law.[14] This argument recurs often in judicial reasoning.[15] The Commission Report[16] isolated it as one of the major obstacles standing in the way of a restitutionary structure for breach of contract. Lord Hobhouse warned in his dissenting speech in *Blake* that

> if some more extensive principle of awarding non-compensatory damages for breach of contract is to be introduced into commercial law the consequences will be very far reaching and disruptive.[17]

Edelman objects to this view that it is unclear why commercial certainty should prevail over valuable contractual rights. As for the risk of commercial uncertainty, this author observes that '[i]t is true that some uncertainty might result … but this is no more uncertain than causation and remoteness tests for compensatory damages'.[18] Edelman appropriately links the 'principle of commercial certainty' to figures such as causation and remoteness. These legal institutions have a policy-driven connotation and can be counterbalanced by different considerations, which in the present case could be the principle *pacta sunt servanda*, as highlighted by Edelman.

In quite a convoluted fashion, the court in *Bredero* did accept in theory the existence of restitution for wrongs, although it confined it to tort law. The problem with this approach is that it is difficult to recognise that breach of contract is a wrong[19] and yet to deny restitutionary damages, which are accepted for other categories of wrongs. Such exclusion requires support, which is lacking

---

[12] *Bredero* (n 6) 1369-1379 (Steyn LJ).
[13] See the previous chapter, I A; and ch 8, IV C ii and iii.
[14] *Bredero* (n 6) 1369-1379.
[15] *Nottingham University v Fishel* [2000] IRLR 471.
[16] Law Commission (n 2) Part III para 1.46.
[17] *Blake* (n 3) 299 (Lord Hobhouse).
[18] *Edelman*, 171.
[19] *Bredero* (n 6) 1371 (Steyn LJ). In *Blake* (n 3) 291, Lord Steyn, without expressing his view on his old opinion, accepted that '[i]t is right to acknowledge that the academic comment has been critical of the decision in *Bredero*'.

in the judgments examined. In fact, the House of Lords has recognised the fragility of this reasoning, clearly stating that the approach in the *Wrotham Park*[20] case ought to be preferred.[21]

Examining the authorities, Gareth Jones observed as far back as 1983 that

> [a] bold court could find ... respectably attractive precedents for a conclusion that the law is now sufficiently mature to recognise a restitutionary claim for damages made from a breach of contract.[22]

Twenty years later, the judiciary decided to make the bold move in *Attorney-General v Blake.*[23] The defendant was an ex-employee of the Secret Intelligence Service. In breach of a contractual undertaking not to divulge any information concerning his service, he published a book without governmental clearance in which he described his life as a spy. The fact that he was a self-confessed traitor who lived in a foreign country after an adventurous escape from a British prison helped him to obtain substantial royalties from his publication. In the Court of Appeal, Lord Woolf MR, giving the judgment of the whole court, after having pointed out that the 'general rule' is that damages for breach of contract are compensatory, observed that:

> If the court is unable to award restitutionary damages for breach of contract, then the law of contract is seriously defective. It means that in many situations the plaintiff is deprived of any effective remedy for breach of contract.[24]

The decision of the Court of Appeal came very shortly after the publication of the Law Commission Report[25] on restitutionary damages and reflected the content of the Report itself, which favoured a common law development rather than statutory intervention.[26] The Report's Recommendation has had a profound impact on the judiciary, as the *Blake* case shows. Restitution for wrongs was regarded as an exceptional instrument, which could have been activated only in those circumstances where other remedies were inadequate. Yet, *Blake* shifted the analysis from the recognition of restitutionary damages for breach of contract to the identification of the requirements for their application. The House of Lords opted for a pragmatic approach:[27] rather than listing a set of prerequisites, their Lordships preferred an analysis based on the circumstances of the case, for no 'fixed rules can be prescribed'.[28] Still, even such case-based approach needs some

---

[20] *Wrotham Park Estate Co v Parkside Homes Ltd* [1974] 1 WLR 798. On this decision, see pp 103-104.

[21] *Blake* (n 3) 283 (Lord Nicholls).

[22] G Jones, 'The Recovery of Benefits Gained from a Breach of Contract' (1983) 99 *LQR* 443-460, 452.

[23] *Blake* (n 3).

[24] *A-G v Blake* [1998] 1 All ER 833 (CA) 845 (Lord Woolf MR).

[25] In fact, only one day separated the Report from the decision in question. See on the latter G Virgo, 'Clarifying Restitution for Wrongs' [1998] *Restitution Law Review* 118-126.

[26] Law Commission (n 2) Part VI, Recommendation No 6.

[27] *Blake* (n 3) 291 (Lord Steyn).

[28] *Ibid* 285 (Lord Nicholls). Morritt V-C in *Esso Petroleum Co v Niad Ltd* (2001) WL 1476190, referred to the passage quoted to justify a decision in favour of the claimant, Esso.

criteria which the courts can follow and upon which the parties can rely. In his analysis of the *Blake* case, and particularly of Lord Nicholls's speech, Edelman identifies two factors which trigger a restitutionary award for breach of contract. The claimant must have a legitimate interest in the performance, and compensation alone must be inadequate.[29] In fact, Lord Nicholls does not refer to the claimant's legitimate interest as a mandatory requirement of the claim. Rather, he emphasises that it is a 'useful general guide, although not exhaustive'.[30] It is still to be seen whether the expression 'general guide' will be construed as 'necessary', as Edelman seems to suggest, or 'opportune', in the sense of an element which should generally, but not necessarily, form part of the evaluation. In effect, even Edelman agrees that '[i]t is very unclear how far the law will recognise a legitimate interest in performance'[31] outside Lord Nicholls's three examples of specific performance, injunctions restraining breaches of negative contractual provisions, and fiduciary relationships. On the other hand, his Lordship's words on the requirement of inadequacy leave little room for doubts: 'It will be only in exceptional cases, where those remedies are inadequate, that any question of accounting for profits will arise.'[32] Despite Edelman's explanation, the decision 'leaves considerable uncertainty over the circumstances in which disgorgement will be available'.[33]

The new rule laid down in *Blake* refers to an 'exception' to the general rule of restitution for breach of contract.[34] An approach in terms of exception is in line with what some scholars have long being asserting. As early as 1985, Alan Farnsworth argued that his

> survey of the disgorgement principle in connection with contracts for goods or services available on a market suggests that the principle is neither justified nor needed.[35]

His argument was that, from the point of view of economic analysis of the law, the principle is not compelling as long as those goods and services are available on the market. Moreover, market rules, if correctly applied, would achieve very similar results to disgorgement. However, Farnsworth admits that there are some exceptional cases in which market rules alone cannot address the issue. One such case would be the 'abuse of contract' if the victim is 'left with a defective performance and no opportunity to use [his] return performance to attempt to obtain a substitute.'[36] Farnsworth's economic analysis of law is not always in line

---

[29] *Edelman*, 150-162, esp 152-155.
[30] *Blake* (n 3) 285.
[31] *Edelman*, 158.
[32] *Blake* (n 3) 285 (Lord Nicholls).
[33] P Jaffey, 'Disgorgement for Breach of Contract' [2000] *Restitution Law Review* 578-587, 579.
[34] Contrast D Campbell, 'The Treatment of *Teacher v Calder* in *AG v Blake*' (2002) 65 *MLR* 256-269, 257: 'It seems unarguable that *Blake* now recognizes a general restitutionary remedy of partial or total disgorgement in "appropriate situations"'.
[35] Farnsworth (n 1) 1378.
[36] *Ibid* 1384.

with the law of obligations. His distinction between a principle of expectation and a principle of disgorgement[37] seems ultimately to refer to two avenues to compensate the victim:

> [I]f the injured party's lost expectation is less than the gain realized by the part in breach, then damages based on expectation do not strip the party in breach of all gain.[38]

When this is the case, according to Farnsworth the courts decline the application of the principle of disgorgement. Whereas his analysis might help to explain the economics behind the principles he discusses, it does not seem able to provide a normative account of restitution for wrongs. Thus, it is implicit in his opinion that expectation might be alternative to restitution – given that expectation damages can strip the defendant of his gains. Yet, Farnsworth does not clarify how and why compensatory damages, linked to expectation, are supposed to share their aim of taking away ill-gotten gains with restitutionary damages. In fact, he confirms his loss-centred view of restitutionary damages when he accepts that property might be a basis for an extension of the disgorgement principle.[39] But if any action founded on the property right aims to restore the right itself to the pre-wrong situation, then that action realises a compensatory goal. Farnsworth therefore mixes various measures of compensation together with proper cases of restitution.

Experience Hendrix[40] offers a post-*Blake* confirmation of the unavailability of restitutionary damages for breach of contract as the general rule. The defendant had breached a settlement agreement previously reached with a record company which prevented the defendant from using some master tapes. The claimant had known of the breaches for a while, but regarded judicial action as financially unviable even if successful. Aware of this, the defendant ignored the settlement in the belief that its behaviour would trigger no consequences. In the first instance, the claimant admitted that it was impossible to quantify the financial loss. Mance LJ, who delivers the leading judgment in the Court of Appeal, observes that *Blake*

> has freed us from some constraints that prior authority in this court (particularly [*Bredero*] and some reasoning in [*Jaggard*]) would have imposed.[41]

---

[37]   For example, *ibid* 1341. D Campbell and P Wylie, 'Ain't No Telling (Which Circumstances are Exceptional)' [2003] 62 *CLJ* 605-630, discuss some recent developments from the perspective of the economic analysis of law posing this alternative between expectation and disgorgement, again without explaining why the two heads of damages ought to be incompatible. They seem to interpret the sources as distinguishing compensation from restitution on the basis of the claimant's 'legitimate interest in preventing the defendant's profit-making activity', which was 'a useful general guide' to assess the opportunity of the restitutionary award according to Lord Nicholls in *Blake* (n 3) 285. *cf* Campbell and Wylie, 611.

[38]   Farnsworth, *ibid.*

[39]   *Ibid* 1368. Yet, he prefers equitable relief to property as a basis for the restitutionary award.

[40]   *Experience Hendrix LLC v PPX Enterprises Inc and E Chalpin* [2003] EWCA Civ 323 (CA).

[41]   *Ibid* para 16 (Mance LJ).

The reference to *Blake* suggests that the Court of Appeal awarded restitutionary damages for breach of contract. This is not the case. The starting point is *Wrotham Park*. There, according to the court, the measure of damages was independent of the profits actually obtained by the wrongdoer. Damages would have been so quantified even if, for instance, the wrongdoer had failed to make any profits owing to his own incompetence.[42] The victim's position seems to be similarly irrelevant: the same measure of damages would have been granted 'whether or not the [victim] would have been better off if the wrong had not been committed'.[43] The guiding principle is the fact that the wrongdoer should not gain any kind of advantage for free.

This measure of damages in *Experience Hendrix* is not restitutionary. According to the circumstances, the defendant might be asked to transfer to the claimant a sum which is independent of its gain. Mance LJ confirms this point when he refuses to order a full account of profits[44] and declares himself in favour of a 'reasonable recompense'.[45] The latter is a matter of 'practical justice'[46] and is described as

> such a sum as might reasonably have demanded … as a quid pro quo to permit the two licences into which [the defendant] entered in breach of the settlement agreement.[47]

Once again, damages are quantified on the basis of the doctrine of the lost opportunity to bargain.[48] *Blake*, which awarded restitution for wrongs, is distinguished, for in *Experience Hendrix* the breach took place in a commercial context. The subject did not concern 'anything like as special or sensitive as national security'.[49] The 'element of artificiality' in the quantification of the damages is not denied by the court. Yet, this solution would have the 'merit to direct the court's attention to the commercial value of the right infringed'.[50]

My analysis of *Hendrix* is rejected by those who consider *Wrotham Park* a proper instance of restitution for wrongs. David Campbell and Philip Wylie, for instance, construe the judicial awards in *Blake* and *Hendrix* as examples of a sliding scale of quantification of restitutionary damages: the former decision would deal with total restitution, whereas the latter decision would contain an instance of partial restitution. They observe that:

[42]   *Ibid* para 26.
[43]   *Ibid.*
[44]   *Ibid* 44.
[45]   *Ibid* 26.
[46]   *Ibid* 42.
[47]   *Ibid* 45.
[48]   See ch 3, n 32 and text thereof. M Graham, 'Restitutionary Damages: The Anvil Struck' [2004] 120 *LQR* 26-30, 28, observes on the basis of the lost opportunity to bargain doctrine that '[i]t may still therefore be open to argue that this remedy aims to compensate a loss rather than disgorge an enrichment.'
[49]   *Experience Hendrix* (n 40) 37.
[50]   *Ibid* 45.

Whilst *Blake* made it more difficult to argue that hypothetical release damages were compensatory rather than restitutionary in nature, it left a residue of serious uncertainty because it did not make it impossible to do so. *Hendrix* goes a long way towards eradicating this particular uncertainty by awarding hypothetical release damages on an unambiguously restitutionary basis and saying that an account of profits, though not justified in the circumstances of the case, might also have been awarded on this basis.[51]

One problem with this approach is that, as the authors correctly conclude, 'the sliding scale which would coherently unite [*Blake* and *Hendrix*] is purest chimera.'[52] Yet, the authors do not justify their conclusion using my argument that these decisions deal with different responses of the law of damages, but rather preferring a 'practical' perspective, which leads them to the define the awards 'a very loose collection of sometimes profoundly arbitrary damages quantifications.'[53] As I endeavour to show in this study, the quantification of damages is not arbitrary at all. A different issue has been raised by Birks, who has observed that a rejection of restitutionary damages in the *Wrotham Park* type of situation might lead to problems in those cases where the breach of contract has been cynically pursued by the wrongdoer and yet the court cannot quantify any damages in favour of the victim. Not all breaches of contract can be construed as giving rise to a continuous violation. A construction in terms of compensation would allow the victim to obtain only nominal damages.[54] The Court of Appeal seems to respond to this objection in *Experience Hendrix*, establishing a reasonable recompense, of compensatory nature, for all cases of intentional breach of contract.

Hendrix strengthens the view that restitutionary damages will generally not be awarded for breach of contract. This construction is preferred to a more progressive interpretation such as the one advanced in *Esso v Niad*[55] a few years earlier. In *Niad*, the Vice-Chancellor applied the rationale in *Blake* to ordinary commercial contracts. The defendant had breached the agreement with the claimant according to which he would not have sold petrol at a higher price than the price offered by the direct competitors in his area. The court awarded restitutionary damages for the breach of an obligation which was essential to the advertising scheme developed by the claimant. *Niad* is distinguished by Mance LJ in *Experience Hendrix* because, to grant restitutionary damages in a commercial context, the breach must go to the roots of the agreement.[56] Furthermore, in *Niad* the wrongdoer had received financial support from the claimant to stick to the contractual rules.[57] In *Experience Hendrix*, the compensatory avenue, albeit

---

[51]   Campbell and Wylie (n 37) 605.
[52]   *Ibid* 606.
[53]   *Ibid.*
[54]   See Birks (n 7) 519: '[t]he law is deficient when a legitimate interest cannot be safeguarded against such opportunism'.
[55]   *Esso v Niad* (n 28).
[56]   *Experience Hendrix* (n 40) 38.
[57]   *Ibid* 31.

based on a fiction, is implicitly preferred. The lost opportunity to bargain theory developed in *Wrotham Park*[58] indicates, according to the court, the correct path of development.

The restrictive approach in *Experience Hendrix* is in line with previous decisions. Deviations from the general rule are rare, as even *Blake* and *Niad* confirm. As Jones put it, the issue of restitution for breach of contract

> has at times been disingenuously concealed in inquires into the measure of the plaintiff's loss from the defendant's failure to do what he promised to do.[59]

Wrotham Park and *Jaggard v Sawyer*[60] are sometimes regarded as two such cases.[61] Often, when the measure of damages is triggered by a breach of contract and appears to be restitutionary, the courts[62] tend to apply the rules on violation of property rights. This tendency is particularly evident in the so-called way-leave cases,[63] in which the breach of contract is regarded as only the occasion to activate the remedy; but the proper ground for granting damages is tortious interference with property rights. Even for *Wrotham Park*[64] and *Jaggard v Sawyer*[65] it is far from obvious that the breach of contract gave rise to restitution for wrongs, because in both cases the courts – in my view, correctly – qualified the damages granted as compensatory.[66]

In *Jaggard v Sawyer,*[67] the defendant was the owner of a plot forming part of a small development. In breach of a covenant which bound all owners, he built an additional house outside the development and connected it through a driveway to the main road of the development. The claimant, who was the owner of another plot, sought an injunction to prevent access to the main road. The court at first instance held that an injunction would have been too oppressive to the defendant. The Court of Appeal agreed and awarded damages in lieu of injunction. To assess the loss, the court applied the 'lost opportunity to bargain' approach of *Wrotham Park,* which the court interpreted as regarding an award of compensatory, not restitutionary, damages. According to Sir Thomas Bingham MR:

---

[58]   *Wrotham Park* (n 20).

[59]   Jones (n 22) 451.

[60]   *Jaggard v Sawyer* [1995] 1 WLR 269 (CA).

[61]   W Goodhart, 'Restitutionary Damages for Breach of Contract' [1995] Restitution Law Review 3-14, 4 and 9.

[62]   *Cf Penarth Dock Engineering Co v Pounds* [1963] 1 Lloyd's Rep 359; *Swordheath Properties Ltd v Tabet* [1979] 1 WLR 285 (CA).

[63]   *Whitwam v Westminster Brimbo Coal & Coke Co* [1896] 2 Ch 538.

[64]   *Wrotham Park* (n 20).

[65]   *Jaggard* (n 60).

[66]   The same applies to Birks's reading of *Moses v Macferlan* (1760) 2 Burr 1005, 97 ER 676, as awarding a restitutionary, instead of compensatory, response. See P Birks 'Restitution for Wrongs' in EJH Schrage (ed), *Unjust Enrichment – The Comparative Legal History of the Law of Restitution* (2nd edn) (Berlin, Duncker & Humblot 1999) 171-195, 181.

[67]   *Jaggard* (n 60).

I cannot ... accept that Brightman J's assessment of damages in *Wrotham Park* was based on other than compensatory principles ...The judge ... had ... to assess the damages necessary to compensate the plaintiffs for this continuing invasion of their right. He paid attention to the profits earned by the defendants, as it seems to me, not in order to strip the defendants of their unjust gains, but because of the obvious relationship between the profits earned by the defendants and the sum which the defendants would reasonably have been willing to pay to secure release from the covenant.[68]

II   German Law

The analysis of restitution for wrongful breach of contract in a civil law system involves three areas of law, which correspond to the division of the law of obligations into contracts, delicts, and unjust enrichment. The first step will be an examination of the law of delict. It will be demonstrated that there is little or no recognition of restitutionary damages within this area of obligations. The law of contract is more promising owing to a remedy which intervenes in particular situations. In the third and final step, it will be examined whether German law applies a restitutionary mechanism which, despite being part of the law of unjustified enrichment, could achieve restitution for breach of contract. Thus, the focus of the analysis shifts from restitutionary damages to restitutionary responses, including the law of contracts and the law of unjust enrichment. Although German law does not know restitution for wrongs as such, still the examination of the restitutionary responses will show the presence of legal institutions which replicate to some extent the mechanism of restitution for wrongs, like para 285 BGB, or achieve similar results through other avenues, which might explain why it is less urgent for German law to adopt restitutionary damages.

A   Law of Delict

Similarly to English law,[69] the view held by the judiciary[70] and scholars[71] is that breach of contract cannot be qualified as a delict, because it concerns a breach of a duty which is owed towards a specific person or group of persons. There are further reasons to exclude a qualification of breach of contract as a delict. German delict law is based principally upon three 'small' general claims. The first, and most important, is contained in para 823 (1) BGB, which states:

---

[68]   *Ibid* 281-282.
[69]   PH Winfield, *The Province of the Law of Tort* (Cambridge, CUP 1931) 40.
[70]   (1961) BGHZ 34 375, 380.
[71]   Staudinger/Schäfer, 'Vorbem zu §§ 823 ff' para 32.

A person who, wilfully or negligently, unlawfully injures the life, body, health, freedom, property or other right of another is bound to compensate him for any damage arising herefrom.[72]

There is no reference to breach of contract in this list of goods protected. The only way in which breach of contract could be included in it is by a wide interpretation of the 'other rights' which are mentioned in the provision. However, such an interpretation would probably overstretch the meaning of the term 'any other right'. Furthermore, since para 823 (1) BGB expressly refers to compensation as the remedy triggered by the breach, the most immediate and common reading of the provision restricts its application exclusively to compensation. It follows that there would be some room for restitutionary damages only if the judiciary identified a different basis for the award.[73] Yet, this construction of the provision would be too far-reaching, given that there is little or no doubt in German law that para 823 (1) regulates delictual liability in general.

Para 823 (2) BGB contains the second delictual cause of action. It establishes a duty to compensate the loss arising from the infringement of statutes which are intended for the protection of others. Finally, the most general clause is to be found in para 826 BGB. It allows compensation for wrongs which are perpetrated wilfully and *contra bonos mores*, that is contrary to public policy. Apart from the fact that these last two provisions are rather seldom applied, there is in both of them an explicit reference to the compensatory function which is linked to their causes of action. Therefore, they are of little avail in an examination of restitutionary damages. The conclusion must be that all three general delictual rules do not help in the individuation of any proper support for granting restitutionary damages for breach of contract.

As has been seen in chapter two,[74] the strongest difficulty to the adoption of restitutionary damages for delict follows from a rule which does not belong uniquely to the law of delict, for it concerns the law of damages in general. This rule is established in para 249 BGB, which states:

A person who is obliged to make compensation shall restore the situation which would have existed if the circumstances rendering him liable to make compensation had not occurred.[75]

This is the basic provision for the law of damages. Read together with para 823 BGB, it creates an obstacle which is difficult to surmount. Para 249 BGB is understood to give rise to two legal principles, which complement each other. The first one is the 'principle of compensation', or *Ausgleichsprinzip*, according to

---

[72] Goren (tr) *The German Civil Code* (revd edn) (Littleton, Colorado, Rothman 1994).
[73] Contrariwise, P Schlechtriem, 'Some Thoughts on the Decision of the BGH concerning Princess Caroline of Monaco' in B Markesinis (ed), *Protecting Privacy – The Clifford Chance Lectures* (Oxford, OUP 1999) vol 4 131-138, 133, seems to think that restitutionary damages could be led back to para 823 (1) BGB. Yet, he does not provide any explanation of the relation which, in his opinion, should link that provision with restitutionary damages.
[74] I B i.
[75] Goren (n 72).

which the law of damages deals solely with the loss of the victim, not of the wrongdoer. The second principle is the so-called *Bereicherungsverbot*, or prohibition of enrichment (at the defendant's expense), which limits the amount of the award to the loss caused by the wrong. The predominance of a rule on compensation presents a serious impasse to a delictual construction of restitution for wrongs. The only way around it would be an extra-codal, judicial development. Yet there are no signals that the judiciary might be prepared, or even just interested, to abandon the solid compensatory tradition.

B   Law of Contract

An analysis of old judicial decisions on contract produces only one instance[76] in which the response granted by the court was not based upon the standard measure of compensation.

A baker was in a contractual relation with the owner of a shop which sold bread. The shop owner provided every day a determinate quantity of dough which the baker was to turn into a certain quantity of bread. After some years, the shop owner discovered that the baker was using part of the dough for himself. The shop owner claimed for damages for breach of contract. The baker admitted that he had diverted part of the dough, but he denied that his conduct had caused any loss to the claimant, because, despite the subtraction of the dough, he had baked always the same quantity of loaves. Although each of those loaves was smaller than it should have been, all loaves were sold by the claimant for the same price as if they had been bread of normal size. This line of defence is not unknown to English courts. Cases like *Strand Electric*[77] show that the English judiciary is not at ease when facing the allegation of the absence of the claimant's loss. Similarly, the German court did not accept the reasoning, but found it difficult to justify the rejection. The judges observed that a loss had undoubtedly occurred to the claimant every time that the defendant had subtracted the dough. At the same time, the subtraction unjustly enriched the defendant. On this basis, the court left both avenues open: restitution for unjust enrichment – what the Romans and even the German judges qualified as a *condictio furtiva* – and damages for breach of contract – *contractlicher Schadensersatzanspruch*. In either case, the court made clear that the measure of restitution or the award of damages would not have been affected by the fact that the claimant could successively mitigate or even completely avoid the loss. Assuming that the court awarded damages, the quantification therefore followed an assessment of the wrongdoer's benefit. Still, the court expressly referred to a contractual form of compensation, or *Schadensersatz*. No mention was made of non-compensatory awards. This approach is correct. The claimant founded his action upon the

---

[76]   OLG Braunschweig (1891) 46 Seuffert's Archiv für Entscheidungen der Oberste Gerichte in den deutschen Staaten No 173 272.

[77]   *Strand Electric & Engineering Co v Brisford Entertainments* [1952] 2 QB 246 (CA). *cf* ch 3, n 46 and text thereof.

violation of his property right to the dough. His aim was the restoration of his right to pristine condition. It follows that this case did not concern restitution for wrongs. Rather, it indicates that German courts were ready even before the introduction of the civil code in vigour to apply in appropriate circumstances a measure of damages which differs from the traditional form of compensation. The modern German contract law on breach of contract is highly complex, and detailed analysis of it is unnecessary here. It is sufficient to point out that, when the law of damages is called upon, contractual provisions always refer to '*Schadensersatz*', or compensation, as para 325 BGB shows. In such cases, para 249 BGB applies. This might seem enough to conclude that contract law has no room for restitutionary damages as such. However, there is an institution of contract law which, although avoiding the language of damages, might be relevant to restitution for wrongs. A breach of contract gives the party not in breach the possibility to terminate the contract (para 323 (1) BGB). Termination triggers a restitutionary claim which is based upon contract law and excludes the application of unjust enrichment.[78] Although the restitutionary claim under para 323 (1) BGB has been only recently introduced, there seems to be no doubt that this response cannot be qualified as restitutionary damages. The gist of the action is the elimination of the effects produced by the invalid contract. Thus, the parties are brought back to the pre-contractual situation (*Rückabwicklung*). However, at least in one particular case some components of the contract will survive. If the party not in breach brings a claim under para 285 (1) BGB, old para 281 (1) BGB, he has to effect counter-performance, para 326 (3) BGB. Para 285 (1) states:

> If the debtor obtains a substitute or a claim to compensation for the subject matter of the obligation as a consequence of the circumstances which, according to para 275 (1) to (3), free the debtor from his obligation to perform, the creditor can require restitution of what has been received as a substitute or the transfer of the compensatory claim.[79]

This situation is commonly described as '*stellvertretendes Commodum*', or 'substitute benefit'. Such benefit can be claimed in any case of subsequent impossibility of the performance, independently of any fault-based liability of the debtor. It is unclear whether it comprises also the gains accruing to the debtor from a breach of contract. Certainly, some cases of breach of contract can give rise to restitution of the benefit, as the following case[80] illustrates.

The claimant and the defendant bought two neighbouring plots of land. The defendant promised that he would register a right of passage through his plot in favour of the claimant, but failed to implement this promise. After some time, the defendant sold his plot to a third party, stating that it was free from rights of

---

[78]   Palandt, '§ 812' para 78.

[79]   Para 285 (1) BGB has been recently modified by a comprehensive reform of the law of obligations which came into force 1 January 2002. However, this reform does not affect the present analysis. Before the reform, this provision was numbered 281 (1). In the following, any reference to the previous para 281 (1) will be converted into para 285 (1) if not otherwise stated.

[80]   (1967) BGHZ 46 260.

other parties. When the third party decided to build some garages on his plot and communicated his intention to the new owner, the latter refused to acknowledge the third party's right. On the basis of old para 281 (1) BGB, the claimant sought restitution of the benefit which the defendant obtained by omitting to register the claimant's right to passage. The claim was accepted by the lower courts, but rejected by the Federal Court (BGH). The BGH held that, in order for old para 281 (1) BGB to operate, both the original and the subsequent obligation, for which the 'substitute benefit' is sought, must deal with the same object.[81] In the present case, the object the performance of which had become impossible was not the same as the one for which a benefit was obtained. The defendant had not promised that he would sell his plot to the claimant, but only that he would register a right of passage in favour of the claimant. On the other hand, the sum which the defendant had received was paid in consideration for the transfer of ownership of the plot. According to the court, old para 281 (1) BGB would have applied if the defendant had promised in a valid contract to convey the property in the land to the claimant, but had instead sold and conveyed the land to a third party. In that situation, the claimant could bring successfully a claim for restitution of the benefit which accrued to the defendant in the form of the purchase price paid by the third party by offering to pay his agreed price to the defendant. The mechanism depicted by the court is commonly referred to as *commodum ex negotiatione*. It is the gain obtained by a defendant who sells and passes to a third party the title in an object which he had previously contractually promised (*schuldrechtlicher Vertrag*) to the claimant. There is general agreement[82] in the judiciary and in the literature that the claimant is entitled to such gain.

The *commodum ex negotiatione* describes a case of restitution for wrongs. Indeed, such link between the law of damages and the *stellvertretendes commodum* is not completely alien to German analysis. It was taken into consideration in older scholarly studies, where it was observed that old para 281 BGB *in concreto* provides 'a kind of compensation'.[83] Yet, a more modern view[84] rejects any connection between this provision and the law of damages. Recently, a new wave of studies which originated in the *Caroline* case[85] has focused on para 285 BGB, which is regarded as being able to provide a solid platform for restitutionary actions.[86] Indeed, para 285 BGB is considered to be 'the only case of application of causes of action which aim at stripping the defendant of ill-gotten gains'.[87] However, the restitutionary actions for which para 285 BGB is invoked

---

[81]   *Ibid* 264: '*Identität zwischen geschuldetem und ersetztem Gegenstand*'.

[82]   Staudinger/Löwisch, '§ 281' para 29; MünchKomm/Emmerich '§ 281' para 16.

[83]   '*Eine Art Schadensersatz*'. Thus G Korsch, 'Der Anspruch auf das Surrogat' (1916) 114 *Archiv für die civilistische Praxis* 1-22, 9.

[84]   Eg H Meyer, *Ersatz und Erlösherausgabe* (Köln, Heymann 1999) 150-151.

[85]   For a detailed analysis of the *Caroline* case, see ch 5, I B iii b.

[86]   Eg C-W Canaris, 'Gewinnabschöpfung bei Verletzung des allgemein Persönlichkeitsrechts' in A-J Ahrens (ed), *Festschrift für E Deutsch zum 70. Geburtstag* (Köln, Heymann 1999) 85-109, 92.

[87]   '[*Der] einzige Anwendungsfall [der Gewinnabschöpfung] ist ... die Pflicht ... zur Herausgabe des commodum ex negotiatione*'. Thus J Köndgen, 'Gewinnabschöpfung als Sanktion unerlaubten Tuns' (2000) 64 *Rabels Zeitschrift* 661-695, 694.

are not wrongful, but claims in unjustified enrichment. According to this recent interpretation, para 285 BGB performs a similar function to restitution for wrongs through a different avenue. Yet, given the compensatory role of the German law of unjustified enrichment, it is questionable whether this area of the law is appropriate to explain the phenomenon at issue. At any rate, the German garage case demonstrates that para 285 BGB does not cover every possible situation of restitution for breach of contract. In fact, the BGH rejected the restitutionary remedy which was sought by the claimant in a context in which restitutionary damages would have been a powerful response to have at the court's disposal. This difference between the *stellvertretendes commodum* and restitutionary damages shows that there is a loophole in the German legal system which cannot be filled with the traditional instruments. Some cases need a different approach if the wrongdoer is not to benefit from his action. Restitution for wrongs would offer an adequate tool to grant a restitutionary claim to the victim in such cases.

C   Law of Unjustified Enrichment

If the contract is void or voidable, unjust, or - more in line with German law - 'unjustified', enrichment provides the main avenue to undo its effects (para 142 BGB in connection with para 812 BGB). On the one hand, the enrichment to be returned will be increased by any benefits which have accrued to the recipient from the use of what he received from the other party (paras 818 (1) and 100 BGB). On the other hand, in an action against the defendant in good faith the award will be limited to the amount of the enrichment which is still in the assets of the enriched party (para 818 (3) BGB). This last rule corresponds to the English defence of change of position. It is unclear whether or to what degree the enriched party will have to return the benefit obtained by selling or using the object of the initial enrichment. In the literature,[88] the view prevails that the gains due to the particular skill of the enriched are not to be given up. The question of restitution of the gains receives an affirmative answer whenever the enriched person has acted in bad faith. In this case, the rules on pure breach of contract come into play.[89] This is due to para 818 (4) BGB, which refers to the 'general provisions' in case of bad faith. While there is some dispute as to what precisely includes these general provisions, there is a widespread consensus[90] that para 285 BGB falls among them. The relationship between unjustified enrichment and the restitutionary mechanism for bad faith is illustrated by the following example.[91]

The claimant sold a lorry to the defendant, who knew that the contract of sale was void. Despite this, the defendant transferred the lorry to a third party at a

---

[88]   P Schlechtriem, *Schuldrecht Besonderer Teil* (6th edn) (Tübingen, Mohr 2003) para 782.
[89]   H Grothe, '§ 347' in Bamberger/Roth (eds), *Kommentar zum Bürgerlichen Gesetzbuch* (München, Beck 2001) para 1.
[90]   MünchKomm/Emmerich, '§ 281' para 5.
[91]   (1980) BGHZ 75 203. The case has been slightly modified for a better understanding of non-German lawyers.

profit. When the claimant found out that the transaction was invalid, he claimed restitution of the lorry. The defendant argued that restitution in kind was impossible and offered the monetary value of the lorry under para 818 (2) BGB. This would have allowed the defendant to keep a profit, that is the difference between the value of the lorry and the price obtained from the sale to the third party. The BGH rejected the defendant's argument. In the opinion of the court, para 818 (1) BGB determines only the starting point for evaluating the measure of restitution. When, consequently to the defendant's bad faith, the so-called stricter liability, or *verschärfte Haftung,* applies, the measure of restitution is increased. There is no reason to privilege the party in bad faith in comparison to the claimant. Therefore, the defendant was ordered to give up the gain accrued to him through his sale to the third party. According to the court, it is *interessen-gerecht,* that is, corresponds to a just evaluation of the interests of the parties, that the assessment of the subject-matter takes also para 285 (former 281) BGB into consideration when the enriched person acted in bad faith. This last statement shows that the judiciary, in line with the German tradition of the *Interessenjuris-prudenz,* is aware of the relevant policy considerations in allocating the benefit.

The lorry case highlights the existence of some points of contact between restitution for wrongs and restitution for unjust enrichment from the point of view of the restitutionary mechanism itself. Para 818 (3) BGB requires bad faith, which can refer to instances of wrongs, as the previous example confirms. In the presence of the stricter liability, the development of restitutionary damages for breach of contract seems a less pressing issue. On the other hand, one could question the mechanism triggered by the bad faith of the defendant as a proper instance of restitution for wrongs, given that the claimant acts on the basis of his violated proprietary right. In support of my thesis, it could be argued that the reference in para 818 (4) BGB to the 'general provisions' entails a departure from the law of unjustified enrichment, which is substituted by purely delictual norms. There is certainly an argument for sustaining that para 818 (4) BGB under certain circumstances transforms the original enrichment claim into a delictual claim if the defendant a wrongful behaviour, or *Verschulden.* Although the commentators[92] do not speculate on the possibility of this transformation of the nature of the claim, still they allow a claim for compensation (*Schadensersatz*) in case of wrongful behaviour when the original subject-matter of the claim cannot be given back to the claimant any longer. In this last case, if the behaviour of the defendant in bad faith was not wrongful, the impoverished loses his claim. The compensatory nature of the delictual claim indicates that restitution for wrongs plays no role in this context.

---

[92]   C Wendehorst, '§ 818' in Bamberger/Roth *Kommentar zum Bürgerlichen Gesetzbuch* (München, Beck 2003) para 126.

Excursus: The scope of para 285 (1) BGB

According to the BGH,[93] para 285 BGB would apply to the entire law of obligations. This statement implies that the provision would not be limited to contract and unjustified enrichment, but would also cover delictual liability. A wide application would provide some support to the case in favour of restitution for wrongs in German law even though, it must be remembered, the norm overlaps, but does not identify with restitutionary damages. Yet, the prevailing view[94] rejects the application of para 285 BGB to delictual events. This point is still controversial. Scholars[95] put forward the instance of the banker who sells the debentures of the claimant. Here, the claimant would have a delictual restitutionary claim based upon para 285 BGB independently of any further duty to compensation in contract or delict. However, this view is generally rejected in favour of the adoption of para 251 (1) BGB, which provides:

> Insofar as restoration is not possible or is not sufficient for indemnifying the obligee, the person obliged to make compensation must indemnify the obligee in money.[96]

This norm points in the opposite direction to para 285 BGB in that it excludes restitution of the substitute as understood by para 285 BGB and limits the subject matter of the claim to the good to be performed or its value in money. Hence, from the perspective of restitution for wrongs, the present situation in German law seems to be that under some circumstances contract and unjustified enrichment might grant more protection to the victim of a wrong than the law of delicts. At any rate, the presence of some mechanism through which a restitutionary response for wrongs is awarded shows that the concept of restitution for wrongs, if not the terminology, is not alien to German legal thought.

III   Italian Law

The following discussion of the Italian law on restitution for breach of contract is based upon the same division into the three pillars of the law of obligations which has been used for German law. In general, Italian law, coherently with the line of strict refusal which has already characterised its response to proprietary wrongs, does not admit any recovery of the gains made by the wrongdoer qua wrongdoer.

---

[93]   (1980) BGHZ 75 203, 206.
[94]   MünchKomm/Emmerich, '§ 281' para 5.
[95]   RGRK/Alff, '§ 281' para 12.
[96]   R Youngs (tr), *Sourcebook on German Law* (repr, London, Cavendish 1998) 309.

A   Law of Delict

The Italian system of delictual liability is built upon the general clause of Art 2043 cc, which states:

> Any fraudulent, malicious, or negligent act which causes an unjust loss to another obliges the person who has committed the act to compensate the loss.

The letter of the law does not exclude that such a general clause could cover also breach of contract. More problematic appears to be an attempt to fit breach of contract within a definition of wrong in the Italian system, which operates in terms of the violation of a victim's right or of a norm which aims to protect the victim.[97] If 'breach of contract' is straightforwardly connected with 'breach of duty', as some English academic writing suggests, then it can be brought under the general roof of the law of wrongs. In a legal system, in which 'breach of contract' is rather linked with 'violation of an interest', the relationship with 'breach of duty' lacks the same immediacy.

Even if it was conceded as a conjectural possibility that Art 2043 cc leaves the door open to restitution for wrongs, there are other obstacles to surmount. One of them is the measure of delictual damages, which is determined in Art 2056 cc. This norm establishes that 'damages must be determined according to articles 1223, 1226, and 1227'. The chain of provisions which starts from Art 2056 cc has already been analysed.[98] In that investigation, I have argued that the model of damages adopted by the code is centred strictly on compensation. In this context, it will be recalled that Art 1223 cc states:

> Compensation for the damage arising from non-performance or delay shall include the loss sustained by the creditor and the lost profits insofar as they are a direct and immediate consequence of the non-performance or delay.

Rebus sic stantibus, scholars and the judiciary do not seem interested in the development of a gain-based remedy in delict. However, nothing in the statute points conclusively towards an exclusion of restitutionary damages. Art 1223 cc, for instance, indicates the heads of damages which 'must' be included in the judicial evaluation of the negative loss. The provision does not contain an exclusive list of the responses for delict, so that the courts are at liberty to add other heads of damages besides the ones mentioned. Indeed, the provision cannot cover restitutionary damages, because it affects solely the regulation of compensatory damages. At any rate, even if the law of delict acknowledged restitutionary damages, the main obstacle remains the one which has been pointed out for English and German law: breach of contract cannot be classified as a delict, for it lacks the characteristic of generality which is required for the activation of delictual responses. Breach of contract concerns the breach of a duty owed to particular persons.

---

[97]   Monateri, *Responsabilità* 225-226.
[98]   Ch 2, I C i.

B   Law of Contract

Art 1218 cc defines contractual liability by stating:

> The debtor who does not exactly render due performance is liable for damages unless he proves that the non-performance or delay was due to impossibility of performance for a cause not imputable to him.[99]

The provisions which help the courts in assessing damages are the same both in delictual and in contractual liability (Art 1223 ff cc). The main difference with delict lies in the fact that, in contract, the defendant who has not acted maliciously is liable only for foreseeable damages (Art 1225 cc). As delict and contract apply the same rules, it would be difficult to justify a discrepancy in the quantification of the respective damages. If restitutionary damages are to be allowed, they should be allowed in both cases.

If one party breaches the contract, Art 1453 cc grants the other party two options: he can choose to demand either performance of the contract or its judicial termination. In case he chooses the first avenue, the law provides various norms to compel the defendant to perform: enforcement by delivery or release (Art 2930 cc); enforcement of obligations to do something (Art 2931 cc); enforcement of obligations not to do something (Art 2933 cc). None of those provisions contemplates the possibility of requiring the defendant to give up the profits which he has derived from the breach of contract.

If, on the other hand, the party not in breach chooses the judicial avenue to terminate the contract, then Art 1223 cc intervenes with the consequences which have already been described. This does not necessarily imply, though, that contract law does not know a mechanism which could cover the same function as restitutionary damages. In fact, if a party opts for termination of the contract, only the party not in breach can claim damages, but both parties can claim back their performances according to the rules on unjust enrichment. As will be discussed in the next section, it could be argued that a faint copy of a restitutionary response for wrongs can be traced in the law of unjust enrichment, so that, under given circumstances, the wrongdoer can be compelled to give up his gain. Yet, this interpretation does not withstand proper legal analysis.

C   Law of Unjust Enrichment

The basic rule is: 'the person who makes a payment which was not due has a right to claim back what he paid' (Art 2033 1st sentence cc). On this basis, there is no room for compelling the wrongdoer, here the enriched party, to give up any part of his benefit which exceeds the performance by the claimant. By contrast with German law, this measure of restitution is not very flexible. Generally, no extension can be made and, strictly speaking, no restriction based on the model of change of position either. This 'defence', which is available primarily for

---

[99]   M Beltramo, G Longo and JH Merryman (trs), *The Italian Civil Code* (New York, Oceana 1969).

restitution of specified thing, bars the claim of 2033 ff cc entirely and triggers the general enrichment action of Art 2041 cc, which has different features. Yet, as was stated above, this strict model of restitution for unjustified enrichment contains a mechanism which links the recovery to the defendant's gain. The following instance will cast some light on the restitutionary mechanism of the law of unjustified enrichment and its relationship with the remedies for breach of contract.

C hands over to the scholar D a precious book for D to use gratuitously for a given period of time. C intends this to be a *comodato*, that is a gratuitous loan for use. Yet, D wilfully sells the book to a bona fide third party T for an extremely high price. As this transaction meets the requirements of Art 1153 cc on transfer of ownership of chattels, title to the book passes to T. Thus, C cannot claim restitution from T. The civil code provides a particular remedy to allow C to claim the benefit accruing to D as a consequence of D's skilful sale of the book. Dealing with the wilful alienation of the unduly received thing, the first two sentences of Art 2038 (2) cc state:

> A person who transferred a thing he received in bad faith, or who transferred it after becoming aware of his duty to return it, is under an obligation to return the thing in kind or to pay its corresponding value. However, the one who made the payment not due can demand what has been given as payment for the transfer and can even take direct action to collect the payment.[100]

Art 2038 (2) cc offers an alternative to C. He can either claim restitution of the monetary value of the book or compel D to give up to him what D obtained from the sale to T. C will opt for the second avenue if it is more beneficial to him, as in this case in which D sold the book at a price which exceeds its value. Thus, C is likely to demand from D what D 'has been given as payment for the transfer'. This payment comprises two elements: the value of the book and the additional money paid by T owing to D's vending skill. The combination of these two elements shows that Art 2038 (2) cc contains a remedial mechanism which uses as its measure the benefit accruing to the defendant. En passant, it might be observed that the same claim is available to the impoverished in para 816 (1) BGB. However, this latter claim is less interesting for restitution for wrongs than the Italian version because German law has the rule in para 285 BGB.

If Art 2038 (2) cc were analysed on the basis of the model advanced by Edelman for English law, which distinguishes two different structures for gain-based remedies, one would be able to conclude that this is a case of restitution for wrongs. According to my own model of analysis, the provision does indeed refer to the defendant's benefit, but it does not contain an example of restitution for wrongs. The basis of the claim ex Art 2038 (2) cc is not the benefit of the defendant; it is rather the loss of the claimant. The latter has been impoverished by the wrongful act of the former and brings an action to make good his loss. Art 2038 (2) cc establishes that a compensatory aim can be achieved through two

---

[100]   *Ibid.*

different avenues, which apply two different measures. But even if that measure is preferred which corresponds to the defendant's gain, the claim remains compensatory. Correctly, the provision at issue offers a choice to the claimant between two compensatory measures which are incompatible because they address alternative situations: the claimant has suffered a loss measured either by the value of the book or by the defendant's enrichment. Unsurprisingly, cases such as *Blake*,[101] which concern truly restitutionary situations, would find no restitutionary response in Art 2038 (2) cc to protect the victim of the wrong. Even if the information obtained by Blake and published by him could be classified as a thing, Blake did not receive it in bad faith; nor had he any duty to return it, which he had breached.

---

[101]   *Blake* (n 3); see n 23 above and text thereof.

5

Comparative Analysis: Other Wrongs and Concluding Observations

T

HIS CHAPTER CONCLUDES the comparative analysis of modern legal systems with an examination of 'other wrongs'. The final observations will be dedicated to a comment upon the parallel evolutionary trends of restitutionary damages in the jurisdictions under comparison.

I Other Wrongs

'Other wrongs' is a residual category for all wrongs which do not fit into the previous categories. The wrongs examined might differ according to the jurisdiction under comparison. The reason for the small discrepancies is not unprincipled. The various topics have been selected owing to their peculiar relevance for the comparative analysis. Hence, if a legal institution brings to light a significant aspect of one particular legal system, it will be examined even if in another legal system its importance might be negligible. In general, however, consistency has been sought as far as possible.

A English Law

In English law, the category 'others' deals mainly with the so-called equitable wrongs. In line with the previous chapters, no distinction will be made between 'torts' and 'equitable wrongs'. All causes of action will be founded just upon 'wrongs'.

i Breach of Fiduciary Duty

With regard to breach of fiduciary duty, the judiciary signals that an 'account of profits' is not based upon the traditional compensatory principle. Lord Wright held in *Regal v Gulliver* that:

> If a person in a fiduciary relationship makes a secret profit out of the relationship, the court will not inquire whether the other person is damnified or has lost a profit which otherwise he would have got.[1]

Many judicial authorities confirm that, in the case of breach of fiduciary duty, the wrongdoer can be compelled to give up the benefits which result from the perpetration of the wrong.[2] The *Regal* case was confirmed as sound law by *Boardman v Phipps*.[3] In this case, a constructive trustee took advantage from some information which he had obtained by virtue of his position. Once it was established that the defendant, who was solicitor to the trustees, was to be treated as fiduciary in relation to some trust matters, it followed that confidential information which he obtained by acting for the trust was to be considered the 'property' of the trust itself. It is arguable whether confidential information should qualify as equitable property.[4] Even without referring to proprietary terminology, a restitutionary duty could be recognised on the stronger base of a breach of a fiduciary relationship.[5] At any rate, the misappropriation of such 'property' was held to be a wrong leading to a duty to make good the loss or to give up the benefit obtained. Restitution was sought and granted. The response took the form of an account of profits.

The courts do not require any particularly blameworthy conduct on the part of the enrichee. The account of profits can be awarded even if the fiduciary has behaved honestly.[6] It is the enrichment itself which, in the context of fiduciaries, paves the way to the restitutionary claim. As Edelman argues, '[t]he institution of trust and confidence is regarded as such an important one that the rule is strict to prevent the possibility of departure from it.'[7] *Murad v Al-Saraj*[8] substantiates this last statement confirming that there is no need for the fiduciary to have suffered a loss. The defendant proposed the joint acquisition of a sound commercial business to the claimants who were foreigners and had to rely on the defendant's expertise. Notwithstanding the good margin of profit obtained by all those involved in the transaction, the Court of Appeal held the defendant liable of breach of fiduciary duty because he had not disclosed to the claimants that he had a personal interest in the business. Arden LJ, with whom Jonathan Parker LJ agreed, awarded an account of profits:

---

[1]   *Regal (Hastings) Ltd v Gulliver* [1942] 1 All ER 378 (HL) 392 (Lord Wright).

[2]   Eg *Bell v Eden Project* [2002] FSR 43 (Ch).

[3]   *Boardman v Phipps* [1967] 2 AC 46 (HL).

[4]   In *Douglas v Hello! (No 6)* [2006] QB 125 (CA) 165, Lord Phillips MR, handing down the judgment of the court, said: 'confidential or private information, which is capable of commercial exploitation but which is only protected by the law of confidence, does not fall to be treated as property that can be owned and transferred.'

[5]   *Cf Industrial Development Consultants v Cooley* [1972] 1 WLR 443 (Roskill J).

[6]   *Ibid* 449 and 453: no moral evaluation takes place, it suffices that the claimant's private interest conflicts grievously with his duty to his employer.

[7]   Edelman, 192.

[8]   *Mohammed Murad and Layla Mohammed Murad v Hashim Ibrahim Khalil Al-Saraj and Westwood Business Inc* [2005] EWCA Civ 959 (CA).

The fact that the fiduciary can show that that party would not have made a loss is, on the authority of the *Regal* case, an irrelevant consideration so far as an account of profits is concerned. Likewise, it follows in my judgment from the *Regal* case that it is no defence for a fiduciary to say that he would have made the profit even if there had been no breach of fiduciary duty.[9]

If, in the face of the recent judicial developments, the proprietary avenue is preferred, then the victim of the breach must be seeking to recover a loss, which corresponds to the defendant's gain. Proprietary language, therefore, implies that the account of profits is alternative to the normal compensatory measure because it offers a different basis to assess the loss itself. If it is accepted that damages are granted on the more appropriate, non-proprietary basis of breach of a fiduciary duty, the qualification of the assessment points towards the opposite direction of a proper case of restitution for wrongs, because, as Arden LJ observed, the claim does not aim to redress the patrimonial disadvantage of the fiduciary.

ii Breach of Confidence

> What has the plaintiff expended on manufacturing these goods? What is the price which he has received on their sale? and the difference is the profit[10].

In *Peter Pan v Corsets Silhouette*, Pennycuick J summarises the judicial view on profits as the result of an account. The defendant manufactured his product using information which was given to him confidentially by the claimant. The latter, who had not authorised the production, sought an injunction to restrain the defendant from producing this particular goods and claimed an account of profits. Both were granted by the court.

In the literature, breach of confidence is sometimes seen as an infringement of intellectual property, although it is acknowledged that the judicial approach in this particular context is different from the general approach in intellectual property cases.[11] As will be seen, this approach is common in some civil law jurisdictions. Yet, in English law it seems that other explanations might be just as, or even more, appropriate, for a relationship between breach of confidence and intellectual property rights is possible but not automatic. Lord Phillips MR observed in *Douglas v Hello! (No 6)*:

> [The claimants'] interest in the private information … did not amount to a right of intellectual property. Their right to protection of that interest does not arise because they have some form of proprietary interest in it. If that were the nature of the right, it would be one that could be exercised against a third party regardless of whether he ought to have been aware that the information was private or confidential. In fact the

---

[9] *Ibid* para 67.
[10] *Peter Pan Manufacturing Corp v Corsets Silhouette Ltd* [1964] 1 WLR 96, 108 (Pennycuick J).
[11] A Burrows, *Remedies for Tort and Breach of Contract* (3rd edn) (Oxford, OUP 2004) 610.

right depends upon the effect on the third party's conscience of the third party's knowledge of the nature of the information and the circumstances in which it was obtained.[12]

In the so-called *Spycatcher* case,[13] a former member of the British Security Service, MI5, wrote a book on his activities as a spy in violation of both his employment contract and the provisions of the Official Secrets Act 1911. The book was published outside the United Kingdom. One of the defendants bought the British newspaper serialisation rights and published an extract of the book some days before the book's publication in the United States. The claimant sought an account of the profits made through the publication of the excerpts in the United Kingdom. Relief was granted on the basis of breach of confidence. As already pointed out, it is questionable whether the wrong committed by the defendant was a consequence of any violation of intellectual property. The preferable explanation classifies the wrong as the result of an infringement of an obligation of confidentiality upon the members of MI5. In this case, this obligation had a contractual nature,[14] for it arose from the employment contract, but it also had roots in the Official Secrets Act 1911. This approach would link breach of confidence to the cases of breach of contract examined in chapter four, so that the award could be classified as a proper instance of restitution for wrongs. Looking for the legal principle which could support the award of an account of profits, Lord Keith applied a well-known formula: '[N]o one should be permitted to gain from his own wrongdoing'.[15] Lord Goff disagreed on this point. The scope of the formula is too wide 'and does not itself provide any sure guidance to the solution of a problem in any particular case'.[16] Suspicious of all-round principles, his Lordship was in favour of a selected application of the formula, whose validity has to be considered on a case-by-case basis.

B   German Law

There are at least three groups of cases in which the quantification of damages differs from the normal approach to compensation. The first group concerns breach of fiduciary duty. This is not German terminology and taxonomy. Yet, it is possible to find constellations which in England would be analysed under that heading. The second group of judicial decisions deals with breach of confidence. The third group concerns the violation of rights to personality.

---

[12]   *Douglas v Hello!* (n 4) 167 (Lord Phillips MR).
[13]   *A-G v Guardian Newspapers Ltd (No 2)* [1990] 1 AC 109 (HL).
[14]   However, the presence of a contract is not an essential requisite of the claim. *Cf Coco v Clark* [1968] FSR 415.
[15]   *Guardian Newspapers* (n 13) 262 (Lord Keith).
[16]   *Ibid* 286 (Lord Goff).

i Breach of Fiduciary Duty

In the analysis of German proprietary wrongs I examined the hypothetical situation in which the claimant attempts to recover in unjustified enrichment a bribe which a third party had paid to the claimant's employee.[17] My conclusion was that the action was doomed to fail. This example served to illustrate that restitution for wrongs and restitution for unjustified enrichment have different areas of application. My view receives further support from those German cases which correspond to the English breach of fiduciary duty. The following instance[18] helps to illuminate the point.

The defendant D was an employee of the company C, which dealt with the transport of industrial waste. D accepted a bribe from the third party T in exchange for transporting metal for T. C, after discovering of the bribe, claimed restitution of the moneys paid to D. According to para 675 BGB,

> [t]he provisions of 663, 665 to 667 … apply *mutatis mutandis* to a contract for service or a contract for work which has for its object the charge of an affair.[19]

The provisions mentioned refer to mandate. Among them, para 667 BGB is of particular relevance for the topic under consideration. It states: 'A mandatary is bound to hand over to his mandator all that … he obtains from the charge of the affair.'[20] This provision has been used by the judiciary as a tool to grant restitution of anything which has been obtained by the 'fiduciary' without the 'beneficiary's' knowledge. The prevailing view among the judiciary[21] and literature[22] is that 'all that the mandatary obtains' is to be interpreted as including everything which has been received in connection with the mandate. This also comprises money paid as a bribe. In the case just described, the BGH followed this doctrine and, applying para 667 BGB, compelled the defendant to give up the benefit accruing to him from the wrong.

As it emerges from the description of the restitutionary duty upon the defendant, the court opted for a restitutionary mechanism based upon the commission of a wrong which was independent of the loss suffered by the claimant. In Germany, this mechanism is not considered to be connected to the law of damages. In fact, if a loss arises to the claimant besides the benefit accruing to the wrongdoer, the latter may be exposed to a concurrent claim for damages.[23] Para 667 BGB contains an autonomous contractual action. The claim allows the victim to recover at least part of the profits which derive to the mandatary from the perpetration of the wrong.

---

[17] See ch 3, n 62 and text thereof.
[18] (1963) BGHZ 38 171. The case has been simplified for explanatory purposes.
[19] CH Wang (tr), *The German Civil Code* (London, Stevens 1907).
[20] *Ibid.*
[21] (1963) BGHZ 39 1; more generally BGH [1991] *Neue Juristische Wochenschrift* 1224.
[22] Staudinger/Wittmann, '§ 667' para 9; contrast MünchKomm/Seiler, '§ 667' para 17.
[23] Staudinger/Wittmann, *ibid.*

ii   Breach of Confidence

In cases involving breach of confidence, the courts see no reason to treat the wrongdoer differently from somebody who has violated intellectual property rights. Secret information pertaining to a company is placed on the same level with patent and copyright.[24] However, the misuse of confidential information is still kept separated from the violation of intellectual property rights even if the two wrongs are held to be similar enough to justify the same kind of response.

In a well-known case,[25] the two defendants, who were employed by a computer manufacturer, resigned from their positions in order to start a new company together with a third person. They revealed to the new company some secret information about a new model of computer which they had obtained when still working for the old employer. As a result of this information and their work for the old employer, the defendants were able to produce and distribute a new computing machine before their old company. The aggrieved company sought delictual relief against its old employees and against the new company. The claimant brought a delictual action, for it could not rely on the criminal law provision in para 17 UWG (Unfair Competition Act), which was barred by limitation. The court allowed the claim on the basis of para 826 BGB, which provides 'compensation', *Schadensersatz,* for damage caused wilfully and contrary to public policy. As regards the measure of damages, the claimant was given the same choice between compensation, a fictional agreement, and an account of profits, which would have been offered for the violation of an intellectual property right. Doubts have been raised in the literature[26] on the appropriateness of a method used for the quantification of damages arising from intellectual property violations. This notwithstanding, the courts do not show any intention of abandoning this line. Therefore, the same rules which apply to infringements of intellectual property can be considered to apply to breach of confidence as well.

iii   Violation of Personality Rights

This topic has attracted the attention of German scholars after a seminal decision of the Federal Court of Justice (BGH) known as the *Caroline* case. To understand this decision, and some of the reactions which it provoked, I shall first present the main developments in the judiciary which have prepared the terrain for the judicial change of direction.

---

[24]   (1972) BGHZ 57 116, 122 (*Wandsteckdose II* case).
[25]   BGH [1977] Gewerblicher Rechtsschutz und Urheberrecht 539 (*Prozeßrechner* case).
[26]   MünchKomm/Oetker, '§ 252' para 55.

a   The Situation before the Caroline Case

Two cases mark this area of the law. The first case is the so-called *Paul Dahlke* case.[27] Mr Dahlke was a German actor who accepted an offer to pose for a photographer. While the set of photographs was taken, the photographer proposed that the actor should pretend to ride a motor scooter, which the photographer happened to have at hand. What the photographer did not disclose to Mr Dahlke was that he had taken photos of other celebrities on the same motor scooter for the purpose of selling them to the company which produced the motor scooters for an advertising campaign. The actor, who knew nothing of the campaign and thought that the photos would be published in a magazine, brought an action for damages against the photographer and the publisher of the advertisements. The court explained that the conduct of the defendants opened two different avenues to the claimant. In this case, both avenues would have produced the same result.

On the one hand, the court granted damages according to the model of the fictional agreement, which is common in the context of intellectual property rights: damages were assessed on the basis of the amount of money which under normal circumstances – *die üblichen Bedingungen* – would have been necessary to buy the publication rights from the claimant.[28] On the other hand, the court stated that the actor could have claimed in unjustified enrichment for restitution. The subject-matter of the claim would have corresponded to the sum for which the claimant would have normally given his permission to publication. Although it was not specified whether this should be pursued in the form of a non-performance-based claim, or *Nichtleistungskondiktion*,[29] it can be inferred from the facts that no performance-based *Kondiktion* would have been possible against the publisher.

A few years after the *Paul Dahlke* case, the court had to decide how to proceed when the violation of the personality right affected someone who was not known to the general public. This is the *Herrenreiter* case.[30] During an equestrian event, a photographer took a picture of one of the competing horsemen. The photo was then sold for advertising purposes without the authorisation of the horseman, who some time later saw his own image on horseback advertising a product which stimulated male virility. The horseman sought delictual relief against the advertising company. In the opinion of the court, the doctrine of the *Paul Dahlke* case could not be applied. A fictional agreement is only possible when the victim has concretely suffered a pecuniary loss. To put it into English terminology, the award required a real loss of the chance to bargain for one's own image. Yet, in the present case, the horseman was not a famous person, so that he could not prove that he had suffered any kind of pecuniary loss deriving from the wrong. He had never had any bargaining power on this matter. Nevertheless, the circumstances

---

[27]   (1956) BGHZ 20 345.
[28]   *Ibid* 353.
[29]   On the *Nichtleistungskondiktion*, see ch 3, II B.
[30]   (1958) BGHZ 26 349.

in which the image of the claimant was published justified compensation, namely for the pain and suffering caused by the use of the image of the victim for this particular kind of product. Thus, the court granted damages in the same amount that the court at first instance had quantified the fictional agreement between the claimant and the defendant. There was absolutely no doubt that the court was awarding compensation, albeit the award was assessed using a less common measure. The legal basis for this form of compensation was found in para 847 (1) BGB, which states:

> In the case of injury to the body or health, or in the case of deprivation of liberty, the injured person may also demand fair compensation in money for damage which is not damage to property.[31]

For the purposes of granting compensation in such cases, the meaning of 'deprivation of liberty' was stretched by the court to encompass 'deprivation of the possibility of taking decisions regarding one's own life'. Thus, alongside the physical deprivation, the court also recognised an 'intellectual' form of deprivation, which gave rise to compensatory damages.[32]

b   The New Scenario

The two previous decisions set the framework for the response triggered by the violation of rights to personality of 'popular' as well as 'unknown' victims.[33] In a more recent case, however, the judiciary introduced a new approach.[34] The claimant was Caroline, Princess of Monaco. She claimed for rectification of some statements made in two magazines, which not only gave the wrong impression that the claimant had granted an exclusive interview to the defendant, but also quoted false statements concerning the core of her private life. In addition to rectification, the claimant sought delictual compensatory relief in the form of damages for non-pecuniary loss. The court granted rectification and damages for the violation of the victim's right to self-determination. The violation of the right to personality, said the court, triggers damages which do not have their legal base in para 847 (1) BGB, a provision which establishes the conditions for an award of damages for non-pecuniary losses. Rather, they have their roots directly in the protection of the person granted by Arts 1 and 2 (1) GG – that is, *Grundgesetz*, the German Constitution – which deal with human dignity and the free development of personality. Para 847 (1) BGB compelled the judges to the use of a more or less 'compensatory' language. Once this head of damages was freed from that restriction, it became possible to go beyond mere compensation. The satisfaction

---

[31]   Goren (tr), *The German Civil Code* (revd edn) (Littleton, Colorado, Rothman 1994).

[32]   (1958) BGHZ 26 349, 355-356.

[33]   See also (1960) BGHZ 30 7 (*Caterina Valente* case); BGH [1971] *Neue Juristische Wochenschrift* 698.

[34]   (1996) BGHZ 128 1 (*Caroline von Monaco* case). An English translation of the case can be read, in summarised form, on the internet: www.iuscomp.org/gla/ (16 June 2006).

of the victim and the function of deterrence were seen by the court as the two main evaluative factors in the assessment of damages in the case of violation of rights to personality.

The main instruments in the hands of the courts were, until the *Caroline* case, the fictional agreement and compensation for non-pecuniary loss. The fictional agreement method is for the judiciary of little use to victims such as 'ordinary people', who from the beginning do not have any bargaining power. The claimant can elect to seek restitution of the unjustified enrichment or delictual compensation, particularly through the mechanism of non-pecuniary loss. It would be incorrect to speak of restitution for wrongs in this context. Damages for a non-pecuniary loss are granted bearing in mind the position of the victim, not the position of the wrongdoer. It does not matter whether the defendant benefited from his wrongdoing, although in practice the judges will tend to take such benefits into account within the assessment of damages.

The *Caroline von Monaco* case changed this framework, but not from the perspective of restitution for wrongs. The emphasis placed on the preventive function of this head of damages seems to suggest that this seminal decision introduced exemplary damages into German law. The court held that the benefit deriving from the wrongdoing is only one of the elements which the court has to consider in granting damages. Yet, the judges rejected any implication that, in the cases of inconsiderate commercialisation of personality, restitution would automatically be allowed for the entire gain.[35] Just as in the case of compensation for non-pecuniary losses, in the restitutionary model depicted by the court the indemnity granted can coincide with the wrongdoer's benefit, but this coincidence is accidental. Thus, despite the fact that it is difficult to deny that judicial authority has introduced a non-compensatory element in the law of damages, it would be incorrect to conclude that this is a restitutionary award.

A definition of the damages awarded in the *Caroline von Monaco* case as aiming to punish the defendant is rejected by the majority view in the literature.[36] A few years before *Caroline*, the German Federal Court had expressly denied recognition to a decision by the Superior Court of the State of California granting exemplary damages to the claimant on the ground that such damages were contrary to German *ordre public*.[37] The German court differentiated the punitive function of exemplary damages from the function of providing satisfaction to the victim, which is recognised to be within the scope of damages ex para 847 BGB. Even so, both the satisfaction and deterrence function of the damages awarded in the *Caroline* case on the one hand, and the way in which such damages are concretely applied on the other, suggest that they are to be classified

---

[35] *Ibid* 16.
[36] W Seitz, 'Prinz und Prinzessin – Wandlungen des Deliktsrechts durch Zwangskommerzialisierung der Persönlichkeit' [1996] *Neue Juristische Wochenschrift* 2848-2850. For a perspective of the *Caroline* case as granting exemplary damages, see J Rosengarten, 'Der Präventionsgedanke im deutschen Zivilrecht' [1996] *Neue Juristische Wochenschrift* 1935-1938.
[37] (1993) BGHZ 118 312, 338.

as exemplary damages. A different explanation would stretch beyond any acceptable standard the definition of *Schmerzensgeld*, or pain and suffering, allowed in some special cases by para 847 BGB. Indeed, more recent analyses[38] of the *Caroline* case accept that there is quite a strict link between the damages awarded and a punitive intent. This is particularly clear if one considers that the quantification of the damages was 'out of proportion' if compared with the damage itself.[39]

c   *Restitutionary Damages and the Caroline Case*

Back in the 1970s, an influential paper by Peter Schlechtriem proposed to use the German law of unjustified enrichment to compel the wrongdoer to give up the benefit actually received in the case of violation of personality rights.[40] In fact, the proposed method was an attempt to enlarge the radius of the *Nichtleistungskondiktion* for policy reasons. This construction provided an explanation dogmatically in harmony with the principles of the law of obligations, without imposing solutions which would enter dangerous grounds, such as noncompensatory damages or alternative measures of compensation. Two decades later,[41] Schlechtriem returned to the topic of his older article. Referring to the *Caroline* case in the context of restitution as an instrument to protect privacy, he states that 'revocation of untrue statements is a kind of granting of restitutionary damages'.[42] Yet, it does not seem that the relationship proposed by Schlechtriem between restitutionary damages and the law of unjustified enrichment is taxonomically correct. The latter does indeed deal with restitution, but not with damages, which pertain to contract and delict. On the other hand, this doctrine, according to which 'the violation of the right to one's personality … gives rise to a restitutionary measure of damages',[43] is irreconcilable with the point made in *Caroline* that the benefit of the wrongdoer is only one among many elements to be taken into consideration when awarding damages for the violation of personality rights, which excludes that the award is purely restitutionary. Mentioning 'a kind of granting restitutionary damages', Schlechtriem, was more likely to refer to a certain overlap of restitution for unjustified enrichment and restitution for wrongs. I have repeatedly argued that this view is in conflict with a correct interpretation of the law of obligations, for restitution for unjustified enrichment applies compensatory reasoning.

---

[38]   C-W Canaris, 'Gewinnabschöpfung bei Verletzung des allgemeinen Persönlichkeitsrechts' in A-J Ahrens (ed), *Festschrift für E Deutsch zum 70. Geburtstag* (Köln, Heymann 1999) 85-109, 106-107; C Siemes, 'Gewinnabschöpfung bei Zwangskommerzialisierung der Persönlichkeit durch die Presse' (2001) 201 *Archiv für die civilistische Praxis* 202-231, 212.

[39]   Thus Canaris, *ibid* 107.

[40]   P Schlechtriem, 'Bereicherungsansprüche wegen Persönlichkeitsverletzung' R Fischer (ed), *Festschrift für W Hefermehl zum 70. Geburtstag* (München, Beck 1976) 445-465.

[41]   P Schlechtriem, 'Some Thoughts on the Decision of the BGH concerning Princess Caroline of Monaco' in B Markesinis (ed), *Protecting Privacy, The Clifford Chance Lectures* (Oxford, OUP 1999) vol 4 131-138.

[42]   *Ibid* 131.

[43]   Schlechtriem (n 41) 133.

Schlechtriem is not the only German author who keeps the two restitutionary models too close together on the basis of a strong similarity of their respective functions. Analysing the restitutionary mechanism activated by a wrong from an economic perspective, Johannes Köndgen concludes that this structure is by no means exceptional. Yet, German lawyers would not be familiar with it because restitutionary responses are scattered in different areas of the law.[44] However, Köndgen himself seems to add to this uncertainty when he refers to this type of response as '*restitutiver Schadensersatz*', which he opposes to a '*kompensatorischer Schadensersatz*'.[45] '*Schadensersatz*' literally means 'substitution for the loss', whereas this expression is used exclusively with the meaning of 'compensation of the loss'.[46] Hence, if my understanding of German law is correct, adding 'compensatory' to substitution does not qualify the response in any further fashion. On the contrary, 'restitutionary substitution', which, on the basis of the mentioned identity between substitution and compensation, sounds very much like 'restitutionary compensation', is a dubious term: a legal response can compel the wrongdoer either to compensate or to give up, but it cannot pursue both aims at the same time.

German authors are dissatisfied with the judge-made response in delict which the BGH has developed *ex novo* in the *Caroline* case. In the literature, there is strong support for a solution which approaches the topic from the avenue of unjustified enrichment. This solution appeals to the scholars, for in their view it fits better within the framework of the German law of obligations. It has the further advantage, one might add, that it moves the focus from a *terra incognita* to an area of the law which – from this perspective – is characterised by a less disruptive content.

C   Italian Law

Questions about the non-compensatory, possibly restitutionary, nature of the award emerge in at least three groups of cases. The first group pertains to the violation of personality rights. Its importance in the present context is more circumscribed than in German law. The second group concerns the so-called environmental damage, which the draftsmen introduced to tackle environmental threats. This institution, some aspects of which might be confused with restitutionary damages, has raised an intense debate in the literature. Finally, a small number of miscellaneous cases are characterised by a non-compensatory response. But first, I shall spend a few words on breach of fiduciary duty.

---

[44]   J Köndgen, 'Gewinnabschöpfung als Sanktion unerlaubten Tuns' (2000) 64 *Rabels Zeitschrift* 661-695, 663.

[45]   *Ibid* 670.

[46]   This point finds wide agreement among German courts and scholars. Para 249 BGB describes the duty to *Schadensersatz* as a duty 'to re-create the situation, which would exist had the event which compels to make *Schadensersatz* not occurred'. There is little or no room for restitutionary damages within this definition: *ex multis* MünchKomm/Oetker, '§ 249' paras 1 and 8.

i   Breach of Fiduciary Duty

Unlike English and German law, breach of fiduciary duty does not have any particularly relevant position in Italian law. A right to restitution of the gain made by the wrongdoer qua wrongdoer is not among the responses available to the victim. Although the Italian legislation on mandate is similar to the German legislation on this point, the question of gain-based awards does not arise. Yet, it would be possible to anchor in the statute a restitutionary mechanism triggered by a breach of such duty. Art 1713 (1) cc states: 'The mandatory … shall turn over to [the mandator] all that he has received as a result of the mandate.'[47] This formula could theoretically justify an obligation to give up the benefit which has accrued to the mandatory, or the 'fiduciary', as a consequence of his wrong, for instance a bribe. Indeed academic commentators[48] have remarked that the mandatory must give up to the mandator every benefit which finds its cause in the mandate. One could contend, with the German scholars, that 'everything' must mean also the gains made from a wrong. However, this point is not argued directly in the literature and judicial decisions, although Art 1713 (1) cc could give an adequate support to the theory of restitution for wrongs.

ii   Violation of Personality Rights

The issues which can be tackled through a restitutionary award for wrongs do not disappear only because restitutionary damages have not found recognition in Italian law. Italian courts address the matter through other avenues, the outcome of which is not always satisfactory. The solutions adopted by the judiciary are similar to the responses which can be found in the other legal systems under comparison. The tools of the Italian law of damages, after all, do not differ greatly from those adopted by the main European systems. Yet, there is little trace of the intense debate on the nature of damages granted by a violation of personality rights which takes place in Germany, although the development of German law is closely monitored in Italy.

The courts award both pecuniary and non-pecuniary damages in case of violations of personality rights. Whenever possible, pecuniary damages are used as first resort for this purpose. The courts define this particular head of damages as the 'price of the consent'. This formula refers to a legal figure which has already been encountered in this analysis while commenting upon English and German law. The Italian variation runs as follows.

Gino Bartali, a very popular cyclist of the past, founded his own bicycle company. For advertising purposes, he used a famous photo showing himself and his main rival, the well-known Fausto Coppi, in the act of passing each other a bottle of water during a race. A few years later, the defendant, another bicycle-producer, utilised the same photo to promote its products. The cyclist claimed

---

[47]   M Beltramo, G Longo and JH Merryman (trs), *The Italian Civil Code* (New York, Oceana 1969).
[48]   G Cian and A Trabucchi, *Commentario breve al codice civile* (5th edn) (Padova, Cedam 1997) Art 1713, III.

compensation for the loss caused by the unauthorised use of his image.[49] At first and second instance, the claim was rejected because the claimant had not been able to prove any loss resulted from the exploitation of his image. The Court of Cassation reversed the decision of the Court of Appeal. It observed that in such cases the damage consists of the loss of the concrete possibility of commercialising one's image for the same kind of advertising. The commercial value of cyclist's image for the purpose of his own advertising was reduced through the use of that image by the competition.

The *Bartali* case shows that the Italian judiciary prefers the German variation of the doctrine of the lost opportunity to bargain rather than the English approach. In fact, in the opinion of the court, the loss arises when the commercial value of the image is concretely affected, and not only as a consequence of the impossibility of the victim – any victim, not just the one who would have a valuable image to bargain with – to sell his image to the very defendant. The courts derive their right to assess damages according to this price of the consent theory from Art 1226 cc, to which Art 2056 cc expressly refers as a source for the measure of delictual damages. Art 1226 cc states: 'If the loss cannot be determined precisely, the judge will quantify damages on an equitable basis.' The necessity of technical discretion is explained with the impossibility of a precise quantification of damages in most of the cases involving a violation of personality rights.[50] The difficulties connected to the individuation of the pecuniary loss can be avoided by granting damages for the non-pecuniary loss instead, which leaves much more room to the courts because of the nature of such damages. The following case demonstrates this point.

A magazine published without authorisation excerpts of letters sent by the Italian writer Elio Vittorini to a person who secretly translated works from English into Italian on his behalf. The magazine used this correspondence as evidence that the author misappropriated work done by others as his own. As the writer himself was already deceased, his daughter claimed in delict against the unauthorised use of the letters relying on the damage to the reputation of the author and the infringement of the right to privacy of correspondence.[51] The court held the defendant liable, but could not find any evidence of a pecuniary loss. Justifying damages as a reduction of the commercial value of the writer's image was considered to be offensive to the memory of the author. Furthermore, a violation of Art 70 *Legge* 22 April 1941 No 633 (Copyright Law) was ruled out, because the excerpts of the letters published were too short to activate the protection given by this statute. The court did not want the wrongdoer to escape liability. An award of 'moral damages'[52] (Art 2059 cc) provided a solution to the impasse. The judgment contains no precise reference to the criteria which apply

---

[49]   Cassazione, 6 February 1993 No 1503 [1995] Foro italiano I 1617 (*Bartali* case).
[50]   Tribunale Roma, 22nd December 1994 [1995] Foro italiano I 2285.
[51]   Tribunale Milano, 30 June 1994 [1995] Foro italiano I 1667 (*Vittorini* case).
[52]   In Italian law, compensatory damages which are awarded for non-pecuniary losses are called 'moral damages'. In the context of Italian law a literal translation has been preferred.

to the quantification of such damages. The court only mentioned 'the parameters which are normally adopted by this court in similar cases'. Yet, such statement provides no information about any such parameters, leaving the court free to assess damages in a manner which the judges deem to be in accordance with justice. The court used indeed the freedom granted by this statement in a way which enabled the judges to identify the measure of moral damages with the benefit accruing to the agent as a consequence of the perpetration of the wrong.

Moral damages cannot be seen as the ideal substitute for a gain-based award. In many cases, they cannot be used to compel the wrongdoer to give up his enrichment. The function of the existing structures, as judicial authority[53] has explicitly, albeit in a subdued fashion, recognised, is mainly to punish the defendant for conduct which is reputed to be particularly blameworthy, or to grant the claimant strong protection for rights which can easily be violated by the agent with minimum risk. Such damages fall within the area of exemplary damages. The Italian judiciary, by contrast with its German counterpart,[54] does not hide behind a definition of compensation which is stretched far beyond its possible limits. Indeed, the courts admit that they are granting a mild form of exemplary damages, in the assessment of which the benefit gained by the wrongdoer can play a significant role.

iii 'Environmental Damage'

An analysis of restitution for wrongs must devote some attention to this topic. It is in this context that the Italian draftsmen for the first time have explicitly included the gain made by the wrongdoer among the criteria which the courts have to take into account when assessing damages. In the following examination, I shall assess the role of the defendant's gain in the quantification of this award for environmental damage, which is a quite unique response in the law of damages. In particular, the question arises whether the wording of the relevant provision suggests the existence of restitutionary damages as a statutory institution.

Art 18 of the *Legge* 8 July 1986 No 349 describes the delictual framework as far as recovery for environmental losses is concerned. Art 18 (1) states:

> Any fraudulent, malicious, or negligent act that, in violating statutory provisions, negatively affects the environment damaging, changing, deteriorating, or destroying it partially or totally obliges the person who has committed the act to pay damages to the State.

This provision has triggered a long debate on the notion of environmental loss, which is still far from settled. The main explanation as to why a specific norm was required in order to protect the environment relates to the fact that the general delictual claim of Art 2043 cc could not cover all environmental issues because

---

[53] Appello Milano, 23 December 1986 [1987] Repertorio Foro italiano Danni civili No 95.
[54] *Cf* the discussion about the *Caroline von Monaco* case, n 36 above and text thereof.

the notion of 'environment' is too abstract. Furthermore, it was often impossible to determine the victim of an environmental wrong. Art 18 L. 346/1986 turns the State into environmental victim qua State, rather than as the owner of the environmentally-damaged area. Consequently, only the State is allowed to claim for damages under this provision.

A seminal decision[55] of the Constitutional Court threw some light on the whole matter shortly after the L 346/1986 was enacted. The court held that the environment is a legal good which is protected by legal norms. The paucity of natural environmental resources justifies and determines the exchange value of this good. Thus, the environment has an economic value, although there is no concrete market value for it. It is not clear whether the response to the environmental damage should be classified under damages for pecuniary or for non-pecuniary loss. The majority view in the literature seems to be oriented towards the second solution because, as Carlo Castronovo has observed,[56] environmental damage does not just consist of destroyed fauna. In fact, environmental damage does not concern concrete parts of the environment and therefore it cannot be quantified according to the *Differenztheorie* as the difference in its value before and after the damaging event.[57] Art 18 (6) L 346/1986 recognises the difficulty in the quantification of environmental damages[58] and consequently allows the judges to assess them by applying technical discretion according to the model depicted in Art 1226 cc. Yet, in comparison to Art 1226 cc, Art 18 (6) L 346/1986 presents some novel factors. In particular, it mentions 'the benefit accrued to the wrongdoer as a consequence of his conduct in violating environmental goods'.

The analysis of environmental damages was prompted by the question whether it is possible to infer from L 386/1986 that restitutionary damages have been codified for the first time. No matter how tempting an answer in the affirmative might be, it does not seem that the environmental loss triggers restitutionary damages. The reasons which compel this denial are the same which have already been put forward in every case in which restitution of the gain was not the only aim of the legal response. In fact, the benefit of the defendant is just one of the elements which the courts may consider in quantifying the consequences of a loss. Hence, the function of Art 18 (6) L 436/1986 on this point is to threaten potential wrongdoers by seeking to ensure that the disadvantages which result from such a wrong exceed the advantages which can be gained. This appears to be another case of exemplary damages.

The punitive role of environmental damages and the deficiencies of the *Differenztheorie* are clearly understood by the judiciary, as the following case[59]

---

[55]   Corte Costituzionale, 30 December 1987 No 641 [1988] Foro italiano I 93.

[56]   C Castronovo, 'Il danno all'ambiente nel sistema di responsabilità civile' in *La nuova responsabilità civile* (2nd edn) (Milano, Giuffrè 1997) 333-347, 337-338.

[57]   Cassazione, 9 April 1992 No 4362 [1992] Massimario Giurisprudenza italiana.

[58]   For a similar view in English law see J Murphy, 'Noxious Emissions and Common Law Liability: Tort in the Shadow of Regulation' in J Lowry and R Edmunds (eds), *Environmental Protection and the Common Law* (Oxford, Hart 2000) 51-76, 51 n 3.

[59]   Cassazione, 1 September 1995 No 9211 [1996] Giustizia civile 777.

demonstrates. A pharmaceutical company delivered some highly noxious substances to a company which provided storage facilities for these products. The container which was used for such purpose had a leak and part of those substances permeated into the earth and thus into the surrounding environment. In consequence, the State had to conduct an emergency intervention to clear the whole area. The State subsequently sued the second company in delict, claiming inter alia environmental damages. As the second company went bankrupt before this trial could begin, the claimant sought to obtain environmental damages from the pharmaceutical company. The claim succeeded. The court recognised the liability of the defendant on the basis of an omission to put in place the necessary control mechanisms, *culpa in vigilando*. The pharmaceutical company was liable in delict even after having delivered the noxious substances to the storage company, for it was held that handing over such substances to another party is not in itself sufficient to fulfil the duties connected with proper disposition. Rather, the pharmaceutical company should have checked the facilities used by the second company for storing such dangerous material before entering into the contract of delivery.

The court pointed out that environmental damages are not to be confused with the more direct damages for pecuniary loss which arise from the perpetration of the wrong, such as the costs of the elimination of the consequences triggered by the inadequacy of the container. Environmental damage is immediate, but its consequences would be evident only as time goes by. More importantly for the present context, the court expressly stated that the *Differenztheorie* could not be applied because environmental damages are a type of 'civil punishment',[60] as is underlined by the elements which concur in the measure of damages: inter alia the malice of the wrongdoer and the benefit gained by him through the wrong. This last judicial statement confirms that there is no room for restitution for wrongs in environmental damages ex Art 18 (6) L 346/1986. The aim of the draftsmen was to punish the transgressor, not to strip him of the gains deriving from the delict.

iv   Other Cases of Restitution in a Delictual Context

A case[61] which has triggered some discussion in academic circles presents aspects of interest as regards the relationship between restitutionary damages and the general enrichment action of Art 2041 cc. Naples City Council found out that some buildings were in such a disastrous condition that they could collapse at any moment. Consequently, it put the claimant in charge of consolidation works which were so urgent that there was no time for the appropriate bureaucratic procedures. After the work was done, the council refused payment on the ground that the contract with the claimant was void due to the lack of the necessary formalities, so that no obligation rested upon the defendant council to fulfil its

---

[60] *Ibid* 780.
[61] Cassazione, 12 April 1995 No 4192 [1995] Foro italiano I 1716.

contractual duties. Such cases of enrichment of public authorities are normally dealt with by the judiciary through the general enrichment claim. From this point of view, the decision is unexceptional. A claim was allowed for restitution of the unjust enrichment of the defendant. Yet, not content with such a traditional solution, the Cassation Court advanced a principle, binding upon the lower court to which the case was referred, according to which the measure of the unjust enrichment was to be calculated by means of the parameters designated by Art 1226 cc.[62]

This last statement has been praised in the literature[63] as an avenue for introducing restitution of the enrichment into delict law. Yet, this use of Art 1226 cc is inconsistent with the function performed by this provision in the law of damages. The norm finds application in the assessment of contractual and, by virtue of Art 2056 cc, of delictual damages.[64] There is no room to establish a link between a rule with only contractual and delictual relevance and unjust enrichment. In fact, there is no real need for such a link. The evaluation of an *unjust* enrichment already implies an amount of judicial discretion for establishing whether the transfer of wealth is unjust. Thus, the criterion of Art 1226 cc cannot add anything meaningful to the task of the courts. Even justifying the application of this provision to unjust enrichment situations by way of an analogical extension of the technical discretion applicable under Art 1226 cc is not helpful. From this extension it cannot be inferred that restitution can all of a sudden be granted in delict law through Art 1226 cc. What the judges attempted to do was to extend some delictual rules to the law of unjust enrichment, not to create a new legal response which applies both to the law of delict and the law of unjust enrichment. Moreover, Art 1226 cc gives technical discretion to the judges only in the context of those situations when damage is certain but cannot easily be proved. So, this norm cannot be used as the sole basis for introducing a new legal response which modifies the 'general rule' of compensation laid down by Art 2043 cc. The difference between the two situations, technical discretion on the one hand and the introduction of a new legal response into the system on the other, is subtle, but clear. Hence, Art 1226 cc does not provide a basis for a theory of restitutionary, or any other kind of non-compensatory, damages. In effect, any development of restitutionary damages on the basis of the existing codal provisions would be difficult, because Art 2043 cc refers exclusively to compensation as the aim of damages in delict. Thus, if restitution for wrongs were to find recognition in the Italian system, the way forward seems to consider Art 2043 cc as relating to compensatory damages alone, and to opt for an extra-codal, judicial development of non-compensatory damages.

---

[62] On this provision, see ch 3, n 72 and text thereof.
[63] Monateri, *Responsabilità* 336-337.
[64] See ch 2, n 52 and text thereof.

II   Concluding Observations

With this chapter, the comparison of the three modern jurisdictions draws to a close. The focus has been on the identification of structures which perform or are considered to perform a restitutionary function for wrongs. It has also been seen how the presence of alternative legal institutions might explain the variable degree of acceptance of restitutionary damages. Finally, the question has been addressed of the level of consistency of restitution for wrongs with the legal systems under comparison. There are some undeniable obstacles to the introduction of restitutionary damages in civil law. Similarly, there are obstacles to their expansion in English law – the only legal system among the three which recognises restitution for wrongs. This notwithstanding, no structural incompatibility between restitutionary damages and the law of obligations has been identified in any of the jurisdictions compared.

One of the reasons for the limited success of the damages at issue has been individuated in the presence of legal structures which partially overlap with restitutionary damages, such as the German *stellvertretendes commodum*. These structures, however, can account neither for the rejection of restitutionary damages *in toto* nor for their merely exceptional role where recognised. An explanation for these phenomena requires an analysis which examines restitution for wrongs from an historical and a theoretical perspective. This task will be undertaken in the next chapters.

A   The Set of Premises

The comparative analysis has required the formulation of a set of premises with the essential function of developing a common frame of research. If the terms 'restitution' and 'wrongs' corresponded to different legal concepts in each system subject to investigation, or if no legal institutions at all could be identified with such terms, comparison would become impossible. While the term 'restitution' bears fundamentally the same meaning in all systems, it has been necessary to elaborate a notion of wrong which is neutral enough to accommodate the differences which, characteristically, mark the divide between common law and civil law. The concept of a wrong has been borrowed from English law, for it is unknown to the other jurisdictions. For the purposes of this analysis, 'wrong' as a breach of duty has different traits in each legal system. For a more precise explanation of the concept of 'breach of duty', it has been referred to the national systems.

The next step has been to define 'tort', 'equitable wrong', 'delict', and 'breach of contract' as breaches of duty. This has enabled 'wrong' to be classed as a generic term comprising the specific categories which share breach of duty as a common element. Hence, the relationship between 'wrong' on the one hand and 'tort', 'equitable wrong', 'delict', and 'breach of contract' on the other hand is one of *genus* to *species*. This understanding has made it possible to engage in a comparison of restitution for wrongs involving legal systems in which not all of those categories form part of 'wrongs'.

B   Two Considerations

The set of premises rests upon two general considerations. First, the law of obligations can be analysed both in common and civil law in the light of the Roman partition in contract, tort/delict, and unjust/unjustified enrichment as has been developed by Peter Birks in his 'event-based classification'. Tort and delict are different concepts but can be treated as equivalent for the purposes of the present study. Secondly, each legal system of obligations can formulate solutions which might not have the form or the external requisites of restitution for wrongs, for instance because they do not belong to the law damages, such as the *commodum ex negotiatione* of German law. This notwithstanding, these national mechanisms achieve a comparable, if not identical, outcome. In some cases, they tend to replicate the modus operandi of restitution for wrongs.

These considerations allow us to compare the different solutions of each legal system within the same framework of the law of obligations. They rest on the idea that restitution for wrongs is a legal institution which is part of the law of damages. Rights to restitutionary damages are secondary rights triggered by the violation of some interest with legal relevance. Restitutionary rights for wrongs may be present in different areas of the law of obligations.

C   The Relationship with Restitution for Unjust Enrichment

As restitution for unjust enrichment does not require the perpetration of a wrong, its requisites do not coincide with those of restitution for wrongs. In my view, bar a few exceptions, in which restitution is based upon the injustice of the enrichment rather than upon the lack of a legal ground for the transfer, there is more to the distinction of the two claims than what emerges from their requirements. Unjust, or rather unjustified,[65] enrichment claims are triggered by a loss to the claimant and therefore tend to apply compensatory reasoning. The impoverished normally brings an action to claim what does belong or should belong to him, and instead is possessed or owned by somebody else. Restitution for wrongs, by contrast, presupposes that the defendant's benefit is linked to the wrong but the claimant's entitlement to it does not follow from a patrimonial damage. There is no compensatory reasoning in operation here.

---

[65] This term is more correct to identify German and Italian claims, for the law of 'unjust' enrichment plays in both legal systems a less relevant role. F Giglio, 'A Systematic Approach to "Unjust" and "Unjustified" Enrichment' (2003) 23 *OJLS* 455-482.

Edelman argues that the two claims could be in concurrence and that, when this is the case, restitution for wrongs would be more helpful than restitution for unjust enrichment. Considering *United Australia*,[66] he observes:

> [A]ssuming that a corresponding action to the wrong of conversion exists in unjust enrichment, the response of restitution for the unjust enrichment will yield a different result to restitutionary damages for the wrong if change of position is not an available defence in the law of wrongs.[67]

It is worth pursuing this line of analysis, because a few words of comment might help to avoid confusion between the two legal responses. I disagree with Edelman's definition of the damages for conversion as an instance of restitution for wrongs.[68] I also disagree that there can be concurrence between restitution for wrong and restitution for unjust enrichment, except in rare circumstances in which a claim in unjust enrichment is based upon equitable principles. On the other hand, in my view Edelman's 'restitutionary damages' realise a compensatory aim, which means that they are not restitutionary at all.[69] On this premiss, his rejection of this defence in the context of restitution for wrongs is appropriate. The defence is based on the innocent behaviour of the recipient, who was not aware of the duty to restitution. The same line of reasoning is followed in German and Italian law. Paras 818 (4), 819 and 820 BGB bar the defence when the recipient knows of his duty to return the benefit. Italian law is even more severe, for the norms on restitution of what has been unduly paid, Arts 2033 and 2036 cc, do not contemplate the possibility of the defence apart in a few particular cases. Only the general enrichment claim of Art 2041 cc lists the enrichment of the recipient as one of the requirements of the action.

It should not be forgotten that the presence of the defence of change of position is strictly linked to the structure of restitution for unjust enrichment. The wrongful recipient should not be able to avoid restitution for wrongs adducing that he is no longer enriched, because restitutionary damages are awarded in tort/delict and for breach of contract only on the basis of a wrong regardless of other considerations. As such cases presuppose the wrongful behaviour of the recipient, the claim is barred if the enrichee did not behave wrongfully, though he is still enriched. As I pointed out at the beginning of this section, this requirement of wrongfulness is alien to restitution for unjust enrichment, which may be awarded even if the recipient has kept an irreproachable behaviour. The absence of the defence in restitution for wrongs is counterbalanced by the need to prove wrongfulness. Still, there should be mechanisms to shape the

---

[66]   *United Australia Ltd v Barclays Bank Ltd* [1941] AC 1 (HL).
[67]   *Edelman*, 97.
[68]   The point is developed in ch 3, II A i.
[69]   See ch 9, VI.

measure of the award in appropriate circumstances. The level of the compensatory damages is affected by the behaviour of both the claimant and the defendant, and even by external elements; the same flexibility should be granted to the courts when assessing restitutionary damages.

D   Restitution for Wrongs in the Three Jurisdictions

In each legal system under comparison there is some mechanism by which the wrongdoer can be compelled to give up to the victim the benefit which the former has derived from the wrong. The identification of these structures is an important step in the analysis of restitution for wrongs. A further relevant step is the investigation of academic and judicial reactions to the introduction of the notion of restitution for wrongs into the legal system. Each jurisdiction appears to have chosen a characteristic way to deal with the topic and thus has produced an original response within the common framework of the law of obligations.

English law is the system most conscious of the presence of a restitutionary structure for wrongs. Only the English judiciary dares to call 'a spade a spade'.[70] The term 'restitution for wrongs' and the like are widely unknown in the two civil jurisdictions under consideration, although in the German literature there is rising attention for this institution. German law resorts to what seems a restitutionary mechanism for wrongs in the area of contractual remedies for breach of contract. Furthermore, there is certainly some ground to argue that breaches of fiduciary duty trigger a restitutionary mechanism for wrongs. It is also worth mentioning the *Caroline* case, which is testimony to an attempt to introduce non-compensatory awards in consequence of the violation of rights to personality, although only with reference to exemplary damages. On its part, Italian law has proven to be more resistant to the introduction of restitutionary remedies for wrongs. Even when the German school of thought adopts such remedies, or other structures which produce an equivalent result, Italian law tends to deny recognition to restitutionary awards. The question is whether there is any rationale behind the more progressive conduct of the English courts, which traditionally are very cautious in their decisions. The following considerations may help to understand this phenomenon.

E   Some Obstacles

There are reasons for the cautious adoption of restitutionary responses for wrongs which are shared by all jurisdictions under comparison. The principal obstacle is seen in the major challenge which a restitutionary award poses to the compensatory principle. In modern legal systems, the paramount function of the law of damages both in tort/delict and in contract is to make good the loss suffered by the victim. All three legal orders deal primarily with this issue when

---

[70]   *Ministry of Defence v Ashman* (1993) 66 P & CR 195 (CA) 201 (Hoffmann LJ).

they define the rights which arise from a breach of duty or the violation of a right. While the concept of a secondary right as a response to a loss suffered by the victim is grasped almost intuitively as the main function of the law of damages, the idea that the wrongdoer could be obliged to give up his benefit is in tension with pre-existing compensatory biases. This puts some strain on the relationship between these two different heads of damages, including questions of concurrent liability.

Another important factor is the worry on the part of courts and draftsmen that the judiciary may not be able to cope with this head of damages in practice. The fear of the consequences engendered by this new category of damages arguably has a strong impact on the courts and hinders the recognition of restitution for wrongs. If the enrichment of the wrongdoer is the key factor in the quantification of damages, the radius of the potential claimants is greatly extended and it becomes difficult to distinguish the claims which deserve an award from all the others. Furthermore, the extension of the claimant's radius increases the workload of the judiciary with repercussions on the whole of the judicial activity. Those difficulties are worsened by the fact that the various instances of restitution for wrongs are scattered across different areas of the law of obligations. This dispersion has prevented the various instances of restitutionary damages from being understood as belonging to one and the same category, and has contributed to the widespread notion that the damages in question should not exist as a category comparable to compensation. The combination of the factors just mentioned leads to a degree of uncertainty especially in the systems of civil law, in which legal dogmatic plays a bigger role. As a result, there is a concrete risk that legal analysis in civilian systems might apply the wrong taxonomy to an autonomous category of restitutionary damages.

Possibly, the main reason for the faster evolution of English law as compared with the civil law jurisdictions is to be found outside the law of wrongs. Both the German and the Italian legal systems have developed mechanisms which are not based on wrongful behaviour, but might overlap with restitution for wrongs to some extent. The Germans have their *Nichtleistungskondiktion* of para 812 (1) BGB. The Italians use as *extrema ratio* the general enrichment claim of Art 2041 cc. Whereas the Italian claim is granted on considerations of justice, and therefore could indeed be applied as an alternative to restitution for wrongs, the *Nichtleistungskondiktion* achieves an effect akin to compensation and has therefore a different nature from restitutionary damages. Although both solutions produce at best only partly satisfactory results when they are utilised as substitutes for restitution for wrongs, their presence eases the pressure upon draftsmen and the judiciary alike. The courts can adapt the existing instruments to the most compelling cases, thus granting at least partial relief to the victim of a wrong where justice requires redress. This is especially true of Italian law, in which the general enrichment claim is much more flexible than the German counterpart and has a wider radius of application. The presence of this claim is likely to furnish the central explanation for the restrained approach taken by Italian law.

6

The Roman Law of Damages

I The Role of Non-Compensatory Responses

ROMAN LAW HAS a considerable influence on modern European legal orders. It furnishes a different yet useful perspective for the study of restitution for wrongs. The investigation will not involve a comprehensive and detailed analysis of the Roman law of damages, for this general overview aims only to facilitate the understanding of the origin and function of the modern law of damages. Both the German and the Italian systems have their roots in the Roman legal science: their law of delict and the legal responses triggered by the perpetration of a wrong owe much to the original model. With the adoption of the law of obligations, the English legal system has forged a link with Roman law which suggests that even English law can benefit from a diachronic comparison.[1]

A recurring argument in support of the pre-eminence of compensatory damages among the legal responses urges that compensation is the principal aim of the law of delict. Yet the analysis of Roman law demonstrates that compensation has not always been the only or most important remedy. In the Roman law of damages, compensation cohabited alongside punishment and – perhaps – restitution for a long period. The evidence that non-compensatory responses were accepted practice in a legal system which supplied the main remedial structures to modern German and Italian, but also English, law challenges the doubts about the consistency of restitutionary damages with modern Roman-rooted or Roman-influenced legal orders. On the other hand, on this evidence alone it cannot be concluded that such legal orders have recognised this type of damages as well. This finding is proof of a theoretical compatibility, not of the existence of this head of damages. The Roman law of damages was developed first to punish the wrongdoer. Different responses came later. Among them, it might be possible to trace examples of restitution for wrongs, although their restitutionary nature is arguable. They are feeble signals that, under some circumstances, the

---

[1] DJ Ibbetson, *A Historical Introduction to the Law of Obligations* (Oxford, OUP 1999) 1, observes: '[t]he Common law of obligations grew out of the intermingling of native ideas and sophisticated Roman learning.'

Roman law of damages might have applied restitutionary mechanisms for wrongs to redress situations which were perceived as unjust.

On the one hand, this chapter looks for instances of restitutionary damages in Roman law. On the other hand, it seeks to demonstrate that the law of obligations, including the English law of obligations, is consistent with legal responses which do not seek to place the victim in a pre-wrong position. The attainment of this second goal would confirm that compensation does not necessarily have to coincide with the concept of damages, as has been commonly held in English law for a long time.[2] There are indeed reasons for the pre-eminence of compensation. But these reasons are mainly historical, rather than legal, as a crucial historical passage in Roman law illustrates: once the criminal trial was assigned to the exclusive competence of the State, punishment faded away from civil trials. I analyse a period which comprises the time span between classical Roman law and the early *ius commune*. The analysis of the philosophical contributions to the law of damages in chapter eight will add Grotius's reflections, which provided the basis for the modern systems of damages.

II   Legal Responses to Wrongs

The classical Roman law of wrongs rested upon the two pillars of compensation and punishment. Although the balance between the two changed considerably during the evolution of the Roman legal system, they characterised most responses to wrongful events until the transition to the *ius commune*. While a detailed analysis of the Roman law of damages would exceed the boundaries of the present study, by following the relationship between punishment and compensation I shall furnish some valid points of reflection for the theory of restitution for wrongs. An investigation of the 'concepts' of compensation and *poena* will not take place here. The analysis will be limited to the identification of the 'role' of compensation and *poena* in Roman law.

The Roman legal system did not have a general principle of compensation,[3] which was substituted by a pragmatic approach. As regards the quantification of the loss, the two main methods of evaluation were the objective value of the damaged thing and the subjective estimation of the thing from the perspective of the claimant.[4] Normally, the preferred criterion took only the objective value of the damaged thing into consideration, ignoring consequential losses or the personal value which the thing had for the specific claimant.[5] As regards the *poena*, or punishment, different methods of quantification were adopted, such as

---

[2]   *McGregor on Damages* (16th edn) (London, Sweet & Maxwell 1997) para 1. McGregor has changed his view in the following edition of his work. See J Edelman, 'Gain-Based Damages and Compensation' in A Burrows and Lord Rodger (eds) *Mapping the Law* (Oxford, OUP 2006) 141-160, 142-144.

[3]   Kaser RP I 498.

[4]   Eg Ulp D 2. 7. 5. I; Paul D 34. 2. 35. pr.

[5]   Kaser RP I 500-501.

the a priori determination of the amount of money due to the claimant for a given loss, or a multiplication of the value of the damaged thing, or even judicial discretion.

Unlike compensation, the idea of punishment is, if not alien, at least suspiciously regarded in most of the modern European jurisdictions. The passage from a prevalently penal to a prevalently compensatory law of delict is paramount to understand the evolution of the law of damages. Particular attention will be dedicated to the Roman penal system for wrongs until the end of the classical period, while post-classical Roman law will be introduced briefly to highlight the passage from the Roman to the modern conception of the law of damages. This approach will enable an assessment of restitution for wrongs as an independent response beyond compensation and punishment.

III   The Punitive Character of the Roman Law of Delict

Roman law was often less concerned with the best way to compensate the loss of the victim and more interested in finding the best way to castigate the wrongdoer.[6] Consistently with this approach, compensation was not always an issue of the law of delict.[7] At times, the measure awarded corresponded to the loss of the claimant. Yet, in some cases, this was not even a certain signal that the action was compensatory in nature. Legal procedure was characterised by the distinction between crime and delict. The former fell within the realm of public law. The wrongdoer was compelled to pay a sum of money to the State as a consequence of his mischief. In any of such proceedings, the trial was in the hands of the Public Administration although a private citizen could sometimes derive some profit from it if the sum of money, which normally exceeded the loss, was awarded by the State to a private individual. The award imposed upon the defendant was called *poena*.[8] The *delictum* did not differ from the *crimen* for the penal character of the monetary award, which, unlike the *crimen*, was always granted to the claimant, but rather in the absence of a State-controlled trial.[9] This trial was exclusively in the hands of private parties, although the monetary award was still called '*poena*' and still normally exceeded the loss of the claimant. Hence, the Roman law of delict, unlike the modern law of delict, dealt with civil law responses to wrongs which were qualified by the application of penal instruments. The distinction between civil law and criminal law became clear only in a later phase of evolution of Roman law. Until classical law, the application radius

---

[6]   Eg *Zimmermann*, 914.

[7]   'Law of delict' meaning here the modern correspondent of the law of torts in civil law countries. Thus, in this instance the expression is not related to the strict Roman sense which will be explained in the next paragraph.

[8]   D Liebs, *Die Klagenkonkurrenz im römischen Recht* (Ruprecht, Göttingen, Vandenhoeck 1972) 266.

[9]   Kaser RP II 425.

of the civil and of the criminal claim tended to overlap.[10] Their boundaries became neatly discernible only starting from post-classical law.

The reason for this peculiar character of the Roman law of delict lies in the fact that it originated in private vengeance,[11] and punishment remained a feature which was never completely abandoned. Certain scholars conclude that the private law of delict is likely to have been developed earlier than the public criminal law.[12] This view is based upon the consideration that, owing to the presence of private punishment, there was less urgency for an intervention through public law. The small number of criminal offences listed in the Twelve Tables by comparison with the delictual sanctions seems to confirm the point. With reference to the punitive aspect, the Twelve Tables offer a lucid picture of the development of the law of delict.[13] At first, the victim was recognised as having a right to take the life of the wrongdoer or, alternatively, to claim the *lex talionis*, that is, retaliation in kind upon the wrongdoer. In a subsequent phase, the victim was offered the choice of accepting a composition in money instead of physical revenge. In due course, this last method of composition became the normal procedure.[14] Table VIII on delict delivers useful pieces of information on the various avenues which were explored by the Roman draftsmen on the issue of the methods used to address and redress delictual situations:

> 2. If he has maimed a part (of a body), unless he settles with him, there is to be talion.[15]

> 3. If he has broken a bone of a free man, 300 pieces, if of a slave, 150 (asses) are to be penalty.[16]

> 10. If a patron shall have done harm to a client, he is to be *sacer*.[17]

The last of these three rules contains no attempt to find any kind of composition. The consequence of this delict is most likely death. The first rule contains a central passage in the evolution of the *poena*: *si membrum rupsit, ni cum eo pacit, talio esto*. Retaliation is here an alternative avenue which is always open to the claimant. Yet, the latter might prefer to find an agreement with the wrongdoer. In this case, a more efficient form of composition substitutes the form of vengeance. This more modern approach does not affect the physical integrity of the *familia*, but only its purse, thus giving the *familia*, and therefore indirectly the whole of society, a better chance to recover. The second passage formalises the acknowledgement that society has nothing to gain from its members killing or wounding each other. The predetermined amount of money with penal function allows

---

[10]   G Rossetti, 'Problemi e prospettive in tema di "struttura" e "funzione" delle azioni penali private' (1993) 35 *Bullettino dell'Istituto di Diritto Romano* 343-394, 344-345.

[11]   JAC Thomas, *Textbook of Roman Law* (Amsterdam, North-Holland 1976) 349.

[12]   B Nicholas, *An Introduction to Roman Law* (Oxford, Clarendon 1962) 208.

[13]   *Cf Zimmermann*, 914.

[14]   This is just a general description. In practice, the line of evolution was not so straightforward.

[15]   MH Crawford (ed), *Roman Statutes* (London, Institute of Classical Studies 1996) vol II 687.

[16]   *Ibid.*

[17]   *Ibid* 689. 'Someone who is *sacer* is too sinister and too polluted to keep in the world', *ibid* 690.

society to solve problems within the group in a fashion which would not affect its efficiency as a united body in front of an external threat.

Another good example of monetary composition is provided by non-manifest theft. According to Gaius,[18] there was some discordance among scholars on the definition of manifest theft. In general, one can state with a reasonable degree of confidence that a theft was manifest if the thief was caught *in flagrante delicto*,[19] that is, in the act. As for the other cases, Gaius says that the Twelve Tables prescribed a *poena in duplum*: the wrongdoer had to pay twice as much as the value of the stolen thing.[20] By comparison with Table VIII, this last situation introduces a further method which is relevant to our analysis. If a thief steals a thing worth 100 pieces, he will have to pay 200 pieces to its owner. In such cases, the monetary composition is higher than the loss, so that the victim will be better off after the assessment than before the delict had been perpetrated. In the legal responses previously considered, this potential advantage for the victim did not emerge as transparently.

In the case of contumely, the Twelve Tables prescribed retaliation. At some point, this form of punishment was felt to be inadequate and the praetor phased it out progressively. This was done by allowing the victim to submit to the judge the claimant's own evaluation of the damage '*ut iudex vel tanti condemnet, quanti iniuriam passus aestimaverit, vel minoris, prout ei visum fuerit*'.[21] Hence, the judge could estimate the loss 'according to what seemed fit to him', using as a basis for his decision the claimant's evaluation. The *actio iniuriarum*, applied in the case of contumely, differed from the previous examples in that it left the judge free to determine the measure of damages using as a main criterion 'what seems fit to him'. This does not necessarily indicate that the judge granted compensation. It could as well mean that the measure of damages was tailored to the situation of the victim, the way the delict was committed, the position of the wrongdoer and so forth. The final quantification could have had as a result compensation or punishment according to what the judge deemed to be appropriate.

This brief overview shows that the draftsmen explored different avenues. The Roman system was based mainly upon the principle of vendetta and self-help. Compensation was only one of the legal responses which could be awarded for wrongs, and probably not even the most important.

IV   Penal and Compensatory Actions

This section examines the main legal responses in Roman law. There is no automatic or necessary relationship between the punitive goal, which was typical of many claims, and exemplary damages. A considerable number of claims with

---

[18]   Gai 3. 184.
[19]   Gai 3. 185.
[20]   Gai 3. 190.
[21]   I. 4. 4. 7.

penal function ended up in a compensatory award against the single wrongdoer without losing their punitive character. The latter was kept despite the award of loss-measured damages in cases, for instance, in which the same 'compensatory' action was allowed against many defendants at the same time, so that the successful claimant would obtain more than his simple loss.

A   *Res* and *Poena*

It emerges from the structure and the nature of the Roman claims that punishment was one of the main goals of the law of damages: '*Agimus autem interdum, ut rem tantum consequamur, interdum ut poenam tantum, alias ut rem et poenam*'.[22] Gaius refers here to a partition of the *actiones* into actions which are aimed at obtaining a thing, actions which are designed to impose a penalty, and actions through which both results may be achieved.[23] The first group collects what is known as reipersecutory actions, *actiones ad rem persequendam*. The second group refers to the penal actions, *actiones ad poenam persequendam*. Finally, the third group concerns the so-called mixed actions, *actiones mixtae*. This tripartite structure was used both in contractual and delictual situations.[24]

Through an *actio ad rem persequendam*, the claimant sought mainly compensation for a loss suffered. Since restitution in kind was not compatible with procedural rules, the claimant could obtain only money.[25] Punishment was the characteristic feature of the *actiones ad poenam persequendam*. The *poena* granted to the victim a sum of money equivalent to the loss. This sum was then normally, but not necessarily, multiplied a given number of times. The multiple award was held to convey the idea that the wrongdoer was being punished for his behaviour. Mere compensation of the damage was probably one of the functions of these actions. In fact, compensation was what the claimant might have obtained in practice if, as will be seen shortly, the *actio ad poenam persequendam* against multiple wrongdoers capped the assessment of damages to the value of the loss, which however each wrongdoer would pay in full. On the meaning and the structure of the *actiones mixtae* there is no general agreement. This term is not of classical origin and was probably coined by Tribonian.[26] Some of them had most

---

[22]   Gai 4. 6.
[23]   The statement quoted is controversial. The major question is whether the partition is due to Gaius's own taxonomy or whether the author reports a common view.
[24]   For an instance of the application of the penal model to breach of contract see the second chapter of the *lex Aquilia* against the *adstipulator* (eg Gai 3.215).
[25]   This was a consequence of the structure of the Roman trial: the *litis contestatio* extinguished the claim brought by the victim and gave rise to a new procedural claim, the *actio iudicati*, which could only have a sum of money as its subject-matter. The situation changed after the enactment of the *cognitio extra ordinem*. cf P Voci, 'Azioni penali e azioni miste' (1998) 64 *Studia et Documenta Historiae et Iuris* 1-46, 6 and 45.
[26]   H Ankum, 'Actions by which we claim a thing (res) and a penalty (poena) in classical Roman law' (1982) 24 *Bullettino dell'Istituto di Diritto Romano* 15-39, 15. In Justinian's Institutes, the Gaian distinction is accepted as a recognised classification: I. 4. 6. 16.

of the features of one of two previous categories.[27] Others were *mixtae ab originem*,[28] truly independent claims from the very beginning.[29].

B   Main Features of the Penal Actions

That punishment was a common response of the law of damages was emphasised by the fact that the claimant obtained an award which was normally higher than the loss sustained. However, it was possible under some circumstances that even an action *in simplum* – a claim which would have granted to the victim merely a sum of money equal to the damage suffered – did not lose its punitive nature.[30] The *actiones in simplum* were a judicial invention. The praetor granted the claimant a sum of money equivalent to his loss.[31] However, other features conveyed the idea of a *poena* independently of the quantification of damages.[32] Thus, when a wrong was committed by many perpetrators, they were all separately liable for the full amount. Furthermore, in normal cases, seeking and being awarded a penal action was no bar to a further reipersecutory action, which had different nature and subject matter.[33] And had the defendant died before the action was brought, the claimant could not sue the heir in application of the principle still recurrent in modern legal systems according to which penal liability is always personal.

V   Restitution in the Roman Law of Damages

The analysis of Roman law casts more than simple doubt on theories which identify the law of damages with the law of compensation. However, from the pre-eminent role of the non compensatory structure with a punitive function it does not necessarily follow that the system developed a restitutionary mechanism for wrongs as well. The Roman claims were oriented towards either punishment or compensation, or a combination of the two outcomes. In any case, the loss sustained by the victim was relevant to the evaluation of damages, the normal quantification being equivalent to the loss itself, be it the value of the thing or the 'interest' of the victim, or to a multiple of the loss. Furthermore, there was also a measure of damages which was independent of the concrete loss of the claimant. Thus, the Twelve Tables provided a fixed sum of money in the case of *os fractum* or *membrum ruptum* with no regard to the actual damage sustained. It is worth

---

[27]   Eg I. 4. 6. 19.
[28]   Ulp D 4. 2. 14. 10.
[29]   Voci (n 25) 38-39.
[30]   *Ibid* 6.
[31]   An instance is provided by the claim *contra mulierem*, D 25. 6; and by the *actio de pauperie*, D 9. 1. 1.
[32]   *Zimmermann*, 915-917.
[33]   There are some important exceptions to this rule, eg in the case of a double *litis aestimatio*, but they are not relevant here.

spending a few words on this last measure of damages. We have seen that Graham Virgo maintains that the judicial award for conversion is

> restitutionary because the defendant must pay the value of the proceeds of sale to the claimant without any inquiry being undertaken as to what the market value of the goods was at the time of sale, which would be the measure of the claimant's loss.[34]

As the legal response of Table VIII 3 uses the same model of assessment depicted by Virgo, applying his argument one has to conclude that this is an instance of restitution for wrongs. I have already expressed my disagreement with this conclusion while I examined Virgo's view in the context of conversion. Roman law confirms rather than denies my point: although the Roman award was independent of the market value of the loss, still it presupposed a patrimonial loss, without which no money payment would have been granted. This measure was linked to a more archaic and less sophisticated method of evaluation of the loss, which, in due course, yielded to more precise compensatory and punitive measures – and not, it should be noted, to restitutionary measures.

An assessment of damages which rests on a loss-based quantification hangs on a criterion which sits uncomfortably beside the one applied in the case of restitutionary damages: to compel the wrongdoer to give up ill-gotten gains. Restitutionary damages are not concerned with an evaluation connected to the loss of the claimant, but exclusively with the enrichment which the defendant has derived from the perpetration of a wrong. The model which has been identified thus far as characteristic of Roman law cannot simply be extended to embrace restitutionary awards. This does not mean, however, that there were no claims which looked at the wrongdoer's gain to quantify the damages.

A   The *actiones in id quod ad eos pervenit*

These actions do not fit easily in the partition punishment-compensation. The starting point of the present reflections is, once again, the *actiones poenales*. It has been shown that they aimed to punish the wrongdoer and that this result was obtained through different avenues, the most important being the quantification of damages in the form of a multiple of the loss. Even other features emphasised the punitive role of these claims. For instance, the action had a strongly personal character so that, generally, at law it could be imposed only upon the wrongdoer himself. In consequence of this personality principle, the praetor found himself before cases in which the wrongdoer had caused a relevant damage to the claimant and yet the latter had no claim because the wrongdoer died before the victim could sue him. This situation, albeit resting on a valid principle of personality of the *poena*, produced an outcome which was unfair to the victim. Beyond the wrongdoer, the heir and other successors could have been called to share in some way the burden placed upon the original defendant. Weighing the

---

[34]   G Virgo, *The Principles of the Law of Restitution* (2nd edn) (Oxford, OUP 2006) 470. See above, ch 3, n 16 and text thereof.

position of the heir on the one hand and of the victim on the other, the praetor decided that it would have been unjust if the heir had derived an undeserved windfall from a wrongful act, even though it was the act of another person. For this reason, the praetor came to the conclusion that, under certain circumstances, other parties should have been held responsible for the behaviour of the wrongdoer. Consequentially, he granted an action against the heir and other successors allowing the claimant at least to mitigate the negative consequences of the wrong.

In the context of the *actio de dolo*, which was a praetorian penal claim, the Roman lawyers debated whether an extension of the application radius of the claim was possible. On this topic, Ulpian said: '*Haec actio in heredem et ceteros successores datur dumtaxat de eo quod ad eos pervenit*'.[35] According to Ulpian, this delictual claim had to be granted not only against the wrongdoer, but also against his heir and other successors. The *actio doli* against the heir had a peculiar characteristic: quite unusually for a delictual claim, its scope was limited to the enrichment obtained from the wrongdoer by the defendant. On this particular action against the heir, a few statements in the Digest (D 4. 3. 26. – 30) have triggered an intense discussion in the Romanistic. The first statement reads:

> *In heredem eatenus daturum se eam actionem proconsul pollicetur, quatenus ad eum pervenerit, id est quatenus es ea re locupletior ad eum hereditas venerit.*[36]

The principle, which is led back to a dictum by Cassius,[37] is the same as the one established by Ulpian:[38] under certain circumstances the heir may stand as a defendant in a trial, but his liability is restricted to his enrichment. Pomponius summarises the gist of the action as follows:

> *Sicuti poena ex delicto defuncti heres teneri non debeat, ita nec lucrum facere, si quid ex ea re ad eum pervenisset.*[39]

This rule applies to the delictual actions, whereas contractual actions were based upon the rule of liability *in solidum*. The difference between the claims is due to the fact that the contractual claims were normally transmissible to the heir. Thus, there was no need to distinguish between the *dolus* and the *culpa* of the wrongdoer as in the *actio de dolo*.[40]

---

[35] D. 4. 3. 17. 1: 'This claim is given against the heir and other successors for no more than what they obtained'.

[36] D. 4. 3. 26: 'the proconsul promises that he will give this action against the heir to the extent that property has fallen into his hands, that is, to the extent that the inheritance reaching the heir has profited from that property'. T Mommsen, P Krueger (eds) and A Watson (tr) *The Digest of Justinian* (Philadelphia, Univ of Pennsylvania Press 1985).

[37] Paul D 44. 7. 35. pr.

[38] Ulp D 4. 3. 17. 1.

[39] Pomp D 50. 17. 38: 'Just as the heir of a dead person cannot be bound to pay the penalty arising from the delict, so he cannot benefit from it either if anything came to him as a result of the affair in question', Mommsen et alia (n 36).

[40] *Cf* G Rotondi, "Dolus ex delicto" e "dolus ex contractu" nelle teorie bizantine sulla trasmissibilità delle azioni' in *Scritti giuridici II* (Padova, Cedam 1922) 371-410, 387.

In the literature,[41] most scholars embrace the view that the claim in point is of classical origin. More controversial is the question of the nature of the claim. Some Romanists[42] prefer to qualify the *actio in id quod ad eum pervenit*, literally 'for what has reached him', as the very same *actio de dolo*, which was a claim triggered by fraud or deceit. The *actio* could have been brought against the wrongdoer, if he had still been alive, and after his death against his successors. A more modern explanation,[43] which however finds some support in older views,[44] rejects any identification of the two actions, and urges that the claim against the heir is to be qualified as an independent action with its own peculiar features.[45] Thus, when this *actio poenalis* was the only means at the victim's disposal to minimise or eliminate his loss, the praetor introduced a new claim to restore justice. This action was triggered by the same delictual event which would have justified a claim against the wrongdoer. Yet, it is probably to be qualified as an action independent of the original *actio doli*. By contrast with the *actio doli*, the action against the heir was reipersecutory, and not penal. As Sabinus put it, the heir was sued *calculi ratione potius quam maleficii*.[46] The only precondition for the award of the claim was that the original wrongdoer acted with *dolus*; the judiciary could then use its own discretion in the determination of the cases in which to allow damages.[47]

The claim *ex dolo defuncti* against the heir or other successors is not the only instance of an *actio* through which the restitution of the enrichment was awarded, or *quanto locupletior factus est*, as the sources sometimes state.[48] Another such action was brought against the minor, who was liable for obligations which the *tutor impuberis* had accepted wilfully in his stead. Again, the liability of the minor was limited to his enrichment.[49] The same restriction to the *id quod ad eum pervenit* applied in the case of children and slaves who were under the control of a *pater familias* and yet enjoyed a certain degree of freedom to act in the name of their master. The *pater familias* would have had limited liability in the case of delicts committed in his name by member of the *familia*.[50]

---

[41]   Rossetti (n 10) 363.

[42]   Kaser RP I 600 n 69. This doctrine is well presented by G Longo (on Albertario's steps), *Contributi alla dottrina del dolo* (Padova, Cedam 1937) *passim* esp 89-94.

[43]   For instance, U Brasiello, 'Delicta' in *Novissimo Digesto italiano* (Torino, Utet 1968) 377-379, 378.

[44]   Longo (n 42) 94-141 with particular reference to Mayer and Betti.

[45]   A Guarino, *Diritto privato romano* (12th edn) (Napoli, Jovene 2001) 979. This latter view presupposes that the fragments of the Digest have not been interpolated.

[46]   Paul D 4. 3. 29: 'for financial reasons rather than as a consequence of his own wrongful behaviour'.

[47]   M Talamanca, *Istituzioni di diritto romano* (Milano, Giuffrè 1990) 238.

[48]   That is, 'for what he has been enriched'. *Cf* Kaser RP I 600.

[49]   Ulp D 14. 4. 3. 1.

[50]   Kaser RP I 605-606.

B   Contractual Restitutionary Damages?

A passage by Julian in the Digest deals with a peculiar case concerning the sale of slaves. There is no consensus in the Romanistic literature about its correct interpretation. From the perspective of the topic at issue, it raises some relevant and remarkable issues.

> *Si quis servum, quem cum peculio vendiderat, manumiserit, non solum peculii nomine, quod servus habuit tempore quo manumittebatur, sed et eorum, quae postea adquirit, tenetur et praeterea cavere debet, quidquid ex hereditate liberti ad eum pervenit, restitutu iri.*[51]

This is the situation depicted here: the defendant sells a slave to the claimant. After the contract is made, but before the execution of the sale, the vendor discharges through *manumissio* the slave with his *peculium*[52] so that the sale cannot be completed. Julian identifies three heads of damages connected to the wrongful behaviour of the vendor. First of all, the vendee can recover the value of the *peculium*; then, he can claim the value of what the slave has acquired after the *manumissio*; finally, he can claim restitution of *quidquid ad eum pervenit*, that is, what the vendor will inherit as patron from the estate of the former slave. At the point in which the claim is brought, the value, if any, of the inheritance is still unknown. Hence, Julian suggests that the vendor would have to give security, or *cautio*, to the vendee.

Unlike the first head of damages, in which the value of the *peculium* does not present particular difficulties to the interpreters, the second and especially the third head of damages have triggered an intense debate on the meaning of the passage and the magnitude of the damages awarded. The quantification of the value of what the slave has acquired has no bearing on the analysis of restitution for wrongs, whereas the third head of damages, the liability *in id quod ad eum pervenit*, offers interesting points for reflection. Some scholars construe this passage as granting damages for what has become part of the *peculium* after judgment was entered for the claimant, otherwise 'Julian's rule would involve the reckoning of some property twice, since part of the *hereditas* would come from the *peculium* which was already charged'.[53] The vendor has to pay damages for the assets present in the *peculium* of the slave. Yet, some of those assets could be in the estate of the slave after his death and therefore among the goods which the vendor inherits *ex hereditate liberti*. In this case, the vendor would pay damages for the very same things for the loss of which the vendee had already recovered under the first head, that is the *peculium*. It seems that, according to Julian, the vendee theoretically could receive a windfall from the vendor's wrong. As it would have potentially allowed double recovery, this solution was dismissed in

---

[51] Iul D 19. 1. 23, the passage continues with Marcellus's remark on Julian's opinion which will be analysed later in this chapter, n 81 and text thereof.
[52] The *peculium* was the complex of assets which a slave could freely manage.
[53] WW Buckland, *The Roman Law of Slavery* (London, CUP 1908, repr 1970) 40.

the Romanistic literature as incompatible with the principle of compensation, which characterises the Roman rules on non-performance of a contract.[54]

However, a different analysis has been advanced more recently. According to Joseph Georg Wolf,[55] there is no need to qualify the case in point as an instance of compensation for non-performance. The breach of contract is not the consequence of the contractual non-performance; rather it is directly a consequence of the discharge of the slave through *manumissio*. This author argues that the interpretative difficulties are due to an attempt to read D 19. 1. 23. as necessarily giving rise only to compensatory damages. Yet, the compensatory approach is not the only way to explain the passage. In reality, the vendor might pay twice for the same goods, but not under the same head of damages.[56] As regards the *peculium*, he pays compensation; as regards the *cautio*, he pays for any possible benefit which he would receive in the future as patron from the perpetration of the wrong. This obligation corresponded to the liability for *negotium gestum*,[57] that is, necessitous intervention. Consequently, on this reading this would be a case of liability *in id quod ad eum pervenit*. Julian deemed it to be necessary to avoid a situation in which the vendor receives an undeserved benefit from his wrong.[58]

The construction of this passage as an instance of necessitous intervention has implications for an examination of D 19. 1. 23 in terms of restitution for wrongs. Wolf suggests that no compensatory mechanism is in operation here. Yet his interpretation of the award as triggered by *negotiorum gestio* still rests on the idea of compensation, for the *gestor* seeks restoration for the losses to his patrimony. This does not seem to be what happens here. Having recovered for the loss of the *peculium* at the moment of judgment and for what has entered the *peculium* after the *manumissio*,[59] the claimant is in a position of neutrality towards the damage. Hence, according to the compensatory principle, the claimant can take no further steps against the defendant. However, after a few years, the slave dies and part of his estate goes to the patron, that is the vendor. The latter, who has already compensated the vendee, receives a benefit thanks to his wrongful behaviour. The benefit is completely independent of the compensated loss. The question is now who is going to profit from the wrongdoing. According to Julian, it is the innocent vendee who ought to receive a windfall, not the wrongful vendor. Thus, Julian let the vendor give security for what he might inherit from the slave as a consequence of the wrong. The reason for providing security seems to be the commission of a wrong rather than an enrichment following the position of the patron qua vendor. A construction of the award as following from liability for necessitous intervention is not able to get around the objections of those who point out the risk of double compensation. An interpretation of the passage as

---

[54]   *Cf* already R von Jhering, *Abhandlungen aus dem römischen Recht* (Leipzig,1844, repr Scientia Aalen 1981) 66.

[55]   JG Wolf, 'Barkauf und Haftung' (1977) 45 *Tijdschrift voor Rechtsgeschiedenis* 1-25.

[56]   *Ibid* 6.

[57]   *Ibid* 12.

[58]   *Ibid* 20.

[59]   This second head required probably a mechanism of estimation.

describing an award of restitutionary damages would overcome the criticism because it accounts for the peculiarity of the claim, which does not compel the defendant to pay twice for the same loss. It also explains the difficulties of the scholars, who are not familiar with the idea of damages which are awarded independently of the loss of the claimant.

VI Evolution of the Law of Damages in the Post-Classical Period

The main characteristics of the law of damages in the post-classical period from the perspective of the topic at issue are the expansion of State influence upon legal procedures and a consequential change in the private nature of the original law of delict. The emperors wanted to exert a tighter control over disputes. This proved to be incompatible with the structure of the classical law of delict. It will be remembered that this type of dispute resolution left the State out of the trial. The proceedings, which could culminate in the award of a *poena*, that is a punishment, were exclusively dealt with by and between private parties. Therefore, the amount of money extracted as a *poena* went to the claimant, and not to the State. The structure of the trial had to change if the State wanted to secure itself a larger degree of control. To respond to this problem, Augustus introduced an alternative, special trial, which could take place at the request of one of the parties.[60] This form of trial was called '*cognitio*' because it allowed a civil servant to 'know' the legal matter so that there was no necessity to send it to a *iudex*, who was a layman, for the decision.[61]

As long as delictual trial was only a private issue, the alternative between crime and delict played an important role, as it differentiated the cases characterised by State intervention from the 'private affairs'. The introduction of the *cognitio* changed the balance, for even delicts became a matter for the State. The judge was a civil servant and the pecuniary punishment benefited the State.[62] The difference between criminal and civil trial tended to become more evanescent, since the judge in criminal proceedings could allow a form of compensation to be awarded to the victim on top of the pecuniary punishment, which went to the State.[63]

The more active role played by the State affected the different responses triggered by the perpetration of a wrong in the civil trial. The ensuing modifications are the historical key to understand the subsequent dominance of compensation among the legal responses. The progressive introduction of the *cognitio* signalled the retreat of the *actiones ad poenam persequendam* from the realm of civil law. More and more, they tended to be confined exclusively to criminal law, which was under the authority of the emperor. The loss of weight of the delictual

---

[60]   *Cf* G Pugliese, *Istituzioni di diritto romano* (Padova, Piccin 1985) 378-379.
[61]   Thomas (n 11) 71-72.
[62]   Kaser RP II 426.
[63]   *Ibid.*

actions did not occur suddenly. It was rather the consequence of a long process which changed the taxonomy of the law of damages. The *delictum*, which could trigger an *actio poenalis*, turned into a purely civil action and was distinguished from the *crimen*, which characterised penal actions.[64] In this fashion, that partition between civil law of delict and criminal law was initiated, which is fundament of living Roman-rooted legal systems.

Even in the cases in which the traditional punitive function of the – now civil – delicts was retained, the sources started to distinguish between what was due as compensation and what exceeded compensation, which was the *poena*. Thus, if the defendant was condemned to pay fourfold, he paid the *simplum* as compensation and the rest as punishment.[65] However, under Justinian this process of expulsion of punishment as a main legal response from the law of damages was far from being completed. In fact, the emperor imposed the State-controlled trial but, along with it, he kept to a large extent the *actiones poenales* with all their traditional features.[66]

The repositioning of the *delictum* in the civil law sphere bears important consequences as regards the further development of the civil law of damages and in particular the new perspectives linked to its increasingly compensatory function. A civil delict is a wrong against the victim, who can claim compensation; yet it is a wrong against society at large as well, because it affects the public interest. The legal response acquires, therefore, social significance of prevention and correction of wrongful behaviour. It appears, then, that some principles related to the idea of criminal punishment transmigrated to civil law, although this penal function of deterrence always remained in a subordinate position.[67] The slow, although progressive, withdrawal of the punitive response from the law of damages does not seem to have affected the liability *in id quod ad eum pervenit*. The heir of the wrongdoer could still be held liable to the limit of what he had obtained from the wrongdoer's estate.[68]

VII   The Law of Damages in the Ius Commune

This part of the analysis covers a very extensive period of time. Since the *ius commune* concerns the reception of Roman law within the medieval, and then the early modern, legal systems, there may be gross variations at local level. Such variations are not considered here. In the context of the topic at issue, it will be

---

[64]   Kaser RP II 426.
[65]   *ex multis* see D 4. 2. 14. 9-10.
[66]   H Coing, *Europäisches Privatrecht Bd I Älteres Gemeines Recht (1500 bis 1800)* (München, Beck 1985) 503.
[67]   The new concept of compensation as a socio-legal response of the law of damages with penal elements is analysed extensively by U Ratti, 'Il risarcimento del danno nel diritto giustinianeo' (1933) 41 *Bullettino dell'Istituto di Diritto Romano* 169-199.
[68]   Kaser RP II 427.

shown which elements of the Roman tradition reached living law and how historical evolution can justify the current views on restitutionary damages.

The Middle Ages saw the consolidation of the divide between civil and criminal claims, the latter being exclusively in the hands of the State. This phenomenon yielded to two major consequences within the law of damages: the establishment of compensation as the foremost legal response in civil proceedings on the one hand, and the withering of the penal component in the traditional Roman delicts on the other hand.[69] The Glossators, who rediscovered the Digest, conducted their analysis in the light of one important consideration: the Justinianic work was strictly based upon Roman law, even though the Commission, led by Tribonian, had the imperial authorisation to interpolate some passages when necessary for better understanding. As Roman law was a source of unquestionable truth, every statement of what became known as the *Corpus Iuris Civilis* had to contain true legal averments. Hence, the theoretical presentation of the law of damages by the Glossators corresponds *grosso modo* to the Justinianic model. Whether analyses of the Glossators were confined to academic disputes, or whether they truly reported what happened in the practice before the courts, is still uncertain. In fact, it is unknown how far the penal delicts, which were investigated extensively in the *glossae*, found judicial recognition. At any rate, it is rather doubtful that private punishment was applied on large scale, given the increasingly stronger weight of the criminal trial in the hands of the State.[70] Furthermore, the measure of punishment did not fit in the new approach of criminal law: whereas the delicts expressed punishment as a fixed measure given by a multiplication of the loss, criminal punishment was more and more tailored upon the person of the offender and the crime which that particular offender had perpetrated.

Compensation became the paramount legal response to a civil delict. The primacy of compensation as the more appropriate dispositive model for disputes between private parties is highlighted by two factors: the legal analysis of the meaning of *interesse* and the transformation of many penal into reipersecutory claims. The concept of *interesse* qualifies one's desire not to see one's position, welfare, patrimony, and other personal interests compromised by somebody else's wrongdoing. It identifies everybody's interest not to be the victim of a wrongful event.[71] That the Glossators recognised the importance of a correct identification of the concept of *interesse* as one of the most difficult and central investigative topics of the *Corpus*[72] signals the profound significance which they attached to

---

[69] *Cf* H Coing, *Europäisches Privatrecht Bd II 19. Jahrhundert* (München, Beck 1989) 512.
[70] *Ibid* 504.
[71] See HJ Wieling, *Interesse und Privatstrafe vom Mittelalter bis zum bürgerlichen Gesetzbuch* (Köln/Wien, Böhlau 1970) 5. On the definition of *interesse* developed by the Glossators see H Lange, *Schadensersatz und Privatstrafe in der mittelalterlichen Rechtstheorie* (Münster/Köln, Böhlau 1955) 13-15.
[72] Wieling (n 71) 3-5.

compensation. The debate on *interesse* found its natural collocation in the context of reipersecutory claims and of the *actiones poenales* which turned into reipersecutory claims.

The transformation of penal claims into reipersecutory actions is part of the wider trend of withdrawal of the pure Roman delicts from the law of civil wrongs owing especially to the pressure of the State-controlled criminal trial. This evolution was not reflected in the works of the Glossators. Instead, they tried to keep such actions alive despite the fact that practising lawyers must probably have increasingly rejected this remedial structure before the courts in favour of more modern criminal claims.[73] On the other hand, part of the spirit of the old *actiones poenales* survived in the reipersecutory claims. These were increasingly permeated by those moralising tendencies which had already qualified the definition of civil wrong put forward in the *Corpus*. The influence of the *Corpus* is to be seen principally in the idea that civil law, like criminal law, performs educational function, showing the citizens that their behaviour is not only legally, but also morally wrong, as it violates the general interest of society at large.[74]

In this extremely fluid situation, in which traditional Roman institutions were apparently kept intact, but in reality altered gradually, it is difficult to follow the events linked to restitutionary responses in a wrongful context. As was to be expected, the Glossators stuck to the indications of the *Corpus* on the *actiones in id quod ad eos pervenit* against the heir or other successor. On this point, Bartolus, while stating the difference with canon law, remarked: '*Nam de iure civili non datur nisi quatenus ad heredem pervenit*'.[75]

The Glossators faced two difficulties in their adhesion to traditional Roman law. First, unlike the Romans, they had to come to terms with a new, very relevant source of law, the *ius canonicum*. Although it was not strictly binding, it proved difficult to resists arguments based upon canon law, as Bartolus' work shows: on the problem of the claim against the heir, Bartolus accepts some times the Roman solution, and other times the solution developed in canon law.[76] Breaking with the pure Roman law tradition, the *ius canonicum* introduced a general principle of liability for wrongful acts which was based upon compensation. This departure from the Roman action-based approach was a strong signal that the situation was changing. In fact, it had a direct effect on the role played by restitutionary damages, especially in combination with the evolution of *actiones poenales* into merely compensatory claims.

The consequence of the combined influence of canon law and criminal law expanded the significance of compensation, which became not just the most

---

[73]   For instance, the *actio legis Aquiliae*, which was the main claim for wrongful damage, became a pure compensatory claim by 17th century. See Coing (n 66) 510.

[74]   Wieling (n 71) 111, remarks that, unlike the Roman way of thinking, strictly based on private law, '*verfolgen spätere Juristen und Byzantiner in steigendem Maße öffentlichrechtliche und moralisierende Tendenzen*', ie the later lawyers pursued increasingly moralising tendencies based upon public law.

[75]   Bartolus, *Glossa* to D 47. 1. 1. n 6.

[76]   Wieling (n 71) 260.

important legal response, but the only possible legal response to wrongdoing. Since the claim was deprived of its punitive function, there was no reason to maintain the set of restrictions which in Roman law limited the applicability of penal actions.[77] The heir was now answerable according to the normal principles of the law of wrongs. Thus, the action *in id quod ad eum pervenit* became unnecessary, especially if one considers that, as the *glossa iuxta facultatem* put it, the heirs '*ultra vires hereditatis non tenetur, si fecerint inventarium*'.[78]

VIII   Some Reflections

From the brief analysis of the Roman law of damages emerges a picture of a constantly changing area of the law, which shows drastic differences between the original formulations and the modern understanding of the function of the law of wrongs. I have tried to show that the reasons for the pre-eminence of compensation are mainly historical: from a legal perspective, nothing points to an exclusive relationship between compensation and the law of damages. I have also examined some legal responses which indicate that the idea, if not the terminology, of restitutionary damages was not necessarily alien to Roman law.

A   The Actions in *id quod ad eos pervenit* as Restitutionary Claims for Wrongs

The Roman law of wrongs was characterised by a tension between two main responses, which correspond to a large extent to compensation and punishment. The *actiones ad poenam persequendam* were to modern eyes peculiar claims. They gave private citizens a power which modern statutes reserve to the State. Under the increasing pressure of a novel concept of punishment as a violation of social order which, as such, affects society as a whole, penal delicts gave way to criminal, State-controlled claims. Yet, the idea of social stigma, originally connected only to the *actiones poenales*, survived in the legal response which increasingly embodied the aim of the law of civil delict, compensation. The *actiones ad rem persequendam* were more than mere compensatory actions. They put the moral blame on the wrongdoer. It is arguable whether restitution for wrongs could find place between the two main aims of the law of damages. The matter is complicated by the fact that no legal-historical studies have examined the law of damages from the particular point of view of restitution for wrongs.

   Valid points of reflection are offered by the Roman action *in id quod ad eos pervenit*, which – be it an independent claim or not – was a delictual action. Even though this claim was founded on the same set of facts which justified the action

---

[77]   See above, IV B, in this chapter.
[78]   'Heirs are not bound beyond the value of the inheritance, if they made an inventory'. *Cf* Wieling (n 71) 260.

against the wrongdoer, a fresh element intervened to change the original frame-work: the wrongdoer died; the claim was rerouted against his heir and other successors. This additional element affected the response which the praetor deemed to be adequate. While in the case of the wrongdoer the award granted to the claimant was meant to punish the defendant, the measure of the victim's secondary right arising from the wrong does not fit the concept of exemplary damages when the claim was directed towards the heir. If, in agreement with the more recent interpretation advanced in the Romanistic literature, the claim is not considered a penal action, the legal response to the wrong cannot be seen as a punishment. In the *actio in id quod ad eum pervenit*, the judge was concerned mainly with the enrichment of the defendant '*ut ex dolo defuncti heres non lucretur*',[79] that is to avoid an enrichment of the heir in consequence of a wrongful behaviour of the deceased wrongdoer. Hence, the function of the claim was to compel the heir to give up to the claimant any enrichment which the defendant might have obtained from the wrongdoer, not to punish him, nor to allow the claimant full compensation for his loss. This characteristic of the claim appears to question its compensatory nature. The situation is all the more anomalous, if one considers that a delictual claim was used against a defendant whose behaviour was largely irrelevant to the determination of the measure of damages. On the other hand, the claim was brought by the victim following a loss sustained by the victim himself, so that compensatory reasoning plays a central role here despite the changes on the side of the defendant. The claim was loss-centred when it was brought against the wrongdoer and remained such even against his heir. The victim would not have been able to claim the defendant's enrichment had the victim not suffered a patrimonial loss in first place. The only novelty factor of the *actio* concerns the limitation of the level of compensation due to the fact that it would be unjust if the heir, who is alien to the wrongdoing, were worse off after having performed compensation. The *actio in id quod ad eum pervenit* is therefore an instance of what I call 'pseudo-restitutionary damages'.

B   The Claim of D 19. 1. 23

The possibility of granting contractual restitutionary damages according to D 19. 1. 23 is more controversial. Not only do many modern legal historians think that Julian's solution was wrong, even certain Roman lawyers seemed to prefer a different outcome. After having reported Julian's opinion, D 19. 1. 23. quotes Marcellus's, which clearly differs from the previous view:

---

[79]   Ulp D 10. 2. 1. 6.

Marcellus notat: illa praestare venditor ex empto debet, quae haberet emptor, si homo manumissus non esset: non continebuntur igitur, quae, si manumissus non fuit, adquisiturus non esset.[80]

Marcellus, therefore, changes the perspective. According to his analysis, it is not what the slave obtained after the *manumissio* which can be claimed by the vendee. Instead, the subject-matter of the claim ought to be what the vendee would have obtained, had the contract been duly performed: expectation damages. This solution excludes that the vendor can be compelled to pay twice for the same goods under two different heads of damages, eliminating the room for speculations on restitutionary damages. Still, it could be objected to Marcellus what I have previously objected to Farnsworth, who proposes the same difference between expectation and restitution damages: there is no ground to conclude that the two forms of damages are incompatible.[81] At any rate, it appears that the controversy about restitutionary damages can be followed back to remote times and it is immaterial to the present analysis to establish which one of the solutions prospected is to be preferred. Even if Marcellus's view were considered more suitable, the value of Julian's opinion would remain unaffected.

An explanation in terms of restitution for wrongs would be able to rely on Wolf's alternative construction, which reads D 19. 1. 23. not as a case of compensation, but as a kind of action *in id quod ad eum pervenit*. While Wolf goes as far as to construe the passage as an example of liability akin to necessitous intervention, it seems that Julian's opinion could be better explained as an instance of restitution for wrongs.

C   Limited Application of Restitution for Wrongs

If my analysis is correct, then it is possible to trace back to Roman law at least one action with characteristics similar to restitution for wrongs. Restitutionary damages might have had a place in the Roman categorisation alongside punishment and compensation, although, as the only detected instance of the damages at issues indicates, they never achieved the importance which was recognised to punishment and compensation. It is also most unlikely that the Romans recognised the award as restitution for wrongs. On the other hand, Julian's opinion suggests that restitutionary damages were consistent with the other responses of the law of damages. A restitutionary award, if ever it existed, redressed situations in which both compensation and punishment could not have achieved an equitable outcome. I therefore conclude that Roman law was likely to acknowledge at least three different responses to the perpetration of a wrong: compensation, punishment, and restitution. The first two constituted the main pillars of the law of damages. The latter was a peculiar remedy of limited relevance.

---

[80]   'Marcellus adds: The seller in an action on purchase should provide what the buyer would have if the slave had not been manumitted; those things he would not have acquired if there had been no manumission are not covered', Mommsen et alia (n 36).
[81]   See ch 4, n 37 and text thereof.

Historical developments, especially the expansion of State authority in private litigation through criminal law and procedure, have progressively restricted the possibility for the parties to solve disputes involving punishment on a private law basis. Together with the influence exerted by the compensatory approach of canon law, State authority determined a gradual withdrawal of punishment from private law. The *actiones ad poenam persequendam* either disappeared or evolved into purely compensatory claims. Mainly compensation benefited from this phenomenon. As there was no necessity to protect third parties against the penal consequences of an action any longer, the *actiones in id quod ad eum pervenit* lost their major area of applicability to the purely compensatory claims.[82] Following the disappearance of these particular actions, the liability of the heir and other successors was not reduced, but expanded. The heir became liable beyond the limits of his enrichment if he did not utilise the *beneficium inventarii*, which would have restricted his liability to the enrichment.

D   An Historical Explanation

The historical analysis, albeit succinct, provides a partial explanation for the absence or the very limited role of restitution for wrongs in modern legal systems. The strong expansion of compensation has probably contributed to form the idea that compensation must inevitably be the only possible answer of the law of damages. Yet, this is not necessarily so. While resistance against exemplary damages can be justified by the view that punishment pertains only to the State and that private revenge should not be supported by civil law – indeed, this is one of the main arguments behind the departure of *actiones poenales* from the civil trial – the same does not, and cannot, apply to restitution for wrongs. Taxonomically, a rejection of restitution on the basis of the same arguments which are applied to punishment would be incorrect. On the other hand, to infer the correctness of restitutionary damages through an a fortiori argumentation where exemplary damages are awarded would be equally incorrect. Restitutionary damages are not just a more lenient version of punishment – as an a fortiori argument would imply. Examined in their historical perspective, the different aims of the legal responses to a wrong and their mutual independence become more evident and help avoiding analytical mistakes.

---

[82]   This evolution is in line with my compensatory explanation of this award.

7

The Law of Damages in the Tradition of Aristotelian Philosophy

I Introduction

IN THIS CHAPTER, I aim to show how Aristotelian philosophy has affected the law of damages and, in particular, what influence it has exerted on the relationship between compensation and restitution. The investigation illustrates how legal philosophy has contributed to our modern understanding of the law of damages. I also introduce the terminology and set the framework which will enable me to discuss some major theories on restitution for wrongs in chapter eight. Furthermore, I shall draw upon the elements which link together the Aristotelian theory of justice with modern explanations of the law of damages. This picture of the influence of Aristotelian philosophy upon legal reasoning will provide the necessary theoretical backdrop against which I shall critically assess some of the leading legal theories of the law of damages in the next chapter, where I shall conclude that no theory of corrective justice has been able properly to account for restitutionary damages. The lack of an adequate theoretical justification extends to both descriptive and prescriptive legal-analytical approaches to restitution for wrongs. So much will be the subject of chapter nine.

The examination of philosophical accounts contributes to explain the pre-eminence of the law of compensation within the legal responses to a wrong. Corrective justice, a central pillar of the Aristotelian theory of justice, has been linked primarily to compensation and punishment for wrongs. The analysis not only of the creation, but also of the evolution, of the Aristotelian theory of justice helps to understand the theoretical underpinnings of those views according to which the law of damages is strictly intertwined with the law of compensation. On this point, legal philosophy will integrate the findings of historical research. The latter established that one of the causes of the wide overlapping of the law of damages with the law of compensation – to the detriment of all non-compensatory measures – is a change in the Roman civil trial. The former will add a further cause: the gradual permeation of the Aristotelian concept of corrective justice into legal reasoning. Aristotle formulated his theory of justice many centuries before the Romans developed a law of damages. Yet, it seems likely that his tenets did not immediately reach Roman legal science. The Aristotelian doctrine was able to exert its full influence on the law only when the force of Roman legal analysis had exhausted its first impetus, so that room happened to be available for the infiltration of new ideas. I argue that the theory of justice which was so influential in legal research was not, however, the pure Aristotelian theory, but rather the Scholastic interpretation of that theory, which in my view emphasised the 'giving back' duty of the wrongdoer and neglected the 'giving up' duty. If this interpretation of the historical and the philosophical data is correct, then the marginalisation of restitution for wrongs is mainly the consequence of historical development; it does not follow from a cogent interpretation of a legal principle. Yet, even if restitution for wrongs were legally compatible with the structure of the law of damages, it is still for each legal system to decide whether to introduce it into the law of damages.

Starting from Aristotle, the development of corrective justice will be followed in St Thomas and the Spanish Late Scholastics. While St Thomas added the Christian perspective to the Aristotelian theories, the Late Scholasticism represents a turning point in the evolution of the law of damages, for the *scholastici* applied moral considerations to legal problems. Their work was widely consulted by Grotius and therefore had a lasting effect upon existing legal systems.

II   The Aristotelian Approach to Responses to Wrongdoing

Aristotle's analysis of the concept of justice is the most influential theoretical explanation of the law of damages from a moral perspective.[1] Although Aristotle investigated the issue from an epistemic point of view, his work furnishes a fundamental starting point to any study of the relationship between compensatory and non-compensatory responses to wrongs.

A   Aristotle's Ethics

Aristotle developed his theory of special justice in his studies on ethics, which have had a strong impact upon the law of damages particularly as regards the definition of corrective justice, although even distributive justice has been used in this context.

---

[1]   Weinrib, *Idea* 56, remarks that '[i]n the history of legal philosophy, private law is Aristotle's discovery'. But contrast P Cane, 'The Anatomy of Private Law Theory: A 25th Anniversary Essay' (2005) 25 *OJLS* 203-217, 203: 'More plausibly, the genesis of private law theory as a discrete area of academic study might be traced to the publication of Ronald Coase's famous article, 'The Problem of Social Costs'.

i The Requirements to Identify the Just Man

'The just', says Aristotle, 'is the lawful and the fair, the unjust the unlawful and the unfair'.[2] This is a political concept according to which just acts tend to produce happiness to the benefit of society.[3] Therefore, the Greek philosopher shapes justice as a relationship which binds the members of society, so that the 'worst man is he who exercises his wickedness not towards himself but towards another'.[4]

Justice is that state of character which makes people disposed to do what is just and makes them act justly and wish for what is just.[5] It requires 'capacity to act'. This concept refers to the distinction, put forward in the third Book of Nicomachean Ethics, between voluntary and involuntary acts.[6] An action is involuntary if the agent acts out of ignorance of the circumstances, or of the consequences, of the action; or if he acts under compulsion. An involuntary action is normally characterised by a feeling of pain and regret on the agent's part. Only voluntary actions can be qualified as just or unjust.[7] Aristotle devotes much attention to the concept of justice, which is necessary to distribute honour and punishment.

ii Particular Justice

In analysing justice from the point of view of the possible responses to moral wrongdoing, Aristotle departs from his previous description of justice as complete virtue. There is another concept of justice, he says, which refers to individual virtues such as courage, generosity and all other components of general justice.[8] Both general and particular, or special, justice concern the relation to one's neighbour. Particular justice rests on the doctrine of the mean, according to which virtue is a state of character which tends to find the mean between extremes.[9] The mean is determined by rational principles so that no act is in itself always good or bad; it all depends on the reason, or the rational principle, which sets the mean. The doctrine of mean requires the recognition of the feeling the extremes of which allow the identification of the mean. In the case of particular justice, this feeling is greed:[10] the unjust man wants more than his equal share. The doctrine of the mean plays a key role in the philosophical explanations of the law of wrongs. As will be seen, compensation is normally

---

[2] *Nic Ethics* V i. If not otherwise stated, the translation adopted is the one by JL Ackrill, *Aristotle's Ethics* (London, Faber 1973).

[3] *Nic Ethics* V i.

[4] *Ibid.*

[5] *Ibid.*

[6] *Ibid* III i, with reference to the draftsmen. For a synthetic description of the Aristotelian position on voluntary and involuntary actions see T Nilstun, *Aristotle on Freedom and Punishment* (Lund, Studentlitteratur 1981).

[7] *Nic Ethics* V viii.

[8] *Ibid* V ii.

[9] See Ackrill (n 2) 22.

[10] R Crisp (ed and trans), *Aristotle Nicomachean Ethics* (Cambridge, CUP 2000) xxii.

perceived by modern legal theorists as the legal response which best translates the principle of corrective justice into a legal institution.

Aristotle identifies two kinds of particular justice:

> One kind is that which is manifested in distributions of honour or money or the other things that fall to be divided among those who have a share in the constitution.[11]

Distributive justice applies a method of geometric proportion to what – with legal terminology – is the quantification of damages: 'the whole has the same ratio to the whole which each part has to the other'.[12] In other words, the same ratio which applies to the persons which compose society must apply to the things to be distributed. Most of the modern theories on the law of torts and delicts are not rooted in the concept of distributive justice. However, a significant attempt to explain some legal structures in these terms has enjoyed wide support in Germany.[13] Analysing the German approach in the next chapter, I shall show that distributive justice does not provide a satisfactory explanation of the modern law of damages and thus of restitution for wrongs.

iii Corrective Justice

Iustitia correctiva, or *commutativa*, is the second model of particular justice. To understand how corrective justice has permeated the law of damages and whether it is incompatible with restitution for wrongs, it is first necessary to comprehend its basic tenets and to follow the general lines of its historical evolution. Note that my aim is to link Aristotelian philosophy to modern conceptions of the law of damages, not to explain Aristotelian principles in a philosophical context.

Aristotle distinguishes between voluntary human transactions, such as sale, and involuntary ones. For their part, involuntary transactions are either clandestine, such as theft and adultery, or violent, such as murder and robbery.[14] Applying legal terminology, corrective justice embraces both the law of contract and the law of torts. The position of the parties is not established by reference to their particular role as members of society. Rather, the parties are regarded as individuals connected by a specific relationship, which identifies them among all members of society. The Greeks called this link '*synallagma*'. A wrongdoing provides a *synallagma* in Aristotelian sense. The theory of mean singles out among all members of society the debtor and creditor of a specific obligation. This result is achieved through an application of this theory in the following fashion. The equal is the mean between the more and the less of a particular feeling. The more of good and the less of pain produce a gain, and the opposite situation triggers a loss.[15] A wrongdoing causes an excess of gain on the agent's

---

[11] *Nic Ethics* V ii.
[12] RW Browne, *The Nicomachean Ethics of Aristotle* (London, Henry Bohn 1850) V iii.
[13] J Esser, *Grundlagen und Entwicklung der Gefährdungshaftung* (2nd edn) (München, Beck 1969).
[14] *Nic Ethics* V ii.
[15] Browne (n 12) V iv.

part and an excess of pain on the victim's part, for the one has done injustice and the other has suffered it. The just is a mean between loss and gain. Doing injustice and suffering injustice forges a link – a *synallagma* – between the parties and nobody else.

The theory of mean requires that both the loss and the gain be nullified. Justice is proportion; but the proportion of distributive justice is not the same as the proportion of corrective justice. Distributive justice is based upon the relationship between an individual and society as a whole. This geometrical model cannot work within the context of a *synallagma* between two given individuals. In this case, the law treats the two persons in a neutral fashion: it 'matters not whether a good man has robbed a bad man'.[16] By contrast with distributive justice, persons and things are considered just as 'monads', that is abstract ones, indivisible and equal to one another.[17] This is arithmetical, as opposed to geometrical, proportion. The theory of mean necessitates the presence of pain, that is a loss, on the victim's part. Significantly for the theory of restitution for wrongs, Aristotle does not explicitly deal with the situation in which the victim has suffered no loss whatsoever, but the agent has obtained a gain. It is for modern legal theory to clarify whether corrective justice can be extended to restitutionary damages.

Aristotle assigns to the judges the task to equalise the difference between gain and pain, between too much and the corresponding too little. The judge takes away from one party what exceeds the just, that is the mean, and gives it to the party who has less than the mean. This function of the judiciary is termed 'diorthotic', an expression which conveys the idea of 'putting straight' what is not in balance. Diorthotic, or judicial, justice applies only to corrective justice. Distributive justice takes into consideration factors which go beyond the mere interest of the parties, whereas the judicial activity of adjudication between conflicting interests does not evaluate the general framework of society.

Within a legal context, 'gain' and 'loss', or 'pain', are ambiguous terms. But they should not be taken literally. Aristotle warns that, in some cases, 'gain' might not be the exact word, as in the case in which a man strikes a blow against another.[18] Whereas it is easy to see the loss, or the pain, of the victim, the agent physically and economically has not gained anything. Yet, a gain is not necessarily a material advantage which can be economically evaluated. However, some form of economic evaluation of gain and loss is necessary, for, if the loss is a wound, the victim will not inflict a wound against his assailant in return. Money is the medium which performs the function of equalising as far as possible the gain and the loss.[19]

---

[16]   *Ibid.*
[17]   J A Stewart, *Notes on the Nicomachean Ethics* Vol I (Oxford, 1892) 425.
[18]   Browne (n 12) V iv.
[19]   *Nic Ethics* V v.

iv Retaliation

Retaliation deals with simple reciprocation: the agent will suffer the same quantity of pain in return, which the other party has suffered. At first, Aristotle seems to reject retaliation as incompatible with corrective justice. Then, he partly changes his mind, accepting retaliation as a special kind of corrective justice.[20] Punishment is a concept at odds with the idea of retaliation, given that it is not a matter of personal revenge, but it is mediated by the diorthotic justice dispensed by the judge.[21] Justice must take into account the fact that the action has caused suffering to the victim but also upset public order. Mere retaliation would grant only a partial balance, because the agent could not suffer in return what society as a whole has suffered.

Retaliation poses an obstacle to an explanation of restitutionary damages in terms of *iustitia commutativa*. Similarly to what has already been observed with reference to corrective justice, 'an eye for an eye' furnishes an evaluation of justice from the point of view of the loss of the victim. This model of loss-centred justice leaves little room to a gain-based analysis.

B   The Expansion of Aristotelian Ideas in Western Europe

Nearly the whole of Aristotle's work was forgotten by Western European civilisation for many centuries. Medieval scholars were Platonists, read Boethius, but largely ignored Aristotle. In fact, the rediscovery of Aristotle was enabled by quite a long process of scholarly research, which began about 1100 AD and only reached completion circa 1270 AD.[22] With the end of the European phase of the armed conflict between Christians and Muslims, European scholars gained access to cultural sources which had been hitherto unavailable to them. Suddenly, Arabic and Greek texts became accessible, and a massive project of their translation into Latin began. This translation work was part of a more general movement of cultural renewal which characterised the intellectual sphere of the time, allowing the expansion of new ideas in general, and the interest for Aristotle in particular.[23]

The *studium generale* in the first universities was intended to prepare the students for their further careers – often in the legal sector. Thus, logic, logical grammar and disputation tended to occupy most of the studies to provide a satisfactory technical education.[24] Following the needs of the labour market, the universities requested translations of Aristotelian works in those areas of knowledge. As a consequence, Aristotle's writings which were not concerned with logic

---

[20]   Probably, this half-convinced turn was due to the pressure exerted by the Pythagoreans, who favoured a concept of justice based upon retaliation. *Nic Ethics* V v. See especially U Manthe, 'Beiträge zur Entwicklung des antiken Gerechtigkeitsbegriffes I: Die Mathematisierung durch Pytagoras und Aristoteles' (1996) 113 Savigny Zeitschrift romanistische Abteilung 1-31, 4.

[21]   *Cf* Stewart (n 17) 446.

[22]   D Knowles, *The Evolution of Medieval Thought* (2nd edn) (London, Longman 1988) 167.

[23]   See Knowles, *ibid* ch 15, on the rediscovery of Aristotle.

[24]   *Ibid.*

became available only from the middle of the 12th century.[25] The historical framework explains why Aristotle's concept of justice did not influence directly Western philosophy for many centuries. It would be inaccurate to affirm that no scholar came in contact with Greek or Arabic, or even a few Latin, versions of Aristotle's work. Equally, not all Western philosophy was free from any direct or indirect link with Aristotelian theories. Indeed, both St Augustine and Boethius discussed Aristotle's works; the latter even translated some of his writings. Yet, it was Plato, not Aristotle, who was seen as the greatest source of philosophical inspiration.

The Aristotelian ideas on distributive and corrective justice, therefore, had been lost for many centuries, at least with respect to the Western philosophical tradition. This is an important contention for the analysis of restitution for wrongs, because it supports the idea according to which the law of damages developed originally with little or no contact with Aristotelian philosophy. If law and Aristotelian philosophy were not in contact until the 12th century, post-Roman legal science produced results which were independent of – or, at best, only indirectly related to – Aristotelian theories. For reasons which will be explained later, corrective justice was used by the Scholastics mainly to support a construction in terms of compensation. One of the great thinkers of that time, who strongly influenced the academic investigations of his epoch and beyond, is St Thomas Aquinas. As will be shown, the Thomistic interpretation of Aristotelian justice has played a major role in every analysis of the law of damages up to the more recent legal theories.

C   The Rediscovery of Aristotle

When St Thomas, born in 1224 AD, went to the University of Naples, the study of Aristotle's metaphysical and ethical treatises was as at a relatively early stage. Although the Italian theologian accepted most of the Greek philosopher's analysis, he reinterpreted it in a personal fashion, which influenced the relationship between law and philosophy, as is evident in the Late Scholasticism. St Thomas refers to 'restitution' in his analysis; but he applies this concept to a mechanism which from a legal perspective performs a 'giving back' function which is akin to compensation.

i   St Thomas and the Aristotelian Doctrine

St Thomas followed Aristotelian thought closely. An identification of the two philosophies *tout court* would, however, be far too simplistic.[26] The major

---

[25]   JA Aertsen, 'Aquinas philosophy in its historical setting' in N Kretzmann and E Stump (eds), *The Cambridge Companion to Aquinas* (Cambridge, CUP 1993) 12-37, 20.

[26]   There are other Neo-Scholastic streams which are founded on Aristotelian philosophy while ignoring, or even opposing St Thomas's, for instance Scotism. See J Owens, 'Aristotle and Aquinas' in Kretzmann and Stump, *The Cambridge Companion* (n 25) 38-39

difference is characterised by the ideas of original sin and grace,[27] which as such are alien to Aristotelian thought. Furthermore, Thomistic philosophy includes Platonic elements.[28] St Thomas re-elaborated the Aristotelian tenets in a distinctive fashion.[29] Aristotle, for instance, did not use the term 'natural law', he just mentioned 'natural rights', which can change with, and adapt to, circumstances.[30] On the contrary, St Thomas interpreted the Aristotelian thought on justice as if the Greek philosopher meant that justice has everywhere the same force and power to induce to good and to prevent evil.[31]

ii   Distributive and Corrective Justice

Commenting on Aristotle's Nicomachean Ethics, St Thomas states that 'justice is explained by the fact that its purpose is to will and perform just actions, and injustice to will and perform unjust actions'.[32] In the *Summa Theologiae*, he interprets this Aristotelian definition from a Christian perspective: justice consists chiefly in God's eternal will and purpose.[33] The definition of justice as 'seated in the will'[34] is coherent with the Aristotelian tenets. Yet, once again, the difference is in the Christian perspective: when St Thomas states that 'men's acts are good inasmuch as they reach the measure of reason'[35] he has a very specific, Christian, goal-oriented definition of reason in mind. Formally, however, Aristotle's and St Thomas's descriptions of justice largely coincide.[36] Thus, St Thomas distinguishes a general and a particular form of justice. The former sets the activities of all the virtues towards the common good; the latter is immediately engaged with the good of one individual.

In the *Summa Theologiae*, St Thomas investigates the concepts of distributive and corrective justice. He bases his reasoning on Aristotle's thought, invariably cited with approval to support his own *responsio*, or reply. In his view, through distributive justice, a thing is transferred from the community to the individual; through corrective justice, a thing is transferred from one person to another.[37] This point is developed in the *Summa*. Corrective justice is concerned with the

---

[27]   This is a one-dimensional explanation. Nonetheless, it highlights a central difference which will influence the subsequent studies of the Late Scholastics. On the concept of grace in St Thomas see B Davies, *The Thought of Thomas Aquinas* (Oxford, Clarendon 1992) 266-296.

[28]   *Cf* Aertsen (n 25) 22.

[29]   PE Sigmund, 'Law and Politics' in Kretzmann and Stump, *The Cambridge Companion* (n 25) 217-231, 224.

[30]   HV Jaffa, *Thomism and Aristotelianism* (Chicago, Univ of Chicago Press 1952) 182-184.

[31]   CI Litzinger (tr), *St Thomas Commentary on Aristotle's Nicomachean Ethics* (Notre Dame, Dumb Ox Books 1993) para 1018.

[32]   *Ibid* para 890.

[33]   ST IIa IIae Qu 58 Art 2.

[34]   *Ibid* Art 4.

[35]   *Ibid* Art 3.

[36]   J Finnis, *Aquinas* (Oxford, OUP 1998) 188, criticises St Thomas's classification of the types of justice as too close to Aristotle, with the consequence that it would 'yield no really clear and stable analytical pattern'.

[37]   St Thomas, *Commentary* (n 31) para 928.

ordering of private persons among themselves, while distributive justice appor-
tions proportionately to each his share from the common stock.[38] The nature of
corrective justice demands that equivalent recompense be made, so that the
reaction matches the action. This might indicate that, according to St Thomas,
the theory of '*contrapassum*', that is retaliation, could be embodied in corrective
justice. In fact, whereas Aristotle appeared to have some doubts about the
relationship between retaliation and the model of justice at issue, St Thomas
rejects any compromise on this point: a theory of justice based upon retaliation
has clear limitations. He makes the case of a subordinate who injures a superior.
Here, even if the ruler were to strike back, no equality would be obtained, for the
action of the subordinate is graver. Accordingly, the subordinate has to be more
severely punished than simply through the application of the same quantity of
suffering.[39] Money furnishes a proportionate standard of measurement.

   In his analysis of the responses which restore justice,[40] that is achieve equality
(*aequalitas*) between the parties, St Thomas introduces the concept of restitution
(*restitutio*) along with punishment. Despite the use of this term, it is far from
obvious that the Thomistic idea of restitution offers support to a legal account of
restitution for wrongs. If the semantic identity were matched by an identity of
content, the theories of restitution for wrongs which are based upon Aristotelico-
Thomistic tenets would find strong theoretical support. However, an identification of '*restitutio*' with 'restitution' in the sense applied to the concept of
restitution for wrongs cannot be confirmed. St Thomas does not use 'restitution'
with the meaning of 'giving up a benefit', but in the sense of 'compensating the
victim for his loss by compelling the wrongdoer to give back his benefit'.

iii   *Restitutio*

The man who acted voluntarily ought to be punished more severely. Punishment
would restore justice whereas simple reciprocation would not. Unlike punishment, restitution[41] is not triggered by an intentional act, but by an act which is
objectively unjust despite the lack of wilfulness on the agent's part.[42] Translated
into legal terminology, the irrelevance of intention means that this response also
can be activated by negligent conduct. St Thomas establishes a direct moral, as
opposed to legal, link between the one who takes and the one from whom it has
been taken. To obtain salvation, the agent has to restore the exact amount of what
has been subtracted, the *simplum*, but will not have to give back what he has not
taken. Restitution has to be performed always to the one from whom something
has been taken: the loss of the one is connected to the gain of the other. For St

---

[38]   ST IIa IIae Qu 61 Art 1.
[39]   *Ibid* Art 4.
[40]   Finnis (n 36) 216, observes that in many cases 'the primary focus of Aquinas' discussions "of
commutative justice" is actually not the duty to recompense, compensation, or restitution but the
prior question whether A's act (eg of killing B in self defence) is or is not a wronging of B. The term
"commutative justice" thus swings back and forth'.
[41]   ST IIa IIae Qu 62 Art 1.
[42]   *Ibid* Art 3.

Thomas and Aristotle, this connection between gain and loss is decisive to identify the parties to the moral obligation which justifies the restitutionary claim. However, once the parties have been determined, in St Thomas's view the loss and the gain are only the occasion for restitution, so that, if the person from whom something has been taken is unknown in his precise identity, the agent will perform his moral obligation to give up what he subtracted even 'by giving alms for [the victim's] welfare, living or dead'.[43] Similarly, the agent also performs his obligation by handing the thing to a third party to keep it instead of the victim if giving it back would harm the receiver.

The moral duty upon the agent confirms that the definition of restitution applied by St Thomas could be of no help to the legal theory of restitution for wrongs. First, the Thomistic concept of restitution does not involve necessarily a direct transfer of wealth from the agent to the victim.[44] This moral approach does not seem compatible with the legal definition of restitution, according to which the gain of the agent must be transferred to the victim.[45] A further point of contrast with the legal definition of restitutionary damages becomes evident in the analysis of the categories of wrongdoers who can be compelled to make restitution: the agent, yet also the so-called *co-operatores*, that is those who co-operate in the wrongful act.[46] The responsibility of the helpers is based upon the moral principle that those who consent are just as involved in the action as those who directly act. Although the direct agent remains the person who is principally responsible for the wrong, the helpers must make restitution even if they have not benefited from the wrong. Thus, the Thomistic moral concept of *restitutio* is loss-centred and does not coincide with the legal concept of 'restitution for wrongs'. Finally, although St Thomas prefers restitution, he does not exclude compensation *per aequivalentem* when what is done cannot be undone or what is taken cannot be given back. Thus, if restitution is not possible, recompense – judicially granted – in its stead will do.[47] When not even the repayment of the equivalent can be achieved, he allows for restoration as far as feasible.

All these signals point toward a moral definition of *restitutio* which corresponds to the legal definition of 'compensation'. Thomistic *restitutio* places the victim in a pre-wrong position, nullifying his loss rather than stripping the agent of his gain. Putting on the same level *restitutio* and compensation *per aequivalentem*, St Thomas indicates that, with *restitutio*, he signifies compensation by means of giving back what has been wrongly subtracted. From a legal perspective, this approach insists upon the victim's loss, not the agent's gain. I argue that this Thomistic interpretation of the concept of restitution has strongly influenced modern Aristotelian philosophers. I shall show in chapter eight that both Ernest

---

[43]   *Ibid* Art 6.
[44]   Finnis (n 36) 211, points out that St Thomas uses the concept of restitution in different contexts.
[45]   Birks, *Restitution* 13.
[46]   ST IIa IIae Qu 62 Art 7.
[47]   *Ibid* Art 2. St Thomas uses 'recompense' in the general sense of 'measure necessary to restore justice'. In the present context, it means 'monetary compensation'.

Weinrib[48] and James Coleman,[49] who developed leading theories related to the law of damages, use the Thomistic concept of restitution. Analysing the modern Aristotelian tradition, James Gordley has observed:

> Corrective justice in the Aristotelian tradition … links the plaintiff's right to compensation and the defendant's duty to compensate: the defendant must pay because he has used up the plaintiff's resources for his own ends.[50]

I concur with this view, although, instead of the expression 'Aristotelian tradition', it seems to me more correct to refer to a 'Thomistic tradition', given that Aristotle himself does not appear to me to be directly related to this evolution. This particular meaning of restitution is the result of Scholastic reflections. The Late Scholastic theologians are responsible just as, if not more than, St Thomas for the transmission of this particular meaning of the term 'restitution' to modern legal theorists.

D   The Spanish Late Scholastics and Grotius

The work of the Spanish natural lawyers of the 16th and 17th centuries has attracted the attention of legal scholarship since the mid 20th century. It has become progressively clear that it was through their contributions that Aristotelico-Thomistic philosophy permeated the analysis of the law of damages.[51] The Late Scholastics deserve a special mention for having transferred moral Aristotelian theories into a legal context. Although much of their analysis was anchored in canon law, so that moral evaluations strongly informed their work, still the Spanish authors who constitute the core of the Late Scholasticism dealt with concrete legal problems, which they examined in detail. As James Gordley has argued, the result of the Scholastics's work 'was a reorganization of Roman law into a systematic doctrinal structure on the basis of Aristotelian philosophical principles.'[52]

The issues which became apparent in the discussion of St Thomas's theory of justice find confirmation in the writings by the Late Scholastics. It is problematic to accommodate restitution for wrongs in a model of damages which follows the Aristotelico-Thomistic tenets, for the authors consider corrective justice mainly, if not exclusively, from the perspective of the loss of the victim. As intimated, St Thomas developed a moral concept of *restitutio* which, within the realm of the law of wrongs, reminds particularly of compensation. Beyond the law of wrongs, this concept also describes the mechanism of restitution for unjust enrichment,

---

[48]   Ch 8, IV C iii.
[49]   Ch 8, III C iv.
[50]   J Gordley, 'Tort Law in the Aristotelian Tradition' in DG Owen (ed), *Philosophical Foundations of Tort Law* (Oxford, Clarendon 1995) 130-158, 139.
[51]   On the role of the Late Scholasticism in the origin of natural law, see especially H Thieme, 'Natürliches Privatrecht und Spätscholastik' (1953) 70 *Savigny Zeitschrift romanistische Abteilung* 230-266, 230-237.
[52]   J Gordley, *Foundations of Private Law* (Oxford, OUP 2006) 4.

which requires the transfer of the agent's gain to the victim independently of the perpetration of any wrong. What does not seem to be comprised in the concept of *restitutio* is restitution as a response for wrongs.

The studies on damages conducted by Franciscus de Vitoria and Dominicus Soto will be taken as representative of this school of thought. The investigation will conclude with a brief introduction to Grotius's views, which were greatly influenced by Scholastic analysis.

i   Restitution according to Franciscus de Vitoria

Vitoria has been called the founder of the Spanish Late Scholasticism.[53] He was a moral theologian with a peculiar interest in legal matters. Unsurprisingly, his method of investigation tends to produce results which are more in line with his views on morality than with legal principle. Sometimes, Vitoria is more interested in saving the soul of the agent than in solving a legal issue.[54] This notwithstanding, Vitoria's legal method and the variety of legal cases which he presents deserves full acknowledgment. His analysis begs more than other authors the question of the meaning of 'restitution'. His view confirms that the Aristotelian moral idea of 'restitution' encounters many difficulties when it has to be translated into legal terms: '*restituere est in dominum pristinum statuere; restitutio enim est aequalitatem reddere, quod pertinet ad iustitiam commutativam*'.[55]

This definition gives a strong indication of the legal function which Vitoria connects to restitution. The idea of reinstating the owner to his proprietary position prior to the event which triggered restitution is compatible only with a meaning of restitution as 'giving back': a proprietary right has been transferred to the agent in violation of the principle of corrective justice. Such principle requires that, through restitution, the new owner retransfer the right to the former owner. Restitution for wrongs seems therefore to be alien to this legal reasoning. If it were construed as meaning 'giving up', 'restitution' would have a wider connotation than the one which Vitoria attaches to this term, as emerges in the example which accompanies the last passage quoted: the thief who steals something from me has more than he deserves. I, on the contrary, have less than I deserve. Restitution brings my position and the thief's back to *aequalitas*. Vitoria confirms the link between 'restitution' and 'giving back' in many passages. For example, he poses the question whether restitution of what has been taken is necessary to attain the salvation of the soul. In agreement with St Augustine's famous dictum according to which there can be no remission of sins without restitution of what has been taken, Vitoria observes that salvation of the agent's soul is imperilled as long as he does not perform restitution.[56] If the same object

[53] No analysis of Vitoria's work can ignore G Otte, *Das Privatrecht bei Francisco de Vitoria* (Köln/Graz, Böhlau 1964) 3.
[54] See Otte, *ibid* 11; and eg Vitoria, *De Iustitia* IIa IIae q 62 art 8 nn 1–8.
[55] Vitoria, IIa IIae q 62 art 1 n 1. 'To make restitution is to reinstate the previous owner in his position; restitution is to achieve equality, which is what pertains to commutative justice'.
[56] Vitoria, IIa IIae q 62 art 2 n 1-2.

cannot be returned, substitutionary restitution must be performed. Thus, if I injure your hand, natural restitution is not a viable solution '*quia debet dare aequivalens*'.[57]

It is difficult to accommodate Vitoria's concept of restitution within modern legal categories. Indeed, even some legal historians think that '*restitutio*' does not have a precise legal equivalent. An approximate translation could be 'to make good an injustice'.[58] Restitution according to Vitoria does not have the meaning which is associated with restitution for wrongs. Vitoria uses restitution only in two specific cases, which in modern terminology correspond to compensation for wrongs and restitution for unjust enrichment. Many passages highlight this two-fold role of the expression at issue. Along with the examples of compensation triggered by a wrong, Vitoria urges that:

> *quomodocumque et quacumque via apud aliquem sit res aliena, qui habet illam, sive pervenerit ad manus suas juste, sive injuste, cum sit aliena, tenetur ad restitutionem vero domino ratione rei alienae.*[59]

It follows from this passage that even when no wrong has been perpetrated, restitution has to be performed to the 'real owner', or *verus dominus*. A still stronger indication that Vitoria does not have restitution for wrongs in mind whilst dealing with the concept of restitution emerges from a variation of Birks' 'thug case'. If T pays A to kill victim V, Vitoria is of the opinion that the payment has to be given back to T, whereas he does not mention a claim of V or his heirs at all.[60] Even the case of the judge who is bribed by one of the parties is not considered from the perspective of restitution for wrongs. The judge helps the agent and therefore is liable *in solidum* with the latter.[61] Once again, this is a normal instance of compensation for wrongs. The possibility of the victim seizing the bribe obtained by the judge in addition to compensation is not examined by Vitoria.

ii   Restitution according to Dominicus Soto

Soto's '*De Iustitia et Iure*'[62] is a major philosophical and legal contribution to Scholastic analysis and natural law. In particular, the fourth Book was highly regarded by Grotius.[63] The sixth question of the fourth Book is titled '*de restitutionis substantia*'. In this *quaestio*, Soto analyses the meaning and the function of restitution. Restitution contains the idea of 'putting something back

---

[57]   *Ibid* n 10: 'because an equivalent thing must be performed'.

[58]   Otte (n 53) 64.

[59]   Vitoria, IIa IIae q 62 art 6 n 2. 'No matter how the thing has reached the one who has it, whether justly or unjustly. If it belongs to another, it must be given back to the real owner because it belongs to another'.

[60]   Vitoria, IIa IIae q 62, art 5, n 7: '[s]*icut de illo qui accepit pecunias ut occideret aliquem, tenetur restituere pecunias illi a quo accepit*'

[61]   Vitoria, IIa IIae q 62 art 8 n 3.

[62]   My analysis is based upon the Latin edition published in Antwerp in 1567.

[63]   Thieme (n 51) 244.

in the right place'.[64] The mechanism of restitution requires the presence of a debt. Without a debt, there is no restitution, and the transfer of wealth is based instead upon an act of liberality. This requirement is already a signal that the concept of restitution is interpreted in the Thomistic sense. Restitution is awarded on the basis of a loss, not a gain. In fact, the *quaestio sexta* deals expressly with the *secunda secundae, quaestio* 62, of St Thomas's *Summa theologiae*. Following Thomistic reasoning, Soto comes to the conclusion that '*restitutio est actus iustitiae commutativae*'.[65] For Soto, restitution can be performed only when its object is unjustly taken or detained by the agent. It is this very object which must be given back: '*restitutio autem importat redditionem illius rei, quae iniuste vel aufertur vel retinetur: quae quidem redditio opus est iustitae commutativae: ergo illa est necessaria*'.[66] This qualification of the object of restitution as the object of the transfer of wealth marks a point of differentiation from punishment, which involves a quantification of the response in terms of the three-fold or four-fold of the value of the thing. Thus, if I sell wine for a price which exceeds what has been established statutorily, the buyer will be immediately able to obtain restitution of the excess; yet, for punishment he will have to wait for the outcome of a trial.[67]

Whenever it is possible, restitution ought to take place between the agent and the victim.[68] However, if the victim himself has no title to receive the object of restitution – for example because he has stolen it – the real owner will be able to claim it: '*restitutio fieri debere vero domino*'.[69] On the other hand, sometimes a person other than the agent might be called on to perform restitution. Soto follows St Thomas's scheme as regards the categories of those who take part into the event which triggers restitution. These *co-operatores* are jointly liable: the performance by one of them will free the others towards the victim, but not towards the one who performed.[70]

With regard to 'illicit giving', or *dationes illicitae*, Soto differentiates three situations which justify a claim for restitution of what has been unduly transferred from the agent to a third party *contra bonos mores*. One such case involves a transfer of money to a judge to decide the trial in favour of the transferor.[71] If the victim, in this case the other party in the trial, were able to recover from the judge what the transferor paid to win the case, the victim's action could be classified as an instance of restitution for wrongs. But this eventuality is not considered by Soto, who only deals with the question of the right to restitution for unjust enrichment between the transferor and the transferee.

---

[64]   *Iustitia,* Lib IV q 6 art I p 117.

[65]   *Ibid*: 'Restitution is an act of commutative justice'.

[66]   *Ibid* q 6 art II p 118. 'Restitution implies the giving back of the very thing which is unjustly subtracted or detained: giving back is necessary because it is indeed an act of commutative justice'.

[67]   *Ibid* q 6 art IIII p 126.

[68]   *Ibid* q 7 art I p 128.

[69]   *Ibid.*

[70]   *Ibid* q 7 art III p 133.

[71]   *Ibid* q 7 art I p 119.

On the whole, Soto follows quite closely St Thomas's philosophical investiga-tions, which he integrates with concrete cases. *De Iustitia et Iure* provides a good example of the interaction between philosophical and legal analysis. However, Soto's work cannot be seen as a piece of legal analysis in proper sense. Soto is more interested in asserting the pre-eminence and the independence of natural law over positive law. His examination has been defined 'metajuridical'.[72]

The works of the Late Scholastics substantiate the thesis that, at some point, Aristotelian thoughts became a component of legal reasoning: Soto shows how philosophical analysis left its purely moral realm to deal with more concrete legal questions. Yet, Soto's idea of restitution is still Thomistic. The victim's loss, not the agent's gain, determines the measure of damages. As such, it is incompatible with the concept of restitution as a response through which the claimant aims to obtain the agent's gain. Indeed, even where there could be room for an analysis in terms of restitutionary damages, like in the case of the bribed judge, Soto – just as Vitoria – does not consider a restitutionary claim for wrongs as a possible avenue.

iii   The concept of damage in Grotius

Grotius's views on the law of damages are testimony to the passage from the predominantly moral analysis of the first and the second Scholasticism to an analysis based upon legal principle. Grotius knew Aristotle and St Thomas. He also knew the doctrines of the Late Scholastics: Soto's and Cajetanus's dicta, for instance, appear in many passages of his analysis of unjust damage in *De iure belli ac pacis*.[73]

Grotius dedicates all of chapter seventeen in the second book of *De iure belli ac pacis* to 'the unjustly caused damage and the obligation which is triggered by it'. The lack of any reference to restitution, to which the expression 'reparation' is preferred,[74] is a striking element of this chapter. However, this difference is mainly terminological. Grotius and the Late Scholastics refer to the same concept: the wrongful act causes a *damnum* to the victim; the consequences of the *damnum* have to be rectified as far as possible. The late Scholastics state that rectification should be achieved by means of 'restitution'. Grotius favours 'repara-tion'. Both refer to the Aristotelico-Thomistic concept of restitution, which is based on the victim's loss. Thus, if the agent kills the victim, the agent will have to pay the fee of the doctor as well as compensation to the parents, wife, and children.[75] Alternatively, if the victim is maimed, the agent will bear – inter alia – the costs of the operation.[76] In the few passages where the term 'restitution'

---

[72]   Thieme (n 51) 250.
[73]   I have consulted the following French edition of Grotius work: *Le droit de la guerre et de la paix*, translated by J Barbeirac (Amsterdam 1724).
[74]   Yet, R Feenstra, 'Grotius' Doctrine of Unjust Enrichment as a Source of Obligation: its Origin and its Influence in Roman-Dutch Law' in EJH Schrage (ed) *Unjust Enrichment – The Comparative Legal History of the Law of Restitution* (2nd edn) (Berlin, Duncker & Humblot 1999) 197-236, 208 n 71, prefers the translation of the function of the claim, *'ut reparetur'*, as 'restitution'.
[75]   Grotius, para 13.
[76]   Grotius, para 14.

appears, it qualifies the duty upon the agent to give back what he obtained through the wrong. Yet the measure of restitution is always the victim's loss. The thief, for instance, has to make restitution of the stolen thing.[77] In this case, restitution has to be performed *in natura*, as also is required by the Scholastics. Only when the thing no longer exists will the agent give back its value, which consists of the just mean between too high and too low a price.[78]

With Grotius, the evolution of the terms used by the law of damages from epistemic concepts to legal institutions is largely complete. Modern lawyers can read Grotius and understand what he means when he uses the expression 'reparation of damages'. In contrast, the Scholastic concept of 'restitution' can hardly be identified with any legal category. In the seventeenth chapter, Grotius separates the law of delict from the law of unjust enrichment and concentrates on the former. In the section on 'damage unjustly caused', the author refers solely to those losses which are a consequence of a wrongful event. This excludes unjust enrichment, for which a wrong is not a requirement. What is more, not only is there no reference to restitution for wrongs in the whole chapter on damages, but also, in line with Thomistic tenets, the response triggered by a wrongful event seems to be exclusively compensation.

Grotius's analysis of the law of damages is the result of the evolution of the Aristotelian theory on justice. The importance of Grotius's view on natural law is such that it is possible to assume that his categorisation provides the scheme for modern accounts of the law of damages. Grotius is not responsible for the modern incapacity to produce a satisfactory theoretical justification of restitution for wrongs. Rather, his work amplifies and imposes the modern interpretation of the theory of corrective justice.[79]

III   Aristotelian Theory and Law of Damages

Roman lawyers were learned persons well versed in Greek philosophy. It would be surprising if, when acting as lawyers, their cultural formation would have not informed their decisions. Yet, a direct link between Roman law and Greek philosophy is probably to be excluded. Thomistic, rather than Aristotelian, philosophy is likely to have played a more concrete role in the shaping of the modern law of damages

The results obtained thus far seem to rule out philosophy as the catalyst of the development of restitutionary damages. In this section, I shall examine from the perspective of restitution for wrongs the philosophical data which I have collected thus far. In the next chapter, I shall use this information to present a theory of restitution for wrongs as corrective justice.

---

[77]   Grotius, para 16.
[78]   *Ibid.*
[79]   The conclusion finds confirmation in Grotius's analysis of the law of unjust enrichment, full of references to Thomistic and Scholastic reasoning. *Cf* Feenstra (n 74) 198-219.

A   Diorthotic Justice

The concept of 'diorthotic justice' is an important contribution of Aristotelian philosophy to legal science. With this notion, Aristotle underlines the significance of justice as mediation between contrasting interests. There must be, in his view, a third, independent party who intervenes to find an equitable solution. For justice to be achieved, this solution cannot be exclusively in the hands of those directly involved in the dispute. The idea of the necessity of mediation seems to have been absorbed by Roman law in the course of its evolution. The original damages *ad poenam persequendam*, for instance, fell progressively under the direct sphere of influence of the State, a passage which is highlighted by the transfer of competence from a lay judge to a professional body of magistrates.

The introduction of a figure who 'puts straight' a wrong, and in so doing keeps an eye on the general framework within which the wrong has been perpetrated, grants corrective justice the necessary degree of flexibility. The diorthotic intervention models the legal response taking account of different factors. Yet, it cannot be stretched so far as to include restitution for wrongs if the response itself is based upon the loss of the victim.

B   The Theory of Mean

Corrective justice establishes a link between the parties to a wrongful action as being in a correlative relationship of doer and sufferer of an injustice. This correlation justifies the application of the theory of mean, which requires a nullification of both gain and loss. St Thomas clarified that the function of justice is to make things proportionally even, 'proportionally' meaning 'according to the correlativity of gain and loss'. Aristotelico-Thomistic doctrines examined the link between the parties primarily from the perspective of the victim's loss. A moral claim arises because there is a loss, which might indicate that there is no room for restitution for wrongs. Still, Aristotle accepted that any form of loss, not only a material one, qualifies for corrective justice. Aristotle's use of metaphorical terminology guarantees to his theory the necessary flexibility which enables an account of restitutionary damages in terms of corrective justice: if even a non-patrimonial loss can be shown, corrective justice can explain the legal phenomenon. Thus, the definition of loss is the key to apply corrective justice to restitution for wrongs. In chapter eight,[80] I shall show how 'loss' can be construed as to comprehend the position of the victim, so that the parties are in the correlative position required by Aristotle. In the present context, I shall only introduce the difficulties faced by any analysis which seeks to justify the damages

[80]   Ch 8, V.

at issue using corrective justice. The idea of proportion based on the principle of mean is a serious obstacle, as the following example shows.[81]

Defendant D has published a book with information on the private life of claimant C in breach of a contract in which he undertook not to divulge any such information. C has suffered no loss from the wrong: neither his reputation nor his assets and well-being have been affected by the publication. C does not feel any particular sense of grievance for D's act. C is indifferent to the publication of the book. Corrective justice seeks the mean between loss and gain. That D has attained a gain is evident; but where is C's loss? Maybe the loss could be justified, in moral as well as normative terms, as a disturbance of social harmony. Thus, diorthotic justice would qualify the offence against the whole of society as a loss which would be compensated allowing C to obtain D's benefit. However, this approach does not seem to fit Aristotle's idea of corrective justice. The loss must affect *in primis* the individual; if it does, then it may be considered in terms of its social relevance. Furthermore, this solution does not explain why, of all possible monetary awards, the benefit of the agent corresponds exactly to the loss suffered by society at large and by the victim. Thus, the theory of mean appears not to be helpful in the present case even if an extremely flexible concept of diorthotic justice were accepted. According to the common understanding of corrective justice – particularly in the Scholastic interpretation – what has been taken from the victim to the advantage of the agent must be given back to the victim. However, in the case under analysis nothing has been taken from the victim which can be given back. Finally, this solution does not justify why it is the particular claimant, and not society as a whole, who obtains the defendant's benefit. In my view, these obstacles can be overcome. Yet, they epitomise the intricacy of a theory of restitution for wrongs founded upon corrective justice.

C   Aristotelian Responses

The relationship between the theory of mean and restitutionary damages is a formidable hindrance for those modern accounts which try to embed restitution for wrongs in the Aristotelian tradition. Building up on the previous section, I shall now highlight some of the reasons for the scholarly difficulties in a brief overview of the Aristotelian responses. Despite the doubts which I express in this section, note that, in my opinion, Aristotelian theory does contain all relevant elements to explain restitutionary damages as an instance of *iustitia commutativa*.

i   Punishment

The Aristotelian description of punishment as a social offence is reflected in the evolution of Roman law. Aristotle and St Thomas are agreed that not any

---

[81]   At this stage, the question of a justification of the link between the parties which explains this imposition of the restitutionary duty on that particular defendant to the advantage of that particular claimant will be ignored.

wrongdoing triggers a punitive response. According to Aristotle, punishment is strongly tied to voluntary actions.[82] The moral character of this evaluation is underlined by the fact that involuntary wrongful behaviour engenders in the agent feelings of pain and regret. Yet, even if I commit a wrong by mistake and do not regret my actions, I will not be punished.

The theory of punishment cannot justify restitution for wrongs. An award of restitutionary damages is independent of any punitive implications. The agent who is stripped of his gain is not worse off after restitution than he was before he committed the wrong. Nor is intention a necessary requirement for the award. Besides, there is no penal element in restitutionary damages. Any a fortiori reasoning, which sought to justify restitution on the basis of the existence of a punitive response in the law of damages, must be rejected. From the existence of exemplary damages, it is not possible to derive an argument in favour of the existence of restitutionary damages, for the two responses have different origins and different functions. They only share their classification within the category of non-compensatory damages.

ii   Restitution

St Thomas classifies restitution as an act of corrective justice. This express mention of restitution seems to be a fortunate event: if he refers to restitution as a response triggered by a wrong, surely there must also be room for restitutionary damages in his theoretical construction. However, this argument is not as straightforward as it appears. 'Restitution' relates to different concepts: it can be used in the sense of restoration of a *status quo ante*, or it can mean 'giving up something'. In the latter sense, it applies to restitution for wrongs, in the former sense it normally denotes an avenue to perform a compensatory duty. Thus, for instance, if I wrongfully take your suit for a ceremonial function, my duty to compensate you will probably include restitution of the suit. In this context, restitution has a compensatory function, so that this term is not used in the sense of stripping you of a windfall which does not correspond to any loss of mine.

In St Thomas's view, *restitutio* is the reverse of *ablatio*, or taking away. Making restitution, the wrongdoer re-establishes the victim in possession of, or dominion over, a thing which, from the perspective of moral philosophy, should belong, or already belongs, to the victim. In this case, restitution means 'to give back'. In legal terms, Thomistic restitution is restoration by means of restitution. What is to be restored is the exact amount of what has been taken. Restitution for St Thomas

> is essentially a matter of restoring to specific losers – to those who now have less than they ought – what they have been deprived of.[83]

---

[82]   *Cf* Nilstun (n 6) 56.
[83]   Finnis (n 36) 210.

Therefore, the 'quantification of damages' is based upon the loss of the victim, and not upon the enrichment of the wrongdoer: *restitutio principaliter ordinetur ad reintegrandam rem ejus qui injuste est damnificatus*.[84] Yet, even St Thomas leaves the door ajar to a different concept of restitution. He describes corrective justice as 'a certain balance of equality'. 'Restitution restores the balance when the taking of something has upset it'.[85] If it can be shown that the enrichment of the wrongdoer has caused an imbalance in his relationship with the victim, then restitution for wrongs should be able to intervene even if the victim has suffered no patrimonial loss.

iii   The co-operatores

The 'standard' function of restitution as restoration emerges in the Thomistic analysis of those who are bound to compensate the victim.[86] In this context, 'restitution' seems to acquire a different meaning, which is larger than 'giving back'. St Thomas considers the situation of those who have consented to the wrongdoing and have helped the agent. If an assistant in the wrongful action is compelled to compensate the defendant's loss although he might have received nothing from the wrongdoing, it appears that this use of 'restitution' is different from the more traditional Thomistic use. The question is whether the enlarged content of the term hints at a different kind of response to the wrong. The *Summa* dispels quickly this impression. The moral connection between gain and loss still provides the base for restitution: the quantification of the obligation is founded upon the loss of the victim. The help and the approval granted to the agent merely extend the area of responsibility to other persons, the *co-operatores*. If one helper performs his obligation, the others will be freed from their own restorative duties in their external relationship, that is towards the victim. St Thomas does not want to enrich the victim; he wants to put the victim in the best possible position at the expense of the agent and his supporters. The same sort of analysis applies to the epigones of St Thomas. Vitoria's view reinforces the Thomistic interpretation when he states that restitution means to give back to the previous owner. He does not mention the victim who would deserve the agent's windfall as a matter of justice.

The treatment of the *co-operatores* is in line with the moral investigation pursued in the *Summa*. The perpetration of a wrong places the moral blame onto the agent, or his *entourage*; the response to this is a moral *poena*, which can assume the form of real punishment when the act has been wilfully performed. St Thomas does not distinguish between criminal and civil liability. Yet, one cannot infer from the Thomistic moral account that punishment is a response belonging to the private law of damages. What St Thomas tells us is that the gain is mirrored

---

[84]   ST IIa IIae Qu 62 Art 7: 'restitution is mainly imposed to return the thing to the person who is unjustly damnified'.

[85]   ST IIa IIae Qu 62 Art 3.

[86]   *Ibid.*

in the loss so that the restoration of the *status quo ante* necessitates all those measures which would eliminate completely the difference between the loss and the gain. Under some circumstances, this result can be reached simply with 'restitution'. In other cases, the seriousness of the matter requires that the agent be punished.

iv Retaliation

Albeit not without doubts, Aristotle accepts that retaliation is a particular response within corrective justice. St Thomas disagrees because in his view *contrapassum* does not guarantee equality of proportions. The discrepancy between the two positions might be affected by the influence of Christian values on social issues. St Thomas is firm in his rejection: by inflicting the same quantity of suffering on the agent which the victim has endured, justice is not achieved, as retaliation is not the result of a diorthotic intervention of the judge. Even accepting the Aristotelian dubitative stance, and thus classifying retaliation as a valid response of corrective justice, the theory of restitution for wrongs derives little or no support from it. 'An eye for an eye' means that the response to the wrongdoing is measured by the loss of the victim. If the loss is, say, £100, retaliation will require that the agent pay £100 to the victim regardless any further evaluation of social kind. Therefore, retaliation is a purely restorative approach, which, as such, is incompatible with a restitutionary solution.

IV The Influence of Philosophical Analysis over Legal Interpretation

The central thesis of the present chapter is that an epistemic analysis of the law of damages on the basis of the theory of corrective justice helps to explain why restitution for wrongs has traditionally been viewed with suspicion. It is doubtful, however, whether Greek philosophy exerted any major influence over Roman legal analysis and thus indirectly over modern legal systems.

A The Historical and the Philosophical Factors

In the previous chapter, it has been ascertained that the modern law of damages is the product of the evolution of an original Roman model. The development of Roman legal procedure in the post-classical period limited the responses available to private parties. In practice, this meant that private parties could only – or mainly – claim compensation for wrongs, whereas the punitive *actiones ad poenam persequendam* were granted solely in the *cognitio* courts before a civil servant.[87] Beside the historical factor, legal theory has influenced the development of the law of damages. The Aristotelian theory of justice has been used primarily to support punishment and compensation for wrongs.

The question which has to be addressed at this point is whether and how far Roman law and his later developments were affected by the Aristotelian tenets. If a link between philosophy and Roman law were positively identified, it would follow that there must be at least two major independent factors accounting for the widespread opinion according to which law of damages and law of compensation are widely overlapping, if not coincident, categories. The historical factor explains, but does not justify, the exclusion of restitution for wrongs from the law of damages. The philosophical factor seems to corroborate the insignificant role of restitutionary damages; yet, this development is the consequence of an historical accident rather than a compelling philosophical reflection. Therefore, neither of the two factors would constitute a legal obstacle to a theory of restitution for wrongs.

B   Greek Philosophy in the Context of Roman Legal Science

Greek philosophy had a different impact on Roman law and on its interpretation by the Glossators. However, in both cases the results are remarkably similar: Aristotelian tenets probably exerted little or no influence on legal analysis – at least, not in a direct fashion. This influence can be observed only at a later stage, especially owing to the Late Scholastics and their impact on Grotius's work.

i   Roman Lawyers

The relationship between philosophy and legal science in ancient Rome is a controversial topic in the Romanistic literature. Although the Roman orators were well versed in Greek philosophy, which they cited to support their argumentation, Roman lawyers did not refer to philosophy in their opinions. One of the few passages in which the importance of philosophy for the study of the law is expressly highlighted can be found at the beginning of the Digest. According to Ulpian, lawyers are 'the priests of the law':

> *Iustitiam namque colimus et boni et aequi notitiam profitemur, aequum ab iniquo separantes …veram nisi fallor philosophiam non simulatam affectantes.*[88]

An analysis of this statement is not directly related to the object of the present study.[89] Yet, the mention of philosophy at the beginning of the Digest is useful to

---

[87] See ch 6, n 61 and text thereof.

[88] D 1.1.1. 'For we cultivate the virtue of justice and claim awareness of what is good and fair, discriminating between fair and unfair … and affecting a philosophy which, if I am not deceived, is genuine, not a sham'. T Mommsen, P Krueger (eds) and A Watson (tr), *The Digest of Justinian* (Pennsylvania, Univ of Pennsylvania 1985).

[89] The possible implications of this passage for Roman legal analysis are investigated by L Winkel, 'Le droit romain et la philosophie grecque, quelques problèmes de méthode' (1997) LXV *Tijdschrift voor Rechtsgeschiedenis* 373-384.

introduce some brief reflections on the relationship between Roman law and legal philosophy. To understand the genesis of restitution for wrongs, it must be investigated whether the development of a legal definition of restitutionary damages – or the lack thereof – is a consequence of the connection between philosophy and legal science. This hypothesis does not seem particularly audacious, given the weight of Aristotelian thought on modern legal thinking. The fact that a link between philosophy and law is widely acknowledged among modern lawyers, however, does not necessarily mean that Greek philosophy and Roman law accepted or recognised it at all.

Helmut Coing argued that Aristotle's philosophy provided an 'atmosphere'[90] within which many different cultural events could thrive: the Roman gentleman would have read Plato, Aristotle and the Stoics. Among the many examples of the contacts between Greek philosophy and Roman culture, one can cite the famous cultural circles of Scipio the Younger and Panaetius, where Greek philosophy was read and discussed; not to mention orators like Cicero. Logic, rhetoric, and ethics attracted great interest in the Roman elite, for they furnished the necessary tools for a career in the Roman civil service. Thus, Greek philosophy was a normal component of Roman education. On the other hand, the connection between Greek philosophy and Roman law is still debated. The function performed by Aristotelian ideas in the shaping of legal institutions is particularly uncertain. However, there seems to be general agreement that at least one aspect of Greek philosophy gave a seminal contribution in the development of Roman law: logic. Roman jurisprudence changed drastically as a consequence of the adoption of Greek dialectic. In the context of the absorption of Greek logical structures, this process led to a systematic study of legal *genera* and *species* which, in turn, transformed Roman jurisprudence into a proper legal science, that is a systematic research of governing principles of the Roman legal order.[91]

The phase of expansion of ideas of Greek origin, which was known as the 'Hellenistic period', takes place around the end of the second century BC and is a central feature of the last two centuries of the Republic.[92] Despite the weight of Greek thought on both general culture and legal knowledge, there is no sign of a parallel development of a legal philosophy. It seems that Roman lawyers were not greatly interested in philosophical inquiries. This fact has been explained through the structure of Roman society and the person of the lawyers; the latter were men 'immersed in practical politics and law',[93] who took little notice of theoretical disputes which did not have an immediate impact upon the development of the law. Indeed, the influence of Greek philosophy is more evident in the periods in which legal discussions took place primarily in the big Roman schools of

---

[90] H Coing, 'Zum Einfluß der Philosophie des Aristoteles auf die Entwicklung des römischen Rechts' (1952) 69 *Savigny Zeitschrift romanistische Abteilung* 24-59, 25.

[91] Thus F Schulz, *History of Roman Legal Science* (Oxford, Clarendon 1946) 63-68.

[92] *Cf* Coing (n 90) 29.

[93] Schulz (n 91) 69.

thought, whereas it was more lenient during the late Classical period, in which the praxis had a more important function in determining the law.[94]

Unlike Greek moral philosophy, logic became an essential trait of Roman legal science, which used it to answer cases on the one hand, and to organise the law in a harmonic structure according to *genera* and *species*, a good instance of which are Gaius's Institutions, on the other. Yet, this evolution never reached a level of abstraction such as the one which qualified the German Pandectist School in the 19th century.[95]

ii The Glossators

Roman pragmatism was a very powerful filter, which is likely to have prevented legal science from the 'contamination' with alien theoretical approaches such as the ones put forward by Greek moral philosophy. The Glossators, on the other hand, started their analysis from a different viewpoint. Although their basic tenet was that Roman sources are never mistaken, so that apparently incompatible passages only needed a correct interpretation to eliminate the contradiction, they were not great pragmatists, but rather legal theorists. It seems, therefore, that they could have been influenced by Aristotelian doctrines. If this were proved to be so, then this result would provide a first indication of a contact between legal development and Aristotelian theories on justice, thus furnishing some arguments in favour of a potential link between Aristotelian corrective justice and the law of damages at a very early stage of its development.[96]

However, legal-historical analysis shows that Greek philosophy, and in particular ethics, had little or no impact on the Glossators. This phenomenon has a clear historical explanation. Aristotelian philosophy was lost to European culture for many centuries and was rediscovered only with the translation of Aristotle's works from Greek and Arabic in southern Europe during the 12th century. Until that moment, what medieval scholars could read on Greek philosophy came from Roman orators like Cicero and later philosophers like Boethius and Plotinus. They were all particularly interested in the dialectic, which means especially logic. Hence, the first Aristotelian works to obtain increasing diffusion were the treaties on logics, the Ethics being translated only from the beginning of the 13th century. The Glossators were likely to know Aristotelian dialectic, but little more. Additionally, the Glossators were lawyers, not philosophers. It is plausible that they had to wait for commentaries on Aristotle's works, which necessarily came long after the translations started circulating.[97] Therefore, the commentaries reached the Glossators at quite a late stage of their research. It is very improbable that the Glossators were acquainted with the Aristotelian non-logical production.

---

[94] Coing (n 90) 26.
[95] *Ibid* 29-30.
[96] The contributions of the Late Scholastics and Grotius indicate the presence of such a link after the 15th century.
[97] *Cf* G Otte, 'Die Aristoteleszitate in der Glosse' (1968) 85 *Savigny Zeitschrift romanistische Abteilung* 368-393, 370-371.

In fact, in the whole of the Accursian Glossa only seven quotations from Aristotle have been identified. Furthermore, legal research has carefully analysed these passages and demonstrated that their authenticity is most doubtful: where Accursius mentioned Aristotle, he normally referred to ideas advanced by Cicero or Boethius.[98]

It seems unlikely that the development of the law of damages was directly influenced by Aristotelian considerations of justice, although a more indirect influence cannot be excluded, or rather is quite possible. If this point is correct, the evolution of the law of damages is a phenomenon which, for a long time, had been relatively immune from contacts with moral philosophy. It follows that, at least until Aristotelian ideas circulated more liberally throughout Europe, the causes for the shape and structure of the law of damages are to be sought primarily within the law itself, intended as statutes, judicial authority and academic opinions. Yet, not any contribution from philosophy or theology was ignored. The evolution of the Roman law of delict into criminal law gathered momentum when the State decided to control the administration of justice. There were legal and political motivations behind this decision, and probably there were philosophical reasons as well, such as the Aristotelian partition in corrective and distributive justice.

On the other hand, through the Late Scholasticism, which involved primarily theologians, and Grotius, important Aristotelian ideas on justice and law have informed legal science. They are now part of the modern conception of the law, as the investigation of normative approaches to the law of damages in the next chapter will demonstrate.

[98] *Ibid* 380-381.

8

Modern Aristotelian Approaches to Restitution for Wrongs

I Introduction

THE INVESTIGATION OF the historical and philosophical sources of the law of damages indicates that restitution for wrongs, at its outset, was probably not influenced by extra-legal factors such as philosophical considerations. A connection between law and philosophy can be established with a certain degree of confidence only from the Late Scholasticism onwards. Building upon the data of the previous chapter, I shall now seek to demonstrate that some of the problems faced by those who apply Aristotelian philosophy to restitution for wrongs follow from the difficulty to link the moral account to legal practice and theory. In my opinion, it is possible to develop a theory of restitutionary damages as corrective justice provided that the concept of 'loss', or 'pain', is not construed as 'patrimonial loss'. Under the influence of Thomistic philosophy, modern analyses which apply corrective justice are often mainly concerned with the victim's loss. Yet a loss-centred perspective is not essential to corrective justice, which can explain a claim for restitution of a benefit if it is shown that the parties to the claim are in a relationship which corresponds to the Aristotelian model of justice. I shall describe my views on this topic after having examined some influential theories.

It is not an oversimplification to assert that most modern Aristotelian approaches to the law of damages can be classified into two groups. A first school of thought denies that the law of torts can be reduced to one single principle. Rather, it is a receptacle of different aims. This account leaves the door open for restitution for wrongs as an independent aim of tort law, although the moral case for awarding some sort of response does not always match the legal case for doing so, as we shall see. The other school of thought rejects the previous approach and traces tort law to one fundamental principle. Ernest Weinrib, a key figure of this school, has adapted this so-called formalist idea to restitution for wrongs. Weinrib's contribution has been the first intervention specifically dedicated to restitutionary damages. The difficulties faced by Weinrib epitomise the formidable obstacles which must be overcome to accommodate restitutionary damages within corrective justice. Chapter seven has already highlighted some of the reasons for these difficulties: particularly since the Scholastics, corrective justice has been mainly used to link the measure of the – moral – response to a wrong with the loss suffered by the victim, whereas an account of restitution for wrongs would need to consider the gain of the wrongdoer.

Before focusing on issues of corrective justice, I shall introduce a German theory which applies distributive justice directly to private relationships, that is to the private law of damages. Whilst offering a good opportunity to examine the correlation between distributive justice and the law of wrongs, this account, developed by Josef Esser, also allows some reflections on the German theory of private law.

II German Legal Theory and Aristotelian Justice

Comparative analysis has shown that restitutionary damages as such are still unknown to German law. However, there are indications that mechanisms which replicate the structure, if not the terminology, of this legal response might find a niche even in that legal system. This recent development is reflected by some academic contributions of German scholars who are aware of the new ideas circulating in the English law of damages, so that even in Germany questions on the nature of restitution for wrongs are newly posed. The analysis of para. 285 (1) BGB[1] and of the action triggered by a breach of fiduciary duty[2] suggests that a restitutionary mechanism founded upon the defendant's wrongdoing is not unfamiliar to the law of obligations.

A The General Studies on Private Law

The studies on the general theory of private law do not seem to link non-compensatory goals to the law of damages. Franz Bydlinski,[3] for example, when examining the German law of damages in his study on the system and principles of private law, focuses only on the law of compensation. German law tends to conflate the concepts of law of damages and law of compensation, so that the central statutory norm on the law of damages, para 249 BGB, is interpreted as giving rise to a 'principle of compensation', according to which the main function of the law of damages is to alleviate the loss of the victim.[4] Although Bydlinski recognises that the principle of compensation alone does not provide a sufficient basis for a claim, he states that 'it belongs to the fundamental values of the law of

---

[1] See ch 4, n 79 and text thereof.
[2] See ch 5, I B i.
[3] F Bydlinski, *System und Prinzipien des Privatrechts* (Wien, Springer 1996) 185-233.
[4] See ch 2, n 37 and text thereof.

damage reparation',[5] so that the principle of compensation takes its place within 'the core of the concept of damage'.[6] The importance of the principle, therefore, is shifted from the law of compensation, the boundaries of which it is supposed to set, to the law of damages as a whole, which is consequently built around the idea of compensation.

The predominant position of the principle of compensation has been questioned in the context of the recently recognised 'function of prevention' of the law of damages. The seminal case of *Caroline von Monaco*[7] justifies the doubts on the exclusivity of compensation among the legal responses.[8] However, most German academics and the judiciary stick to the traditional dogmatic construction, which explains the *Caroline* case as a peculiar application of constitutional principles not susceptible of extension to other situations.

The Aristotelian partition of justice is well known to German legal theorists. A particular feature of their analysis is the attention given to the social function of distributive justice.[9] Helmut Coing observes that distributive justice intervenes whenever a burden or a benefit ought to be allocated within the community and the rules of corrective justice would be of no avail.[10] In his view, *iustitia distributiva* is characterised by an element of dynamism. In the name of social justice, it can be used to shape actively a community, such as in the case of participation of workers in pension schemes partly sustained by the financial output created by their own work.[11] Yet, without questioning the use of distributive justice for experiments of social engineering, it is the supposedly exclusive relationship between this kind of justice and society which raises some doubts. Aristotle considers man a 'social animal'. From this perspective, every aspect of human activity contains relevant social factors. Both distributive justice and corrective justice intervene to establish social harmony which has been or could be imperilled by a wrongful allocation of resources and social honours. Even the 'dynamic advantage' of distributive justice is dubious. It ignores the role of diorthotic justice. More than simple retaliation, it is mediation which shapes the measurement of the loss to be compensated. The louder the 'public outcry' due to the commission of a certain wrong, the more substantial the measure of damages will be, for the person who strikes the ruler will be punished more severely than the one who strikes a private citizen.[12]

---

5 Bydlinski (n 3) 187: '*es gehört ... zu den Grundwertungen des Schadensersatzrechts*'.
6 *Ibid* 188.
7 See ch 5, I B iii b.
8 On this Bydlinski as well agrees, (n 3) 190.
9 H Coing, *Grundzüge der Rechtsphilosophie* (2nd edn) (Berlin, De Gruyter 1969) 211-213.
10 *Ibid* 213.
11 *Ibid* 214-215.
12 *Cf* ch 7, text to n 39.

B   Esser's Theory of Distributive Justice

The idea of a particularly strict connection between social issues and distributive justice provides the foundation for Josef Esser's influential study on the law of delict,[13] which is arguably one of the first attempts to relate substantive rules of delictual liability to the Aristotelian concept of justice.[14] The question is whether Esser's model offers room for the development of restitutionary damages. His starting point is that the law of delict cannot restrict itself to rules on fault-based liability, because the victim of an accident has not deserved his bad luck, even if the accident happens without the agent's fault. If the contrary position were correct, Esser argues, delict law would rest on the following principles: 1) everybody has to bear the consequences of his own fault; and 2) the victim alone bears the consequences of bad luck.[15] Against this outcome, Esser rejects a concept of justice according to which there can be no compensation without corresponding fault.

In Esser's view, the law of compensation performs a double function. On the one hand, it attempts to bring to equilibrium a situation which has been unbalanced by a wrong.[16] Moral philosophy normally links this function to a form of punishment or expiation. On the other hand, through compensation the negative consequences of a wrongdoing are allocated according to a criterion of just distribution. The relationship between fair allocation and society refers to the social task which has to be performed by the law of delict. Esser observes that corrective justice is strictly limited to the parties to the wrong. Society is not involved in the evaluation of gain and pain which, from the perspective of corrective justice, isolates the agent and the victim from all other individuals. Only distributive justice concerns society, for it has to balance the interests of everyone in the community and of the community as a whole. Esser concludes that when there is no fault, but just allocation is called for, as in the case of strict liability, then only distributive justice will do to justify such allocation.[17]

Esser's analysis is a pillar of German legal science in so far as it has contributed to shaping a vision of the law of delict which, despite being questioned, is still considered the academic orthodoxy.[18] Esser deals exclusively with compensatory issues. It is doubtful whether, in the light of the social engineering task of the law of delict, restitution for wrongs could be accommodated in his theory. One avenue could be to qualify as socially unjust the agent's retention of the proceedings of his wrongful behaviour, so that *iustitia distributiva* could intervene to re-establish harmony within the community. However, as regards restitution for wrongs, this theory has different hurdles to surmount. First, an

---

[13]   J Esser, *Grundlagen und Entwicklung der Gefährdungshaftung* (2nd edn) (München, Beck 1969).

[14]   Thus I Englard, *The Philosophy of Tort Law* (Aldershot, Dartmouth 1993) 11.

[15]   Esser (n 13) 72-73.

[16]   Esser would rather use the term 'delict', but there is no reason not to extend his approach to wrongs in general.

[17]   *Ibid* 69-74.

[18]   *Cf* P Schlechtriem, *Schuldrecht Besonderer Teil* (6th edn) (Tübingen, Mohr 2003) paras 937-938.

application of distributive justice to the private law of damages encounters difficulties in explaining the moral and normative reasons for the transfer of a benefit from a specific wrongdoer to a specific victim. The agent has to perform restitution because he is responsible for the wrong and has benefited from it. Yet, it is unclear why the victim ought to receive the payment in pursuance of distributive justice. Aristotle and St Thomas leave open the categories of criteria on the basis of which allocation can take place. If the victim has been impoverished by the wrong, he ought to be compensated by the wrongdoer. But if one applies the divide 'rich/poor' as a criterion to establish a right to compensation, then the benefit derived to the agent from the wrong should be distributed among all poor persons, regardless of whether they were involved in the wrongful action or not. If one takes the whole community into consideration, the victim is only one case of poverty among many.[19] The situation becomes even more complicated if the victim was very rich and the agent very poor. It would be difficult to explain why strict liability for, say, a nuclear accident affects the poor and rich people equally, for, applying the rich-poor divide, rich people should receive less compensation than the poor. One could say that those victims who have suffered bad luck from a wrong ought to recover their losses. Yet, as I have already observed, all sufferers from bad luck ought to be compensated regardless their relationship with the wrong. Even the agent could claim compensation if he had suffered bad luck from another, totally unrelated, wrong. Esser's legal analysis ignores this problem.

A further difficulty lies in the statement 'distributive justice equals social justice'. Diorthotic justice, which applies only in the context of corrective justice, goes beyond automatic retaliation. The judge should consider the general implications of the wrong as regards society and should assess the damage in that context. Judicial intervention guarantees that social issues are properly considered even in corrective justice. Through the involvement of the courts, the element of 'evaluation in a social context' becomes as relevant for corrective as it is for distributive justice.

The complex questions raised in the context of an application of distributive justice to the law of wrongs are not the only obstacle to an account of restitutionary damages on the basis of the model proposed by Esser. German legal science leaves little room for the category 'restitution' among the responses of the law of damages. The dogmatic distinction between the law of delict, which deals with compensation, and law of unjust enrichment, which deals with restitution, still holds true for German academics.[20] The role of a restitutionary response for wrongs is not questioned. Legal-theoretical analyses, such as the ones developed by Bydlinski and Esser, do not recognise any further model of response beyond

---

[19]   D Klimchuk, 'On the Autonomy of Corrective Justice' (2003) 23 *OJLS* 49-64, 55-56.
[20]   *Cf* H Hagen, 'Funktionale und dogmatische Zusammenhänge zwischen Schadens- und Bereicherungsrecht' in G Paulus, U Diederichsen and C-W Canaris (eds) *Festschrift Larenz zum 70. Geburtstag* (München, Beck 1973) 867-884.

compensation. Esser, for example, mentions almost indifferently the law of compensation (*Schadensersatzrecht*) and the law of damages as if they were synonymous.

III   A Moral Instrumentalist Theory on the Law of Damages

This investigation does not deal with all possible accounts of justice, but only with those accounts which are based upon Aristotelian tenets. My reason for the reduction of the analytical spectrum to a particular philosophical approach – that Aristotle's theory has had a unique impact on the fashion in which legal science considers the law of damages – is not universally accepted.[21] Still, it finds its justification, I think, in the historical presentation of Aristotelian theory in chapter seven.

Jules Coleman and Ernest Weinrib have developed two particularly influential theories on the relationship between corrective justice and restitutionary damages. This section opens with Coleman's work on the law of torts, in which restitution for wrongs itself represents only a minor part. By contrast, Weinrib has formulated a theory of justice which is specifically related to restitutionary damages. His contribution raises the question of the role which corrective justice can play in a non-compensatory context.

A   A 'Moral' and 'Instrumentalist' Theory

The outcome of the historical-philosophical analysis suggests that, for many centuries, the law of damages was not directly shaped according to Greek moral tenets, but varied in line with political views and with the weight accorded to Roman legal science by its interpreters. However, moral theories crept in by degrees, progressively informing the law of damages, for which some legal theorists have been seeking a justification on the basis of moral principles. The qualification of these descriptions of the law of torts as 'moral', alone, does not identify sufficiently their philosophical features. The common law tradition groups moral explanations of tort law into two categories: instrumentalist and formalist.

Instrumentalism rejects the idea that the law of torts aims at a single goal. This is a pragmatic approach[22] which recognises that tort law is an amalgam of many, sometimes diverging, interests and defines it on the basis of those interests. For

---

[21]   Not all recent accounts of justice are based upon the Aristotelian classification. *Cf* for instance RA Posner, 'Wealth Maximisation and Tort Law: A Philosophical Inquiry' in DG Owen (ed), *Philosophical Foundations of Tort Law* (Oxford, Clarendon 1995) 99-111. See an overview of the main theoretical approaches to private law in P Cane, 'The Anatomy of Private Law Theory: A 25th Anniversary Essay' (2005) 25 *OJLS* 203-217.

[22]   England (n 14) 30

instrumentalism, the various aims which tort law serves determine its structure. As Coleman put it, '[t]ort law is justifiable provided it turns out to be a good way of pursuing those human ends and ambitions it is designed to achieve'.[23] For instance, the duty upon the agent to compensate the victim does not depend on the relationship between the parties, but on their – agent and victim – relationship to the external aims of tort law. For Coleman, these aims correspond to moral principles.[24]

B Agent-Specific and Agent-General Duties

Tort law is, for Coleman, a question between agent and victim. An account of tort law which fails to provide a persuasive explanation of the relationship between agent and victim 'simply does not understand tort law.'[25] In his view, the core of tort law lies in the practice of holding individuals liable for the wrongful losses for which they are responsible. Tort law concentrates on losses because its main feature is the allocation of risks. It affects risks *ex ante* by assigning liability *ex post*.[26] Coleman recognises pragmatically that his analysis is rooted in the current nature of tort law. From the identification of its contemporary core, no inference can be drawn as regards the shape of tort law in the future.[27]

Coleman's starting point is that civil liability can emerge in two forms. If a hurricane devastates a community, the duty of helping the victims in the moment of need is on the whole community rather than on its members. If one member gives a certain amount of money directly to one of the victims instead of devolving it to common funds, he has not discharged his duty and therefore he will have to pay again, but this time to the fund. Conversely, if somebody injures another person in a car crash, he cannot discharge his duty by paying a sum equivalent to the damage caused to a fund which helps the victims of car accidents. These different situations correspond, according to Coleman, to different duties of the agents. In the hurricane case, the duty is 'agent-general', for it applies to every member of that community. In the second case, the accident creates 'agent-specific' reasons for acting, which apply only to a particular agent.[28] Although Coleman does not exclude the possibility that agent-general duties could be based on a principle of distributive justice, he does not rule out different justifying principles. By contrast, he argues that the 'principle of corrective justice imposes agent-specific reasons for acting.'[29]

---

[23] Coleman, *Risks* 202.
[24] *Ibid* 204.
[25] *Ibid* 198.
[26] *Ibid* 223.
[27] *Ibid* 198.
[28] J Coleman, 'The Practice of Corrective Justice' in D Owen (ed), *Philosophical Foundations of Tort Law* (Oxford, Clarendon 1995) 53-72, 54-55.
[29] *Ibid* 56.

C   Corrective Justice and Legal Analysis of Tort Law

Coleman's transition from moral to legal analysis is not always smooth.[30] His investigation of tort law from the perspective of corrective justice is prevalently loss-centred. As regards the concept of restitution, he seems to follow the line traced by Thomistic philosophy: 'restitution' is mainly used with a compensatory connotation.[31]

i   Conceptions of corrective justice

Coleman has developed two theories to account for the compensatory duty which links the defendant to the claimant. He calls his first conception 'annulment theory'. 'According to the annulment thesis the point of corrective justice is to eliminate, rectify, or annul wrongful (or unjust) losses'.[32] Coleman has come to the conclusion that the annulment theory is flawed, as it does not furnish a satisfactory account of what happens in tort law. The annulment thesis provides grounds of recovery, but cannot furnish an overarching theory of the reasons which connect the parties to the compensatory duty. This theory maintains only that wrongful losses ought to be redressed. It does not explain why it is the agent who has to redress them. He therefore accepts the criticism advanced by theorists who insist on the wrong itself rather than on the wrongful losses, as the basis of responsibility:

> The existence of a *loss* is not necessarily to trigger claims based on corrective justice… it is the wrong, not the loss that must be annulled, that specifies the content of the relevant duty.[33]

Focusing on the wrong instead of the loss, this relational conception distinguishes two positions. On the one hand, there are those individuals for whom the duty to compensate is a consequence of their own liability. On the other hand, there are all potential individuals who could be called to repair the loss without, by doing so, creating further wrongful losses. Unlike the annulment theory, the relational theory individuates 'specific, agent-relative reasons for acting',[34] for it builds a special relation between the agent and the victim.

On the basis of the issues highlighted by the relational theory, Coleman develops a 'mixed conception of corrective justice'. The relational view cannot explain, according to Coleman, why the reparation of a wrong involves the reparation of its attendant losses. If agent A drives negligently and causes an

---

[30]   In his book review of *Risks and Wrongs*: 'Markets and Morals in Contract and Tort' (1993) 13 Legal Studies 396-415, 396, P Cane remarks that "[t]he author's main aim seems to be to develop arguments which are philosophically 'interesting' … but at the price of working with a very sketchy, not to say impoverished, analysis of the law."

[31]   See J Gordley's reflections on this point in 'Tort Law in the Aristotelian Tradition' in DG Owen (ed) *Philosophical Foundations of Tort Law* (Clarendon, Oxford, 1995) 130-158, 138-140.

[32]   Coleman, *Risks* 306.

[33]   *Ibid* 314, emphasis in the original text.

[34]   *Ibid* 315.

injury to the victim V, there are many possible ways to repair a wrong and not all involve compensation. If corrective justice requires only repairing the wrong, A could avoid compensating V for his loss by apologising to him or in any other way deemed to be suitable. V will have to bear his loss despite the fact that it was caused by a negligent infringement of his right of personal integrity. The mixed view would bridge the leap from wrong to loss. The difference between the position of A and that of any other negligent driver, T, is that, although both parties are acting wrongfully, third party T's behaviour causes no harm.

In his mixed conception, Coleman points out the necessity to annul the wrong. 'To annul a wrong is to eliminate its effects in the world, as much as feasible'.[35] Yet, this annulment does not involve the elimination of every effect: if V misses the plane because of a car accident caused by A and the plane crashes, one of the consequences of the car accident is that V is still alive. To apply the relational view strictly, A ought to kill V. Therefore, not all results have to be annulled, but only the wrongful consequences of the wrong. The mixed view is summed up thus: '[c]orrective justice imposes on wrongdoers the duty to repair the wrongful losses their conduct occasions, losses for which they are responsible'.[36]

ii   Coleman's theory in a legal context

In Coleman's view, corrective justice deals with the wrongful consequences of a wrong. Coleman uses the term 'wrong' with a double connotation. Each person has a moral right not to be treated in such a way which would be incompatible with the principles of tort law. Beyond this moral value, 'wrong' acquires a legal value in the sense of violation of legal rights. A legal wrong is the difference between standard behaviour, which is required under the law, and the actual behaviour of the agent.[37] When the two diverge, because the agent's behaviour falls below the standard required and a legal right is violated, the agent will be held liable independently of the breach of a moral duty on his part.[38]

The transition from a moral to a legal analysis of justice is crucial. Coleman claims that, from a moral perspective, the law of torts can achieve different results. There are goals, he says, which are satisfied by basic substantive, as opposed to formal, rules of liability. 'Compensation simpliciter is not a goal of tort law',[39] because not all victims deserve to be compensated. Anglo-American practice is concerned mainly with vindicating rightful claims to repair:

[T]he best explanation of current Anglo-American tort law sees the practice primarily in terms of its efforts to meet these demands of justice – what I call corrective justice.[40]

---

[35]   *Ibid* 322.
[36]   *Ibid* 325.
[37]   On the 'objective standard of competence' see T Honoré, 'Responsibility and Luck' (1988) 104 *LQR* 530-553, 531-537.
[38]   Coleman, *Risks* 367: 'at its core, tort law is a matter of corrective justice'.
[39]   *Ibid* 209.
[40]   *Ibid.*

Coleman's central claim seems to be, therefore, that the law of torts deals mainly with 'reparation' of a loss. From a legal perspective, Coleman observes pragmatically that tort law does concern mostly compensatory claims – if this is what he means with 'reparation'. Yet, his analysis does not bar a priori a restitutionary avenue for wrongs. Indeed, since Coleman agrees that the aims of tort law cannot possibly be decided in the abstract, one has to conclude that the transfer of the agent's benefit to the victim would be a legitimate aim of tort law if the legal system recognised it as such. Hence, there is, for Coleman, no theoretical identity between law of damages and law of compensation.

Distinguishing between moral and legal wrongs, Coleman leaves the world of moral philosophy and propounds legal evaluations. His view reinforces the theory – common among English lawyers – according to which non-compensatory damages are exceptional measures of the law of damages. Coleman does not make this claim explicitly. However, he states that the main actual aim of tort law is corrective justice, and tort law is mostly concerned with 'reparation of losses'. This reasoning seems to suggest[41] that, in his view, the law of damages offers primarily compensatory responses, for only compensation provides reparation of the victim's loss and the tort law system – at least at present – deals primarily with such reparatory issues. Building on the 'primary' function of compensation, one could conclude that non-compensatory damages are at best secondary.[42]

Independently of the dispute on the exceptionality of non-compensatory damages, Coleman's methodological approach indicates an avenue which could lead to a theoretical justification of restitution for wrongs. Following his line of reasoning, one could say that restitution for wrongs is part of the law of damages if stripping the agent of ill-gotten gains to the benefit of the victim realises one of the aims of tort law. It is irrelevant whether such non-compensatory damages have wide or limited application: if they perform a basic function which corresponds to an aim of tort law, restitution must have the same significance as compensation.[43] If I am correct in construing Coleman's concept of 'reparation' as compensation, given that his vision of corrective justice is loss-centred[44] non-compensatory awards can be part of the law of torts, but do not fall within corrective justice. Yet Coleman identifies another model of justice, termed 'restitutionary', which strives to strip the agent of ill-gotten gains to the benefit of the victim, focusing on the agent's gain instead of the victim's loss. The problem is, as will be shown shortly, that Coleman seems to place his restitutionary justice

---

[41]   Coleman's legal terminology is sometimes imprecise. My reading of his philosophy from a legal perspective is necessarily tentative.

[42]   This line of thought is not alien to English law. See ch 2, n 12 and text thereof.

[43]   I shall develop this idea in my explanation of restitution for wrongs as corrective justice. See section V in this chapter.

[44]   Coleman, *Risks* 370.

both outside the scope of tort law and outside corrective justice. It is difficult to follow his reasoning on both these conclusions.[45]

iii   Restitutionary justice

Coleman does not deny the immorality of the gains accrued to the agent through wrongdoing. He only excludes that corrective justice can supply a justification of restitution for wrongs. This exclusion leaves him with the problem of finding a different explanation for non-compensatory damages. In *Risks and Wrongs*, he analyses wrongful gains starting from the following example.

Somebody drives negligently. By this action, he imperils the lives of all the persons on the street, but injures only one pedestrian. The agent saves the money he ought to have invested in safety. According to Coleman, every person who is put at risk by the negligent driving has a claim in justice to obtain a part of the driver's profit. As the injured pedestrian belongs to the group of persons whose personal integrity has been imperilled, he too has that claim. Thus, the victim will have two claims, one for his wrongful loss, and the other for the agent's wrongful gain.[46] If the agent secures a further wrongful gain specifically through his negligent harm of the pedestrian, the latter will have three claims: beyond the two actions already mentioned, he will be able to claim restitution of the gain which is a consequence of his injury. The moral right to obtain the agent's gain is founded upon restitutionary, rather than corrective, justice. 'Restitutionary justice gives the victim the right to the wrongdoer's gains secured at her expense'.[47] Where gains and losses coincide, compensation according to corrective justice will satisfy the demands of restitutionary justice as well, and vice versa.[48]

iv   Coleman's legal analysis and restitution for wrongs

'Tort law is the central institution for discharging the duty to repair wrongful losses; restitution is the legal remedy for repairing wrongful gains.'[49] This statement, which sums up Coleman's view on restitutionary justice, triggers some fundamental interpretative problems of both terminological and taxonomical nature. 'Restitution' is regarded by Coleman as belonging to the same category as 'tort law': tort law would deal with compensation and 'restitution' with restitution. Both would furnish legal responses to wrongdoing. By using the term 'restitution', Coleman is probably referring to unjust enrichment, which together with contract and tort constitutes the largest part of the law of obligations. However, he qualifies 'restitution' as a 'remedy'. This classification raises some questions. Taxonomically, unjust enrichment occupies the same position as tort and contract: it is an event which gives rise to a legal response, which in this

---

[45]   Cane (n 30) observes that Coleman's assertions on restitutionary justice as a separate body from corrective justice are made 'without argument'.
[46]   Coleman *Risks* 370.
[47]   *Ibid* 371.
[48]   The correctness of this statement will be tested in ch 9, n 53 and text thereof.
[49]   Coleman, *Risks* 371.

context has to be restitution. Yet 'restitution' as an event is incompatible with Coleman's words, for the statement 'restitution is the legal remedy for repairing wrongful gains' suggests a different idea of restitution: not as an event, but as a response to an event. In this last meaning, restitution aligns with compensation, punishment and so forth. In this sense, the statement quoted above tells us nothing about the event which triggers restitution.[50]

Applying the correct legal terminology, the quotation is likely to bear the following meaning: 'the application ambit of corrective justice is tort law, whereas the realm of restitutionary justice is unjust enrichment'. If my interpretation of Coleman's thought is not mistaken, this statement, placed in the context of the analysis of wrongful losses and gains, suggests that wrongdoing is an essential requirement of the unjust enrichment claim, which is incorrect. When a wrongful event elicits a response which is linked to restitutionary justice, this response must be restitution for wrongs, not restitution for unjust enrichment. If restitutionary justice required a wrongful event and were linked only to restitution for unjust enrichment, from a theoretical perspective the event 'unjust enrichment' would be connected to two different forms of justice: wrongful unjust enrichment activates a response in the area of restitutionary justice, whereas in all other, non-wrongful cases of unjust enrichment the response is independent of restitutionary justice. Coleman does not address this point. Furthermore, it should be clarified on which theoretical basis the non-wrongful transfers of wealth would lead to restitution. Still, Coleman's statement can be accepted with some qualification, for restitution for unjust enrichment might be triggered by wrongdoing not qua wrongdoing, but as a behaviour which causes an unjust enrichment. Possibly the statement under examination refers to this particular situation using an incorrect legal terminology. This interpretation, however, causes other difficulties. If Coleman refers to restitution for unjust enrichment, then his statement according to which corrective justice concerns tort law and not unjust enrichment does not answer the question of the position of restitution for wrongs, which is not part of unjust enrichment and still involves restitution.[51] An alternative reading of his tenet could be that Coleman does not consider unjust enrichment at all, but only restitution for wrongs. This approach seems to be confirmed by his constant reference to the agent's 'wrongdoing'. This interpretation would not necessarily exclude restitutionary damages from tort law; but it would definitely bar any account of such damages in terms of corrective justice and would leave restitution for unjust enrichment outside restitutionary justice. On the basis of Scholastic tenets, one can conclude that corrective justice aims to make good the victim's loss, rather than to compel the agent to disgorge his

---

[50] See Birks' 'event-based classification' in *Unjust Enrichment* (2nd edn) (Oxford, OUP 2005) 21-28.

[51] The insufficient attention paid by Coleman to strict legal issues is stressed by Cane (n 30) 399, although Cane's criticism is probably too strong when he says that Coleman 'has given us an interpretative theory of that part of tort law which he considers quintessential. In so doing he has made life far too easy for himself and has left us to wonder how his theory of the parts relates to the whole' (413).

benefit. Yet, any interpretation of Coleman's statement which were consistent with the law of obligations paves the way to a series of questions which remain unanswered.

IV   A Moral Formalist Theory on the Law of Damages

The moral formalist theories on the law of damages, like the instrumentalist views, give an Aristotelian account of justice. Beyond this common element, there are fundamental disagreements on the fashion in which the two approaches describe tort law. For instrumentalism, tort law is a mixture of different aims. It is designed to achieve certain results. Consequently, every legal institution which helps to accomplish one of the aims of tort law falls under the roof of tort law. Instrumentalists express this idea saying that 'the criteria of justification are extrinsic to the practice'.[52] This approach is rejected by formalists. In their view, every element of tort law is so organised as to answer to one common principle. The characteristic aspects of tort law ordering 'are intelligible only through the integrated whole that they form as an ensemble'.[53]

For Coleman,

[w]hereas the instrumentalist believes that the substantive aims of tort law determine its structure, the formalist believes that the structure of tort law determines the extent to which various goals can be pursued through it.[54]

Weinrib replies that 'an intrinsic ordering is coherent whereas conventional ordering is not.'[55] Coherence is considered by formalists as a value which explains the scope of tort law: if the latter is governed by only one principle, it is necessarily coextensive with the scope of its justification.

Weinrib has been hailed as 'the leading formalist of modern private law'.[56] His work is particularly relevant to the topic at issue because he has developed a theory of justice with particular reference to restitution for wrongs. I shall examine this theory after having placed it in the proper context of Weinrib's thought.

A   A Kantian Approach to Corrective Justice

Weinrib draws his theory from the Kantian tenet of practical reason,[57] which refers to the importance of freedom of will. Humans decide freely; the law links

---

[52] Coleman, *Risks* 202.
[53] E Weinrib, 'Understanding Tort Law' (1989) 23 *Valparaiso University Law Review* 485-526, 495.
[54] Coleman, *Risks* 200.
[55] Weinrib (n 53) 496.
[56] Coleman, *Risks* 200.
[57] England (n 14) 8-9.

the free choice of one person to the free choice of another. Individual relationships are therefore regulated by a universal law of freedom.[58] This view, which
favours the centrality of individual volition, is incompatible with a description of
tort law as a sum of different aims. The individuality of persons, sustained by the
law of freedom, does not allow for the imposition on one person of a duty if this
duty is seen as a mere attempt to achieve another person's aim. Instead, the key
element is provided by the concept of correlativity. In the Kantian perspective,
this concept connects rights and duties:

> The requirement that one's action be consistent with the other's freedom means that
> every actor is obligated not to violate the rights of others. In Kantian theory, rights are
> the juridical manifestation of the freedom inherent in self-determining agency.[59]

Correlativity, explains Weinrib, is not to be seen as a factor which delimits the
Aristotelian conception of corrective justice. If it were so, then gain and loss
would have to be equal for any application of this model of justice to be viable. It
is not a factual correlativity which matters to the justificatory structure of
corrective justice, but rather a normative definition of it. Weinrib links normative
correlativity and the Aristotelian concept of harm suffered by the victim by
giving to the latter the meaning of 'injury that is actionable'.[60] To satisfy the
dimension of correlativity, Weinrib's concept of corrective justice requires the
justificatory consideration to be unifying, bipolar, and expressive of transactional
equality.[61] Unity is provided by the infringement of a Kantian right. It is the
violation of another's freedom of choice which furnishes the baseline for both
loss and gain. Loss and gain are regarded as normative rather than factual values.
They are bipolar, so that one party's loss is another party's gain. Loss and gain are
not independent of one another, because in corrective justice 'a single liability
links the particular person who gained to the particular person who lost'.[62]
Finally, corrective justice is characterised by transactional equality. It is neutral
with respect to either party. Compensation, for instance, is a response which takes
the position of the victim into consideration, whereas the agent's gain is, from
this perspective, irrelevant. As compensation does not forge a bilateral link
between the parties to the wrong, it excludes one party from the evaluation of
justice. For this reason, as a goal it does not respect the requirement of neutrality
between the parties. This does not mean, however, that compensation is immaterial to tort law. The latter reflects corrective justice in some, but not all aspects.
One of the main points of contact between compensation and tort law is to be
seen in the fact that the perpetration of the wrong compels the agent to place the
victim in a position which is as close as possible to the one in which he would

---

[58]   *Ibid.*
[59]   Weinrib, *Idea* 122.
[60]   *Ibid* 119 n 8.
[61]   *Ibid* 120.
[62]   *Ibid* 63.

have been had the wrong not been committed. Hence, 'under corrective justice damages are compensatory, not punitive'.[63]

In this context, it appears that there is little room for restitutionary damages. Yet, in a recent series of studies dedicated to restitution for wrongs Weinrib formulates a theory of corrective justice which in his view is able to accommodate restitutionary damages.[64]

B   Restitutionary Damages as Corrective Justice

Having stated in his previous work that compensation is the normal response to a wrong, Weinrib looks now for 'special arguments'[65] which would furnish adequate support for a restitutionary structure for wrongs according to the principles of corrective justice. 'Correlativity' is a central element in Weinrib's doctrine: the agent and the victim are related, for they are opposite parties to the same injustice. This relationship is expressed by the categories of right and duty, that is violated right of the victim and breached duty upon the agent not to interfere. Justice is obtained if rectification is granted. Rectification, through which the victim's right is vindicated, requires a monetary payment. Single aims of tort law, such as compensation and restitution, do not offer a satisfactory explanation: any justification must include both the reason for imposing on the agent a duty to rectify and the reason for entitling the victim to the benefit of rectification.[66]

Weinrib deals first with compensatory damages; he then applies the same line of reasoning mutatis mutandis to restitutionary damages. Compensation is granted in tort law when the connection between the wrongfulness and the loss is normative and not merely historical. Among all possible negative consequences, the law takes into consideration only those which are wrongful by virtue of their inherent normative quality. Thus, tort law will not be activated if the claimant is outside the ambit of the foreseeable victims, like in *Palsgraf v Long Island Railroad*.[67] In that case,

> the prospect of [the claimant's] loss was not a reason for thinking that the defendant's conduct was wrongful. Because the conduct was not a wrong relative to her, the defendant was held not to have been under a duty with respect to her loss.[68]

Furthermore, the mere existence of a wrongful loss does not automatically mean that the gain realised by the agent is wrongful as well:

---

[63]   *Ibid* 135 n 25.

[64]   E Weinrib, *Restitutionary damages*, and 'Punishment and Disgorgement as Contract Remedies', (2003) 78 *Chicago-Kent Law Review* 55-103. This later article applies to contract law the ideas developed in the previous article.

[65]   Weinrib, *Restitutionary damages* 2.

[66]   *Ibid* 3-6.

[67]   248 NY 339, 162 NE 99 (1928).

[68]   Weinrib, *Restitutionary damages* 9.

> What matters is not the historical connection of gain to wrong, but rather the nature of the wrong and whether the gain partakes of the wrong's normative quality.[69]

The central issue concerns therefore the individuation of the cases in which a gain is wrongful and thus can give rise to restitutionary damages. According to Weinrib,

> restitutionary damages should be available when the defendant's gain is the materialization of a favorable possibility – the opportunity to gain – that rightfully belonged to the plaintiff.[70]

This definition restricts the applicability of restitution for wrongs to a specific set of cases related to the violation of property rights, either through the alienation or through the use of another's property.

The correlativity of the victim's violated property right and the agent's breach of duty to abstain from intermeddling with alien property is for Weinrib not in line with the principles of corrective justice. If this correlativity is linked to the realisation of profits, the law achieves justice by allowing restitution for wrongs. In so doing, it 'reverses the wrong',[71] rejecting the agent's assertion of ownership. The assertion is an expression of the will of the agent, who intentionally, and unlawfully, acts to change a proprietary situation in his favour. It follows that no restitutionary award can be granted where there is lack of intention and the action produces inadvertently the wrongful result. Only intentional torts against property trigger restitution for wrongs.[72]

In the case of violation of property rights, the agent's gain belongs to the victim according to justice. Weinrib expresses this concept in a central passage in which he states that restitutionary damages for proprietary wrongs are 'an entitlement of the proprietor':

> One's rights provide the baseline for measuring injury. If those rights include the possibility of gain, then the defendant's gain measures the extent of the plaintiff's injury.[73]

As regards the method of assessment of the damage, in the case of alienation Weinrib offers the claimant a choice between the value of the thing alienated and the price which the defendant received,[74] both possibilities being within the victim's entitlement.

The law differentiates the innocent from the wilful wrongdoer, giving the first a right to recover the expenses for improvements which benefit the property, and thus the victim. Weinrib discards a description of the higher damages which the

---

[69]   *Ibid* 11.
[70]   *Ibid* 12.
[71]   *Ibid* 13.
[72]   Compare St Thomas, ST IIa IIae Qu 62 Art 3, who did not consider intentionality as a requirement of restitution. But with 'restitution', he meant compensation for wrongs. Yet, for Aristotle, Nic Ethics V viii, only intentional actions could be qualified as just or unjust.
[73]   Weinrib, *Restitutionary damages* 13.
[74]   *Ibid* 16.

wilful wrongdoer has to pay as punitive. The wilful wrongdoer denies the owner's right; the law recognises the implication of wilful conduct and interprets the improvements as a manifestation of a donative intent. It is not an instance of a punitive legal response; rather, the law respects the intention of the wilful wrongdoer and gives legal value to it by holding the agent to what his conduct implies.[75]

Beyond property rights, Weinrib allows an award of restitutionary damages in some particular circumstances, which he terms 'property-like rights'. These are rights which share either or both features of property rights: validity *erga omnes* and a subject matter which is morally capable of being acquired or alienated.[76] A paradigm of the property-like rights is provided by the violation of fiduciary duty.

> The other property-like wrongs are those characterized by action of the defendant that … treats the plaintiff's right as an asset whose value the defendant can appropriate.[77]

The well-known Birksian example[78] of the thug who is given money to beat the victim up falls into this category, for the thug will not be able to resist the victim's restitutionary claim on the argument that bodily integrity is not an alienable thing.

C Weinrib's Analysis and Restitution for Wrongs

In this section, I shall argue that Weinrib's attempt to develop a theory of restitution for wrongs fails because what he describes as restitutionary damages is a legal response which does not realise restitution, but compensation. Still, his account raises a series of important issues which cannot be ignored. In particular, Weinrib's explanation for 'restitutionary damages' is useful to provide a theoretical support to what I have called 'pseudo-restitution'.

i Corrective justice according to Weinrib

Aristotle examines the responses to wrongs from a moral perspective. St Thomas follows the same approach. He identifies two main moral responses to a wrong. If the agent intentionally performs a wrongful act, this act upsets the equilibrium in the relationship between the agent and the victim on the one hand, and within society on the other hand. Corrective justice requires that equilibrium in both areas be restored. Compensation eliminates the loss and therefore sets the relationship with the victim. Yet, intentional wrongdoing also affects society at large. In this case, compensation alone might not be an adequate response; punishment might be required.[79]

---

[75] *Ibid* 30.
[76] *Ibid* 32.
[77] *Ibid* 34.
[78] Birks, *Restitution* 319.
[79] ST IIa IIae, Qu 62, Art 1.

Weinrib propounds a normative interpretation of corrective justice. Acknowledging punishment as a legal response accountable in corrective justice would destabilise his approach based on the Kantian distinction of moral rights and duties. His argument is that punishment is not party-related. As in a punitive relationship correlativity is absent, the situation which triggers a punitive response only grants the claimant a windfall.[80] On the other hand, in his studies specifically dedicated to restitution for wrongs Weinrib accepts that corrective justice can account for restitution. Yet, like the Scholastics before him, in his analysis of the concept of restitution he does not abandon a loss-centred perspective: by referring to 'the potential for gain' as a part of the victim's violated right which determines the measure of the victim's claim he implicitly accepts that, in the end, restitutionary damages are quantified on the basis of the loss of the victim rather than the agent's benefit. He allows restitution within the limit of the benefit which the agent obtained, but which would have gone to the victim had the wrong not distorted the correct proprietary allocation. From the viewpoint of legal analysis, Weinrib's theory cannot apply to restitutionary damages. In the next sections I shall endeavour to provide arguments in support of my last statement.

ii   Proprietary rights and tortious protection of property

Weinrib revives an old idea according to which the law of unjust enrichment and the law of property are strongly interrelated, for the claim in unjust enrichment is but the bringing of a proprietary claim by other means. When vindication, that is the main civil proprietary claim, is no longer available, unjust enrichment intervenes. Weinrib would award wrongful claims for restitution with the function of proprietary claims. To achieve this result, he applies the restitutionary structure of unjust enrichment to the law of wrongs. In so doing, he gives his personal answer to two central questions concerning restitution for wrongs.

The first question states: Why should restitutionary damages be allowed? According to Weinrib, it is because they are included in the definition of property. In claiming restitution, the owner is just asserting his own proprietary right: 'This benefit is mine!' The owner claims back what is his according to corrective justice, but also according to the law.

The second question asks: When should restitutionary damages be allowed? For Weinrib, it is when a proprietary interest is violated. The violation is the consequence of the agent's intromission into the proprietary relationship between the owner and the thing defined as valid *erga omnes*. Conversely, any violation of non-proprietary rights ought not to trigger a restitutionary tortious response.

Weinrib must acknowledge that his theory is not free from sharp edges: there are cases in which restitutionary damages are awarded, or ought to be awarded, and yet they are unrelated to proprietary situations, so that his construction

---

[80]   Eg Weinrib, Punishment and Disgorgement (n 64) 86.

cannot explain why they are granted. One such case would be *Attorney-General v Blake*. To accommodate some of these situations within his theoretical framework, Weinrib argues that not only proprietary claims, but also quasi-proprietary claims, can justify restitution for wrongs.

The proprietary approach is strict, but provides a clear-cut rule to distinguish the cases in which – in Weinrib's view – restitution for wrongs is a viable response from all the others. The enlargement of the restitutionary sphere breaks the rigidity of the proprietary rule, allowing for some flexibility. Yet, it also creates problems as regards the definition of quasi-proprietary rights and questions the very meaning of the proprietary rule, which *in concreto* is disallowed. The risk is that the discussion shifts from the definition of restitutionary damages to the definition of quasi-proprietary rights. Weinrib faces a dilemma: either applying a strict rule, which would exclude some situations where justice – or at least the courts – would require restitution, or applying a more lenient rule, which might create difficulties as regards the identification of the rights affected by his theory. He chooses the second alternative and accepts that the answers to some fundamental questions on the nature of quasi-proprietary rights and on the application of restitutionary damages are necessarily vague. He recognises the problem and admits that his classification 'may appear to provide a convenient black box into which to stuff the residual instances that do not fit what a property-based approach requires.'[81] However, he cuts off the issue, remarking that 'difficult questions are unavoidable'.[82]

There is another, more fundamental, difficulty with this approach. Using a proprietary structure suggests that the claim rests upon a compensatory mechanism. If the owner says: 'the benefit is mine', he is implicitly asserting that the wrongdoer has taken advantage of what belongs to him. If, as Weinrib put it, 'the defendant's gain is of something that lies within the right of the plaintiff', then the claimant's action must be directed towards the reintegration of the claimant's position before the wrongful event. Once again, it emerges that Weinrib's approach is loss-centred: the victim is in reality claiming compensation for a loss because the victim is deprived of a benefit to which he was entitled. The agent has no such entitlement. The situation is brought back to equilibrium through a transfer of wealth which allocates the benefit to the victim, who has a right to claim and keep it, and takes it away from the agent, who cannot oppose to the claimant's action what German lawyers would call a '*Behaltensgrund*', that is a legal justification to keep what has been obtained.

As intimated, this construction conceals a compensatory response because Weinrib adopts a restitutionary mechanism which is akin to the model implemented by the law of unjust enrichment. The connection between this remedial mechanism and the law of unjust enrichment is explicitly recognised by Weinrib in several passages of his study on restitutionary damages as corrective justice.[83]

---

[81]   Weinrib, *Restitutionary Damages* 33 n 50.
[82]   *Ibid.*
[83]   For instance, see Weinrib, *Restitutionary damages*, 6 n 6, and 25–26.

Yet transferring a proprietary structure from the law of unjust enrichment to the law of wrongs can only be done at a cost. The first problem is that it provides a framework only for ownership-related situations:[84] unjust enrichment gives to the former owner a restitutionary – quasi-proprietary – claim once the owner lost his proprietary title. The second problem is that this theory cannot explain those cases in which the perpetration of the wrong is unrelated to proprietary rights, such as in *Attorney-General v Blake*.[85] The duty of silence, which Blake breached, did not belong to the victim according to the proprietary construction. In reality, this theory provides a solid argument in favour of an enlargement of compensation to the claimant's benefit which has been taken by the defendant, rather than in favour of the application of a restitutionary mechanism to compel the defendant to give up his benefit regardless of the loss of the claimant.

iii   Pseudo-restitutionary damages

If my line of reasoning is correct, Weinrib's theory does not account for restitution for wrongs. Yet, his explanation provides theoretical support to a different legal response which has caused some interpretative difficulties in both judicial and academic analysis. I have called it 'pseudo-restitutionary damages'. In my opinion, these damages have a compensatory aim, but are assessed on the basis of criteria which diverge from the traditional form of compensation, for the gain of the wrongdoer plays a major role in the quantification of the compensatory award. In the course of the present study, I have come across many instances of pseudo-restitution, particularly with reference to property cases, including intellectual property wrongs.

My contention that compensation can be measured by the gain of the wrongdoer, instead of the loss of the victim, might appear confusing. Weinrib explains the idea behind this mechanism:

> [R]estitutionary damages should be available when the defendant's gain is the materialization of a favorable possibility – the opportunity to gain – that rightfully belonged to the plaintiff. Then the gain to be nullified by the award of restitutionary damages represents an injustice both committed by the defendant and suffered by the plaintiff.[86]

If we substitute the expression 'restitutionary damages' with 'pseudo-restitutionary damages', Weinrib's view depicts clearly what I mean by 'pseudo-restitution'. The victim claims back something of which he has wrongfully been deprived. This is a loss. The measure of this loss is obtained by quantifying the wrongdoer's gain. What appears to be restitution for wrongs is in reality a case of compensation for wrongs. Weinrib unveils the theoretical foundation of this

---

[84]   It would be interesting to explore whether the same scheme applied to possessory situations as well. It is now widely recognised in civilian systems that, from the point of view of restitution for unjust enrichment, possession can be treated in a similar way to property with the so-called *condictio possessoria*. It does not seem that Weinrib's quasi-proprietary right would also include possession.

[85]   *A-G v Blake* [2001] 1 AC 268 (HL). See ch 4, n 23 and text thereof.

[86]   Weinrib, *Restitutionary damages* 12.

measure of damages. The doctrine of lost opportunity to bargain, developed by Sharpe and Waddams,[87] provides further information from the viewpoint of legal analysis. In chapter three,[88] I have shown that their doctrine is able to explain the allocation of *losses* triggered by property wrongs. The loss corresponds to the price which the claimant would have accepted to relinquish his right to third parties. Sharpe and Waddams's analysis refers to one of the main alternative measures of compensation. But there are other measures of quantification of losses even in the context of property wrongs. Thus, in the analysis of the violation of intellectual property rights I have examined the possibility for the victim to claim an account of profits. Weinrib's account embraces such award too.

V   Corrective Justice and Restitution for Wrongs

Despite my rejection of Weinrib's explanation, I do think that it is possible to account for the damages at issue as corrective justice. My contribution to the ongoing discussion starts from the Aristotelian theory of justice. I have shown that the gist of Aristotle's idea was the need to restore the balance in a relationship impaired by an unjust action. The theory of mean requires that the party who has more gives to the party who has less. The two parties are connected by the concept of *synallagma* as the doer and the sufferer of the wrong. To justify a restitutionary duty upon the wrongdoer, it is necessary to establish such connection between the parties. The starting point must be an analysis of the concepts of loss and gain.

Restitution for wrongs cannot be explained by a theory which focuses upon the concept of 'loss'. Thus, Coleman states explicitly that his analysis concentrates on 'events that negatively or adversely affect welfare ("losses" or misfortunes)'.[89] An analysis which seeks to understand 'the moral character of the loss' and 'the relationship between the loss and those thought to have reason to act in virtue of it'[90] suggests that corrective justice issues are examined from a Thomistic, loss-centred perspective. Coleman himself recognises expressly that '[w]rongful loss is the concern of corrective justice'.[91] In his book review of Coleman's *Risks and Wrongs*, Peter Cane observes that 'at no stage does Coleman discuss at any length what he means by "losses"'.[92] In fact, I would argue that Coleman's approach, centred on the nullification of the victim's loss, is Aristotelico-Thomistic, rather than purely Aristotelian.

---

[87]   RJ Sharpe and SM Waddams 'Damages for Lost Opportunity to Bargain' [1982] 2 *OJLS* 290-297.
[88]   Ch 3, n 32 and text thereof.
[89]   Coleman, 'The Practice of Corrective Justice' (n 28) 54.
[90]   *Ibid.*
[91]   Coleman, *Risks* 370.
[92]   Cane (n 30) 408.

By placing his restitutionary justice outside corrective justice, Coleman is coherent with his Aristotelico-Thomistic premises. Yet, in my opinion, this ostracism of 'restitutionary justice' from corrective justice does not necessarily follow from the principles of corrective justice. I have pointed out repeatedly that St Thomas and then the Late Scholastics have imposed an idea of corrective justice which focuses on the wrongdoer. But Aristotle kept a more neutral stance. In his construction, the loss does not seem to acquire a higher status than the gain. What is required is only that loss and gain are linked by a *synallagma* – Weinrib would probably refer to the concept of correlativity. Aristotle's use of terms like 'pain' and 'gain' was metaphorical. With these expressions, he wanted to indicate that the parties are identified as the doer and the sufferer of an injustice. Yet the injustice does not necessarily have to bring about the same quantity of gain and pain. Consider Aristotle's example of a man who strikes a blow against another: the gain and the pain are correlative, but they are not identical, for a gain can also consist in the agent's satisfaction for having performed the action which caused pain. Aristotle did not refer to patrimonial advantages or disadvantages. If justice can be attained if the victim has suffered a financial loss but the agent has not obtained a corresponding financial gain, one can infer that it will also be attained if the agent has obtained a financial gain which does not correspond to a patrimonial loss of the agent.

The next passage requires me to explain why, in the case of restitution for wrongs, the loss and the gain are correlative. If I demonstrate the existence of a *synallagma* between the parties, I am much closer to an account of the damages at issue as corrective justice. The prohibition of enrichment goes back to Roman law. Various passages of the Digest confirm that nobody should become richer to the detriment and by the injury of another.[93] This equitable principle is the key for a normative analysis of restitution for wrongs from the perspective of corrective justice. 'Detriment' does not mean 'patrimonial loss'. A wrongful behaviour is detrimental to the defendant not because it causes a patrimonial loss, but because it places the victim in the position of sufferer from an injustice. English law knows many examples of the difference between legal, actionable loss – in the sense of patrimonial loss – and detriment, which may or may not be a form of actionable harm.[94] Detriment is the normative translation of the moral concept of 'pain' adopted by Aristotle and does not presuppose a patrimonial loss. The two concepts are completely independent. 'Loss' is a technical legal term normally used in the context of a form of harm which is susceptible of pecuniary quantification. 'Detriment' is a normative term which qualifies the victim as the sufferer from a legal wrong. It follows that a wrongful action can be detrimental to the victim even though it has caused no patrimonial loss. If a wrong can be detrimental in the absence of a patrimonial loss, then a wrong which has caused

---

[93]　Thus the Roman jurist Pomponius in D 50. 17. 206, which is likely to be the most famous formulation of the prohibition.

[94]　Consider for instance the torts actionable per se and the loss of a chance caused by wilful conduct in the absence of an affirmative duty on the agent.

no patrimonial loss, but has enriched the wrongdoer, must be detrimental too. And both the enrichment and the detriment are wrongful. Thus, the wrongful enrichment is a consequence of a wrong which has created a *synallagma* between the wrongdoer and his victim as the doer and the sufferer of an injustice. The *synallagma* binds only doer and sufferer, because the gain is the consequence of a wrongful action which targets the victim and nobody else.[95]

At this point, I still need to clarify why the wrongful enrichment should be an entitlement of the victim. The perpetration of a civil wrong creates a relationship between the parties to the wrong from which all other members of society are excluded. As it is a matter between agent and victim, nobody else but the victim has a connection to the wrongdoer's gain. If the victim cannot claim the wrongdoer's benefit, nobody else can – at least, not on the basis of corrective justice. Before the alternative between the doer and the sufferer, the innocent sufferer must have a stronger moral claim to the wrongful gain than the wrongdoer. The wrong creates party-related reasons to act so that the agent would benefit from his own wrongful conduct if the victim's claim to seize the wrongful gain were barred.

---

[95]   Coleman, *Risks* 370, refers to 'the additional gain the [wrongdoer] secures as a consequence of injuring [the victim].'

9

Wrongs and Restitution

I Introduction

THE ROMAN LAW of damages offered to the victim of a wrong two main instruments to react to the injustice suffered: punishment and compensation. An opinion delivered by Julian, which could be read as introducing a restitutionary model for wrongs, does not seem to have left many traces in the evolution of the law of the following centuries. The marginal role played by restitution for wrongs through the centuries might partly be explained by the presence of the non-wrongful restitutionary response of unjust enrichment as the third pillar of the law of obligations. Comparative analysis has revealed that restitution for wrongs is an issue mostly in English law, that is a legal system in which the law of unjust enrichment has been developed only recently. On the other hand, the analysis has also shown that the law of unjust enrichment cannot normally be used to strip the wrongdoer of those gains which are unrelated to the violation of the victim's proprietary or quasi-proprietary right. Moreover, the expansion of Aristotelian ideas in the Scholastic interpretation is likely to have diverted the attention from the concept of restitution as taking away the wrongdoer's profits independently of the victim's loss to a concept of restitution as transferring to the victim that gain which is directly connected to a financial loss.

In this chapter, I try to achieve two aims. First, I shall critically examine some explanations of restitution for wrongs which rest on the legislative and judicial data, rather than on moral philosophy. It will soon become clear that I disagree – on various grounds – with all the theories which I am going to introduce. Descriptive accounts are particularly problematic, because the comparative analysis has shown that the law still contains some incongruence, so that the judicial cases do not always fit into one single model of analysis. This first part opens with the examination of some of the leading studies of the concept of restitution for wrongs conducted by Birks, Jackman, Goff and Jones, and the Law Commission. Particular attention will be dedicated to Edelman's recent, innovative approach. These proposals contain important contributions for the development of a legal concept of restitution for wrongs and have the great merit of fostering much needed discussion even though, in my opinion, they are unable to capture the idea of restitutionary damages in its entirety.

In the second part of this chapter, I shall examine the concept of restitution for wrongs which has emerged from the historical-philosophical analysis. It is not a goal of my research to establish whether English law should adopt restitutionary damages and, in so doing, how far it should go. The main questions debated here concern their level of compatibility with the law of damages and the ascertainment of their main characters. The starting point for my position will be offered by the Law Commission's definition of restitutionary damages as stripping the defendant of ill-gotten gains. This widely accepted description is of little avail in the understanding of the damages at issue, for it does not provide any guidance as to their boundaries and nature. My analysis will focus on the relationship between compensation and restitution, and particularly on those judicial awards which are seen as performing a compensatory and a restitutionary role at the same time. I reject the possibility of 'multitask' responses. The solution which I propose distinguishes restitution from compensation on the basis of their respective connection with the damaging event: nullifying the patrimonial loss does not eliminate the defendant's benefit which is the object of a claim for restitutionary damages; it only eliminates that particular gain which is directly connected with the loss.

One of the corollaries of this position is that I consider compensatory and restitutionary damages as specular: whereas compensation places the victim in the same position in which the victim would be had the wrong never happened, restitution places the agent in the same position in which the agent would be had the wrong never happened. If this approach is correct, then specular rules apply to the responses at issue, which means that, as there is no substantial legal objection to compensation, there can be no substantial legal objection to restitution. Any rejection of restitutionary damages would be based on policy considerations only.

II   Birks' Three Tests

In his *Introduction to the Law of Restitution*,[1] Peter Birks examines the set of criteria which triggers an award of restitutionary damages. He distinguishes three different situations, to which correspond three tests. A positive reaction to one of the tests is enough to justify the award.

The first test is the deliberate exploitation of wrongdoing:

> Where a defendant has deliberately set out to enrich himself by committing a wrong against the plaintiff, he ought to be liable to make restitution of that profit.[2]

---

[1]   Birks, *Restitution* 326-333.
[2]   *Ibid* 326.

His well-known 'thug case' exemplifies this situation: agent A is paid by third party T to beat up victim V. There is no connection between the transfer of wealth from T to A on the one hand, and the loss sustained by V on the other, beyond the fact that A's assets have increased owing to A's perpetrating a wrongful action. From the perspective of the law of unjust enrichment, A is not enriched at the expense of V: A does not interrupt a transfer of wealth which should flow from T to V. A's benefit does not belong to V or ought to be V's in any way.[3] From the perspective of the law of wrongs, V cannot claim A's benefit as part of compensatory damages, for the gain of the wrongdoer is independent of the victim's loss. As both the law of unjust enrichment and the law of compensation are ruled out, the only way for V to reach A's benefit is through an award of restitutionary damages.

In this context, Birks compares the restitutionary response for wrongs with the criteria for the application of exemplary damages set by Lord Devlin in *Rookes v Barnard*,[4] the latter being a blunter instrument than the former. But this connection between exemplary and restitutionary damages is not convincing. Since exemplary damages are linked to the wickedness of the wrongdoer, there is no direct relationship between the agent's actual gain and the victim's recovery: the award of damages could be higher or lower than the gain according to the court's perception of the degree of wickedness. Yet, Birks is forced into it by the lack of suitable authorities to support his theory of restitution for wrongs, which aims to provide a descriptive analysis of the judicial data. In fact, he admits the difficulty of proving the degree of acceptability of this test and remarks that exemplary damages provide the strongest, but not the only, argument in its favour. I would argue that behind this supposed link of punishment to restitution hides the danger of falling into the trap of the a fortiori argument: as exemplary damages are allowed, restitutionary damages must be allowed as well. Yet, historically, theoretically and taxonomically the two legal responses are independent of one another. The a fortiori argument only leads to an unclear classification of the law of damages.

The second Birksian test distinguishes between duties which are 'designed to prevent enrichment',[5] the breach of which triggers a restitutionary response, and other duties. Birks acknowledges that to differentiate between the two classes of wrongs is not always an easy task. Yet, he urges that this test provides a clear explanation for the differences among torts, only some of which are related to a restitutionary mechanism. Nuisance and defamation, for instance, have never been linked to restitutionary awards; this, in his view, stems from the fact that they do not perform an anti-enrichment function. Once again, Birks tries to reconcile the existing authorities with his general theory of restitution for

---

[3]   Birks *ibid*, however, seems to prefer the opposite view.
[4]   *Rookes v Barnard* [1964] AC 1129 (HL).
[5]   Birks, *Restitution* 328.

wrongs. Consequently, he has to admit that not every breach of an 'anti-enrichment wrong' will give rise to restitutionary damages.[6] This criterion does not explain when the damages in point are to be granted; it only says that, given a specific framework, they might be granted. It is therefore unable to illustrate why some legal events trigger restitution and others do not. Furthermore, the test is limited by historical constraints: the fact alone that restitutionary damages have never been granted for a certain tort does not mean that they could not be granted in the future.

The last of the three tests stresses the importance of prophylaxis in the evaluation of the restitutionary claim. The idea is 'not to bring about a situation in which the mischief in question *might* happen'.[7] Birks sees an application for this test especially in trust cases: the imposition of a restitutionary duty reduces the opportunities for the fiduciary to obtain personal profit. If the fiduciary enriches himself instead of pursuing the beneficiary's interest, the beneficiary will compel the fiduciary to give up the benefit. The prophylactic approach operates to prevent the fiduciary acting in his own interest because he knows that he will have to transfer his profit to the beneficiary. One might object that this particular approach highlights a characteristic common to all wrongs, not only to restitutionary cases. The main aim of the law of wrongs might be seen in the rectification of injustice. Yet, a secondary, important, function consists of prevention: the agent knows that the consequences of his wrongful behaviour will be undone as far as possible by the reparatory measures. This is as true of restitution as it is of compensation. This criterion, therefore, is as vague as the one concerning anti-enrichment wrongs. It just states that restitutionary damages ought to be awarded when the agent has benefited from the perpetration of a wrong. It does not explain which one, among all possible breaches which have granted the agent an underserved windfall, ought to trigger restitution, for a prophylactic approach could apply to all categories of the law of damages without any particular selection.

III   Protection of Facilitative Institutions

Instead of examining the wrong itself to see whether it is compatible with a restitutionary measure, the 'facilitative institutions' hypothesis, advanced by Jackman, suggests an alternative avenue. Jackman investigates the right to restitution for wrongs and propounds a theory which explains the function of the restitutionary response itself rather than taking into account the protective sphere of the wrong, as Birks does. In Jackman's view,

---

[6]   *Ibid* 329.
[7]   *Ibid* 332; italics in original.

the rationale for the right to restitution for wrongs is the protection of a variety of private legal facilities, or facilitative institutions, namely private property, relationships of trust and confidence, and (with some qualification) contracts.[8]

Subsequently, Jackman identifies a need for 'a criterion to determine which wrongs do, and which do not, trigger the right to restitution.'[9] According to Jackman, restitution for wrongs can be explained by examining the 'power-conferring facilities' which the law makes available to private individuals for the creation of arrangements between them.[10] His view is supported by an investigation of the three facilitative institutions which endeavours to answer two questions: 'first, which facilitative institution is at stake in any given case, and secondly, what is required to fulfil the rights and duties which exist by virtue of it.'[11] He concludes that, indeed, restitutionary damages are granted to protect 'facilitative institutions'.

Jackman's central idea is that the aim of restitutionary damages is to preserve some legal institutions rather than to protect the victims of a wrong.[12] This account has the advantage of simplicity – despite the fact that its appeal is partially lost when Jackman mentions the necessity for a 'hierarchy of moral fault' to supplement his rule.[13] But even leaving aside the – not insignificant – question of the opportunity to refer to moral issues in that context, the 'facilitative institution' theory raises some concerns. As the author himself admits, his theory alone cannot provide a justification for the whole phenomenon of restitution for wrongs. Protection against institutional harm ought to be combined with other criteria. From what emerges in his contribution, Jackman's analysis seeks to be descriptive rather than prescriptive. This is hard to reconcile with the admission that his description cannot furnish a systematic account of the law.

Another difficulty of Jackman's theory is that it does not cover all situations in which the wrongdoer obtains a benefit from his action and it would be unjust if the victim could not claim it. This is the same obstacle which Weinrib's account of restitution for wrongs is unable to surmount. There are cases in which restitutionary damages should be awarded, but not to protect one of Jackman's legal institutions. Bodily integrity is such a case: the 'facilitative institution' rule cannot justify a restitutionary claim in Birks' 'thug case'. Another good example would be a variation of the *Caroline von Monaco* case. If journalist A publishes blatantly incorrect news on princess V, knowing that his profit will be higher than any compensation he will have to pay to V, the latter cannot seize A's enrichment on the basis of the protection of a facilitative institution, for no institution is to

---

[8]   IM Jackman, 'Restitution for Wrongs' (1989) 48 *CLJ* 302-321, 302.
[9]   *Ibid* 303.
[10] *Ibid* 304.
[11] *Ibid.*
[12] See for instance *ibid* 313 and 320.
[13] *Ibid* 320.

be protected which falls under Jackman's categories, provided that the information was not published in breach of a duty of confidence. An ad hoc enlargement of the number of institutions protected would leave Jackman's theory without content: if all institutions were potentially facilitative, this theory would be deprived of any value.

Finally, there are serious difficulties with the theoretical underpinnings of this position. If it is said that the function of the wrong is to protect legal institutions, it is easy to see why the wrongdoer should perform restitution. What is not clear, however, is why the right-holder should benefit from the restitutionary duty imposed upon the defendant. The institutional harm does not create any particular link between the parties to the claim which would identify the right-holder and the wrongdoer as doer and sufferer from the same wrong. If the function of the judicial award is to protect an institution, this might as well be achieved by compelling the wrongdoer to transfer his enrichment to a fund for the protection of certain legal institutions. In other words, the protection argument does not create party-related reasons to act.[14]

IV   General Acceptance

The most radical proposal on the extent to which restitutionary damages ought to be recognised in the English legal system has been advanced by Lord Goff and Gareth Jones in their seminal treaty on the 'law of restitution'. They submit that English courts should adopt a clear-cut rule:

> [I]f it can be demonstrated that a tortfeasor has gained a benefit and that benefit would not have been gained but for the tort, he should be required to make restitution.[15]

This is a very straightforward approach, of which Weinrib recognises 'the twin virtues of simplicity of formulation and comprehensiveness of application'.[16] Its consequences are far-reaching: every benefit ought to be transferred to the victim simply on the basis of causative evaluation.

The role which Goff and Jones ascribe to the causal link has been subject to criticism. Weinrib remarks that it would be impossible and unjust to put on the agent's shoulders such a heavy burden as the duty to transfer all gains to the victim, whatever the relation of the gains with the victim might be. He opposes a theoretical construction which limits restitution to those gains which depend upon 'the wrong's normative quality'.[17] Yet, the two visions are not as incompatible as it may appear. It is unlikely that Goff and Jones suggest the use of a concept of natural causation. Legal causation offers to the courts the possibility

---

[14]   See especially Weinrib, *Restitutionary damages* 2.
[15]   Goff of Chieveley and G Jones, *The Law of Restitution* (6th edn) (London, Sweet & Maxwell 2002) para 36-004.
[16]   Weinrib, *Restitutionary damages* 12.
[17]   *Ibid* 11.

to select the legally relevant elements of the chain of causation which in turn would allow the judges to link the award to the wrong's normative quality.

Still, Weinrib is right when he points out the risks connected to the width of this principle. Goff and Jones' treatise is mainly descriptive, whereas the principle sets a line of future development. Yet, the authors manage to avoid any accusation of surreptitiously imposing their own view within a merely descriptive context, for they never pretend to state the law on this point; they simply advance a proposal. Their idea, however, mainly shifts the contentious issue from the identification of the restitution-yielding wrongs to the definition of restitutionary damages and to causative issues. Saying that such damages are always to be awarded tells us little of why and in which circumstances they should be awarded, for the requirements to identify cases of restitution for wrongs are not specified. Some gains can be the result of the agent's bargaining skills; they might be only extremely loosely connected to the wrong. Furthermore, the wrong might not have been intentional, but merely negligent, or not even that, as in the case of strict liability. Applying the Goff and Jones principle, a non-intentional wrong-doer could be called to transfer to the victim a gain which is hardly related to the wrong itself. It is unclear whether Goff and Jones would extend restitutionary damages to such cases as well. They place a very sharp weapon into the victim's hands. Although the wrongdoer ought not to keep an undeserved windfall, neither should he be automatically deprived of a gain owing to the simple existence of any sort of link with the wrong.

V Position of the Law Commission

In the Law Commission proposal[18] there are recognisable elements of both Birks' and Goff and Jones' views. Yet, the Commission combines those elements in such a fashion that the final outcome is characterised by a degree of originality. The Commission's basic view is 'that the development of the law on restitution for wrongs is most appropriately left to the courts'.[19] In deciding whether to allow restitution, the judiciary ought to be guided by the principle according to which 'no man shall profit from his own wrong'. The Commission justifies the preference for a purely judicial avenue on the basis of two arguments. On the one hand, it remarks that the law of restitution for wrongs has attracted the interest of legal science too recently to allow sufficient consensus to be built around any one set of application requirements. Incremental judicial development would obviate the problem.[20] On the other hand, in the case of restitution for breach of contract the lack of agreement among commentators would suggest 'that it would be danger-ous to "freeze" in legislative form the extent to which, if at all, restitutionary

---

[18] Law Commission, *Aggravated, Exemplary and Restitutionary Damages* (Law Com No 247, 1997) Part III paras 1.38-1.57.

[19] *Ibid* 1.38.

[20] *Ibid* 1.41.

damages should be available.'[21] However, the Commission admits an exception to its basic position in favour of a purely judicial development: a legislative reform ought to deal with restitutionary damages for the case in which the agent's conduct shows a 'deliberate and outrageous disregard of the plaintiff's rights.'[22] This exception is considered to be necessary to bring restitutionary damages in line with the Commission proposal on exemplary damages, which should be available on such an occasion.

Hence, according to the Commission, the judiciary should be free to decide when and why to award restitutionary damages. This approach is partially compatible with the Goff and Jones proposal, which states that in principle there should be no limitation to the application of restitution for wrongs; yet it differs from it because it leaves to the courts the possibility of denying restitution for wrongs in concrete cases. The only exception to the general rule of judicial discretion reminds us of Birks' concept of deliberate exploitation of wrongdoing. Both avenues recommended by the Commission share the difficulties which have been examined in relation to the original models. In transferring the decisional responsibility to the judiciary, the Commission recognises the impossibility of reconciling the different views expressed by the commentators. This solution provides an answer to some immediate technical problems. However, the Commission does not lay down any criteria which explain what restitutionary damages are and when, if at all, they ought to be granted.

The exception to the general rule of judicial decision provides an example of this lack of theoretical structure. The Commission justifies it by reference to a need for harmony and co-ordination with the proposed regulation on exemplary damages: to have situations in which restitution is not available, but punishment is, would be 'unacceptable'.[23] Although not expressly stated, this line of reasoning is based upon the old a fortiori argument. I have repeatedly pointed out the weakness of this argument. Neither historical nor theoretical analysis provides any support to this thesis. The only common element shared by exemplary and restitutionary damages is their position within non-compensatory responses. But their aims, their structure, their history and their nature are so different that from the award of the one it cannot be inferred that the other is part of the law of damages too. In fact, the Commission itself realises that its argument is not as straightforward as it might appear when it admits that it is possible 'that a statute could be held to be consistent with an award of punitive damages, but not restitutionary damages'.[24]

---

[21]   *Ibid* 1.47.
[22]   *Ibid* 1.49.
[23]   *Ibid* 1.51.
[24]   *Ibid* 1.51 n 270.

VI   Restitution Disgorgement and Deterrence

James Edelman has recently advanced an innovative proposal for restitution for wrongs which casts new light on the topic. In Edelman's view, the origin of the uncertainty concerning the availability of the restitutionary claim lies in a systematic mistake. The traditionally accepted view is that there is only one legal response which concerns restitutionary damages for wrongs. Edelman proposes a model based upon two responses. He labels the first restitutionary response 'restitutionary damages'. Such damages, he suggests, constitute 'a monetary award which reverses a transfer of value. It is an award which gives back value transferred from a claimant to a defendant as a result of a defendant's wrong and is almost always measured by the objective gain received by the defendant.'[25] The second restitutionary response is aimed at a result different from the mere reversal of a transfer of wealth. The function of this response is 'disgorgement'. Unlike the previous group, here 'the measure of the gain ignores whether or not any transfer has occurred and is measured by the actual profit accruing to the defendant from the wrong.'[26]

The two awards cover separate areas of the law of damages and differ both in their structure and in their aim. 'Restitutionary' damages perform within the law of wrongs a function similar to restitution for unjust enrichment. According to Edelman, 'restitution' for wrongs and restitution for unjust enrichment run parallel,[27] although the requirements of the law of wrongs and of the law of unjust enrichment do not coincide, and therefore shape the respective claims in a dissimilar fashion. 'Disgorgement' damages are directly related to the pure benefit obtained by the wrongdoer. They strip the wrongdoer of ill-gotten gains independently of any further evaluation. On the basis of this dichotomy, the author concludes that 'by separating these two different measures of damages it is simple to explain both when gain-based awards should be available for wrongdoing and the measure of such awards.'[28] 'Restitutionary' damages should always be awarded for wrongs; 'disgorgement' damages should be awarded when deterrence is required and compensation alone would be inadequate.[29]

The great merit of Edelman's explanation is that it forces us to reconsider the role of the two different measures which he connects to restitutionary awards for wrongs. One measure, says Edelman, reverses a transfer of value. Thus, where £100 should have stayed with C, but instead went to D due to D's wrongful behaviour, C can claim 'restitutionary' damages from D. Edelman provides theoretical backing to his construction. 'Restitutionary' damages aim 'to restore both the claimant and the defendant to their respective positions before the

---

[25]   *Edelman*, 66.
[26]   *Ibid* 72.
[27]   *Ibid* eg 70.
[28]   *Ibid* 65.
[29]   *Ibid* 81 and 83.

wrong occurred'.[30] Edelman properly identifies corrective justice as the philosophical account which supports his construction of 'restitutionary' damages.[31] He then confutes any link between corrective justice and 'disgorgement' damages.[32]

Edelman's 'restitutionary' damages are a modern version of a time-honoured legal institution which goes back to the Thomistic concept of restitution. St Thomas then, and Edelman now, base their construction on the traditional, loss-centred perspective of Aristotle's corrective justice: when there is an imbalance, the one who has more has to give the excess to the one who has less. At the end of the operation, both parties will be in a position of neutrality in respect of the *status quo ante* the damaging event. The 'Aristotelian claimant' – but the term 'Thomistic claimant' would probably be more correct – is often seen by legal theorists and academic lawyers, and Edelman is no exception, as seeking to mitigate, or possibly eliminate, the negative impact of the damaging event on his own assets. He does not claim the agent's benefit qua benefit, but as part of his own loss.

The true nature of Edelman 'restitutionary' award emerges clearly from the link which Edelman establishes between his 'restitutionary' damages and restitution for unjust enrichment. The claimant in unjust enrichment asserts his right over the thing which is in the hands of the enriched party: 'the thing is/should be mine!' The claim is based on a misplacement of wealth. What the claimant should have had, the defendant received instead. Therefore, and independently of any subsequent event which affects his wealth, the claimant acts on the basis of a loss. But to accept this outcome would undermine Edelman's approach, for it would compel the conclusion that his 'restitutionary' damages are in reality a particular measure of compensation – that is what I have called 'pseudo-restitution'.[33] To avoid this result, he distinguishes between the financial loss sustained by the claimant and the claim-yielding transfer of value, which he relates to the concept of 'subtraction from the claimant's *dominium*',[34] meaning that 'the generation of value has come from the assets of the claimant even though the claimant may not have suffered any financial loss'.[35] Yet, the divide between the concept of loss and the concept of subtraction – already tenuous from an analytical point of view – is questionable from a theoretical perspective. There is no need to refute this point in detail, for Edelman's explanation faces the same objections which I have discussed whilst examining Weinrib's theory of restitution for wrongs, and

---

[30]   *Ibid* 82.

[31]   *Ibid* 86.

[32]   Later in his investigation, Edelman seems to change his mind, for he brings even 'disgorgement' damages under the roof of corrective justice. Yet, this result appears to be more the consequence of Weinrib's influential work, to which Edelman refers, than a fully developed theoretical analysis. In fact, the only reference to corrective justice within the context of 'disgorgement' damages is confined to one line, *ibid* 246.

[33]   See ch 8, IV C iii.

[34]   *Edelman*, 67.

[35]   *Ibid*.

particularly the role of this theory for pseudo-restitution.[36] Edelman follows the same line of reasoning and his analysis is vitiated by the same analytical mistake which affects Weinrib's work. The points of contact between Edelman's and Weinrib's approaches are clear: not only refers the former expressly to the explanation provided by the latter, but Edelman uses also a parallel between restitution for unjust enrichment and 'restitutionary' damages which is stated by Weinrib too.[37]

The compensatory nature of Edelman's 'restitutionary' damages finds further confirmation in the aim which, according to Edelman, these damages should achieve: they *restore* both parties in the position in which they were before the wrong was committed. If the victim is restored to a pre-wrong position, this must be a loss-centred perspective which owes much to the Scholastics and creates a problem of congruence with the other responses of the law of damages. The aim which Edelman ascribes to his 'restitutionary' damages is in reality what a compensatory award seeks to realise. If restitutionary damages, following Edelman's formula, were characterised by the same aim as compensatory damages, there will be two different responses, compensatory and 'restitutionary' damages, which would perform an identical function. The legal system has no particular need for such a multiplication of responses. Edelman's 'restitutionary' damages are compensatory damages with a different label.

The problems of taxonomy inherent in Edelman's classification have recently emerged in Mitchell McInnes' analysis of the user principle. Considering the remedial consequences of the violation of the ownership right, McInnes argues that 'ownership entails a number of rights, including the right of *dominium* (*ie* the right to control access and use of a thing) … A loss of *dominium* is considered reparable through the payment of a price at which a reasonable purchaser would buy, and a reasonable vendor would sell, such a right.'[38] The idea of *dominium* is not alien to Edelman's account of 'restitutionary' damages. McInnes develops this idea implicitly highlighting the inappositeness of Edelman's restitutionary reading of a compensatory award. Edelman's reply emphasises the difficulty of applying this 'right-based measure of compensation', as he calls it, to infringements of rights held for commercial purposes.[39] Yet, the authorities which he uses in support of his view are not unequivocal. Furthermore, his defence does not tackle the issues of legal theory raised by McInnes. At any rate, what counts for my analysis is that this is a first step back from the 'pure' dual theory, for 'restitutionary' damages are confined to particular constellations, that is they are no longer able to account for any reversal of value transferred by the claimant to the defendant on the basis of a wrong.

---

[36]   Ch 8, IV C ii and iii.
[37]   With reference to a German claim in unjustified enrichment, Weinrib, *Restitutionary damages* 6 n 6, observes: '[t]he basic idea of this article is identical to the one that has animated the analysis of the *Eingriffskondiktion* in German law'.
[38]   M McInnes, 'Gain, Loss and the User Principle' [2006] Restitution LR 76-92, 81.
[39]   J Edelman, 'Gain-Based Damages and Compensation' in A Burrows and Lord Rodger (eds) *Mapping the Law* (Oxford, OUP 2006) 141-160, 153-158.

Edelman's 'disgorgement' damages, by contrast, are a true instance of restitutionary damages. Edelman justifies their award with 'the need to ensure deterrence of wrongdoing'.[40] This explanation is not satisfactory. Let us assume that D wilfully publishes a book containing a false account of C's private life. D is ready to pay compensation because he thinks that the profits from the sale will exceed the compensatory award. Thus, the risk of having to pay damages will not deter D from publishing the book. According to Edelman, a 'disgorgement' award would lead to a more appropriate result. D will not publish the book for fear of having to disgorge his profit. However, it is not quite clear why this should happen. If D were aware that he might be compelled to pay 'disgorgement' damages, he would know that, in the worst scenario, the publication of the book would leave him in the same position in which he would be had he never published it, for 'disgorgement' damages would deprive him of the profit, not punish him.[41] Hence, publication may still be worth taking the risk of paying 'disgorgement' damages. The agent is all the more likely to commit the wrong in a system in which the award of restitutionary damages is disputed or is left to the discretion of the courts.[42] Edelman does not explain why this position of indifference should have any deterrent effect upon the wrongdoer, or indeed secure a 'greater level of deterrence ... than compensatory damages can produce.'[43]

On the other hand, a mild deterring effect can be recognised to any legal response. As Edelman agrees, a stronger deterring effect can be attached to exemplary damages. Yet, even nominal damages could work as a deterrent, for instance by flagging some inadequacies in the defendant's conduct.[44] And although deterrence is likely to work in a particularly effective fashion in the case of intentional behaviour,[45] there is no reason to exclude that even negligent behaviour might be affected by the – maybe unconscious – thought of the possible consequences of a certain course of conduct.

It follows that deterrence cannot be seen as the peculiar element of 'disgorgement' damages. But Edelman utilises two further arguments to support his view. The first set of circumstances is the deliberate and cynical perpetration of a wrong. The reasoning runs similarly to Birks' deliberate exploitation of wrongdoing and is subject to the same criticism. Edelman applies the Birksian a fortiori argument, which is neither historically nor theoretically grounded.[46] The second

---

[40]   *Edelman*, 83. This point is addressed more in detail later in this chapter, n 68 and text thereof.

[41]   A similar argument is advanced in the context of violation of intellectual property rights by J Köndgen, 'Gewinnabschöpfung als Sanktion unerlaubten Tuns' (2000) 64 *Rabels Zeitschrift* 661-695, 685.

[42]   See D Fox, 'Restitutionary Damages to Deter Breach of Contract' (2000) 60 *CLJ* 33-35, 35.

[43]   *Edelman*, 83.

[44]   Fox (n 42), observes that '[r]estitutionary damages indirectly protect the claimant's interest in performance by removing any financial incentive for the defendant to renege on his bargain'. Yet, a similar argument might apply to other areas of the law of damages.

[45]   Thus A Tettenborn (ed), *The Law of Damages* (London, LexisNexis UK 2003) paras 1.40-1.41.

[46]   *Edelman*, 84-85: 'The rules applicable under ... exemplary damages should also apply to disgorgement damages'.

set of circumstances is related to the need to protect the fiduciary relationship, which is seen as a particularly deserving institution. The reason for this special treatment is individuated in the vulnerability and susceptibility to abuse of fiduciary relationships. Why only these relationships deserve particular protection is, however, not sufficiently clarified. Although Edelman distances himself from Jackman's 'protection of facilitative institutions' theory, his analysis is not dissimilar from Jackman's and encounters analogous obstacles.

Edelman's thesis is compensatory-centred. 'Disgorgement' damages, he claims, should be awarded only when more traditional responses are inadequate. This approach does not provide a theoretical explanation for restitution for wrongs; it only shifts the analysis from restitution for wrongs to a definition of inadequacy of other responses, especially compensation. Compensatory damages must be considered first. If they fail, 'disgorgement' damages might be called upon. Consequently, 'disgorgement' damages have no autonomous life. Although Edelman correctly insists that their 'rationale is not compensation',[47] they depend on compensation.

It is arguable, therefore, whether Edelman has achieved his stated, worthy goal of simplifying this troublesome area of law. Through his 'restitutionary' damages, he introduces a response with a legal aim which sits uncomfortably between compensation and restitution. Still, Edelman's analysis has the merit of highlighting the various avenues to measure compensation for wrongs. 'Restitutionary' damages do realise a compensatory aim; but their quantification differs from the traditional measure of compensation and this is the main reason why they have caused considerable trouble in the assessment of their nature. My terminology of 'pseudo-restitutionary damages' reflects these difficulties: damages which might be easily confused with restitution. Pseudo-restitution means proper compensation, which, however, is hard to recognise as such. Different measurement criteria do not necessarily imply the existence of different forms of damages with independent aims within restitution for wrongs. Damages might be assessed in different fashion, according to what the court intends to achieve. But the multifarious forms of assessment do not alter the nature of the awards. It is the aim underlying the award which determines the categorisation. Thus, compensatory damages are subject to various forms of assessment, all aiming to make good the claimant's loss.

VII   The Requirements of the Claim

Having rejected the previous explanations, especially the dichotomy 'restitutionary'/'disgorgement' damages, the question of the structure of restitution for wrongs remains open. Let me set the framework of my investigation with an example.

---

[47]   *Ibid* 82.

Agent A takes wrongfully victim V's bicycle. Let us assume that the legal system requires that all legal responses be based on a monetary evaluation. The court will award damages in the amount which is likely to correspond to the value of the bicycle, say £100. The circumstances of the case seem to point to the conclusion that the court allows compensation. Yet, the coincidence of the monetary award with the value of the thing does not necessarily exclude the possibility of other responses. In Roman law, for instance, the punitive element was not automatically linked to the measure of the award. Thus, there might be room for conceiving the remedy as non-compensatory. In this context, it may be asked whether the £100 can qualify as restitutionary damages owing to the fact that the agent has been enriched to that amount through the wrong. The analysis of this question requires an investigation of the elements which characterise restitution for wrongs as an independent legal response. In granting restitution for wrongs, the courts strip the wrongdoer of ill-gotten gains: this standard definition, correct as it might be, does not provide a satisfactory description of the fashion in which restitutionary damages operate. It is necessary, therefore, to identify the boundaries of restitutionary responses by explaining why, in a particular case, the award is restitutionary in nature rather than compensatory, punitive, or anything else. In fact, in the case of non-restitutionary responses, there are different sets of criteria which permit us to say: 'The court is awarding exemplary damages'; or: 'The court is awarding compensation'. On the contrary, no such certainty surrounds restitution for wrongs. This phenomenon has given rise to some confusion about the structure of restitutionary damages.

In restitution for wrongs, as opposed to compensation, the benefit of the agent is indeed directly linked to the wrong, but – unlike the bicycle example – is independent of the victim's loss. It is immaterial to the restitutionary award whether the victim has suffered any financially quantifiable harm, that is any negative modification of his patrimonial sphere. On the contrary, the existence of a financially quantifiable harm is essential to a compensatory award, for the function of compensation is to put the victim in the same position in which the victim would be had the wrongful event never happened. The wrongdoer is regarded as taking something away from the patrimonial sphere of the victim. Compensation ought to reintegrate the victim in the *status quo ante* as far as possible, whereas restitution deals exclusively with the patrimonial position of the agent. This position has been improved and the modification is the direct consequence of the commission of a wrong. This time, it is the patrimonial status of the victim which does not influence the quantification of the judicial award. Discussing a case of breach of fiduciary duty, Arden LJ explained my point with considerable force with reference to the account of profits, which in that context was a restitutionary measure:[48]

---

[48]   In my view, the function of an account of profits can be restitutionary or compensatory according to the situation. *Cf* ch 3, n 83 and test thereof.

The fact that the fiduciary can show that that party would not have made a loss is ... an irrelevant consideration so far as an account of profits is concerned. Likewise ... it is no defence for a fiduciary to say that he would have made the profit even if there had been no breach of fiduciary duty.[49]

Thus, compensation and restitution as legal responses concentrate on the patrimonial position of different parties in the quantification of the damages. On this premiss, it seems odd that there could be any confusion as regards the nature of the judicial award. Still, in some cases the aim of a legal response is disputed, as the following example demonstrates.

If A wrongfully takes V's bicycle, and the court awards V £100 as damages, is the court using a restitutionary measure? The agent's patrimonial position is indeed improved by – the value of – the bicycle. At the same time, the patrimonial position of the victim is reduced, or affected, by the same amount: the victim has suffered a pecuniary loss. There is a direct connection between the two modifications in this bicycle example which makes it difficult to see a difference between compensation and restitution. It might be possible to say that V can claim £100 either as compensation, or as restitution, or as a combination of compensation and restitution. I contend that, in this scenario, the victim can only claim compensation. This reasoning needs some elucidation.

The victim's loss is a necessary element of the wrong, whereas the agent's gain is purely accidental. If A had taken away the bicycle and then damaged it, V would have suffered the same loss, £100, but A would not have had a gain of £100. In this case, the agent might have had a different gain, but the intensity of A's gain would not have mirrored V's loss from a patrimonial perspective. The agent might have a gain or not, and this gain might coincide with the victim's loss or not, but this is irrelevant in the quantification of the judicial award. This conclusion is all the more clear if we assume that a friend of the agent pays £50 by way of compensation for A's wrong to the victim. The agent would still have a £100 profit, but the victim would not be able to claim it. V's compensatory right after the donation by A's friend is now restricted to £50. It follows that, in the bicycle case described, if A had made a profit of £100 – the value of the bicycle – V would not bring a restitutionary action for wrongs. The victim claims the wrongdoer's gain on the basis of the victim's loss, not because A made a profit. In the case of compensation, the connection between the victim's loss and the agent's gain,[50] whatever this gain might be, is immediate: the agent has a gain because the victim has a loss. In other words, the gain is a direct consequence of the loss. This connection between loss and gain is typical of compensation and distinguishes it from restitution, which does not rest upon a loss. We have already encountered the constellation examined here when I introduced the concept of

---

[49] *Mohammed Murad and Layla Mohammed Murad v. Hashim Ibrahim Khalil Al-Saraj and Westwood Business Inc* [2005] EWCA Civ 959 (CA) para 67 (Arden LJ).

[50] The term 'gain' is used in Aristotelian sense: it does not refer strictly to cases where the defendant has obtained an advantage which is economically quantifiable.

'pseudo-restitution'. In chapter eight, I provided a normative theory which accounts for this very same situation as a case of compensation.[51]

In the case of restitution for wrongs, the positive improvement in the agent's patrimonial sphere is unconnected to the victim's loss. When the agent's gain is reflected in the victim's loss, it disappears as soon as the loss is nullified by the agent – just as in the bicycle case. Rather than depriving the defendant of a benefit, the nullification of the loss mirrored in the defendant's gain rectifies the negative consequences of the wrongdoing upon the victim. It follows that the proper aim of such a claim is compensatory, not restitutionary. In my bicycle example, when the agent, who wrongfully took the bicycle worth £100, and thus made a 'gain' of £100, compensates the victim's loss, the agent's benefit vanishes with compensation, for the gain is a direct consequence of the loss. Conversely, if I bribe judge A so that he wrongfully decides in my favour in the proceedings against innocent victim V, V's loss and A's gain are not corresponding. A transfer of wealth from me or from A to V in terms of compensation would leave the question of A's benefit untouched. A's benefit is unrelated to V's loss, although both are related to the same wrong. Hence, V will have two claims, one for compensation and one for restitution. For this reason, Coleman's assertion that when 'the wrongful gains and losses exactly coincide, satisfying the demands of corrective justice suffices to satisfy the demands of restitutionary justice as well, and vice versa'[52] cannot be accepted. In the situation depicted by Coleman, there are no demands of restitutionary justice to be satisfied, for the necessary correspondence of loss and gain signals the presence of a compensatory mechanism. Simply put, wrongful gains and wrongful losses might coincide, but redressing the latter leaves the former unaffected.

In Birks' 'thug-case', the victim is physically harmed by the agent, who receives a payment by a third party for his wrongful action. This situation triggers two legal responses in accordance with the model just described. As regards the victim's physical loss, the agent will have to restore the *status quo ante* as far as possible. It is here immaterial whether the agent's patrimonial sphere has been positively or negatively affected by the perpetration of the wrong. Yet, the victim also wants to seize the benefit which the agent obtained by the third party. The agent's wealth is directly related to the wrong, that is it is not mediated by the agent's loss. Just as compensation, even restitution requires a connection to the wrong. Yet, to paraphrase Birks,[53] as regards restitution for wrongs the victim has to rely on the wrong, and not on the loss, to connect himself to the agent's profit. As Lionel Smith put it, '[t]he plaintiff's connection to the defendant's gain is that

---

[51]   Ch 8, IV C iii.

[52]   Coleman, *Risks* 371. This is quite a common view; see eg P Jaffey, *The Nature and Scope of Restitution* (Oxford, Hart 2000) 375 n 61: 'A liability for compensation may have the effect of removing part or all of the benefit obtained through a wrong. ... [I]n so far as the defendant's profit is reduced by a remedial liability, the need for disgorgement is reduced also'.

[53]   Birks, *Restitution* 320.

the gain was realized via a wrong done by the defendant to the plaintiff.'[54] Hence, the situation which leads to an award of restitutionary damages is triggered by a gain in the agent's wealth and an immediate connection between the agent's behaviour and the wrong suffered by the victim on which the gain is dependent.

My view finds support in the so-called doctrine of the lost opportunity to bargain,[55] a good example of which is provided by the *Wrotham Park* case.[56] There, the court awarded damages corresponding to the amount which the claimant would have reasonably paid to relax a covenant. As I have intimated in the discussion of this method of damages quantification,[57] the doctrine at issue cannot be related to restitutionary damages because it presupposes that the victim has suffered a loss and that damages were evaluated on the basis of that loss. Examining situations where the patrimonial spheres of agent and victim have seen a positive and a negative modification, and there is a direct link between loss and gain in the sense that the latter is a consequence of the former, Sharpe and Waddams pointed out that the victim suffered a concrete loss and proposed a measure to quantify it. The mechanism in operation is the same as in my bicycle case, although the measure of compensation may vary. On the contrary, the *Mahesan* case[58] furnishes an instance of restitution for wrongs. The bribe obtained by the agent is wrongful. The agent's receiving the bribe does not cause a patrimonial loss to the victim; it is independent of this loss. The money is not something which legally belongs to the claimant, and which the latter claims back. However, a connection can be traced between the bribe and the wrong on the one hand, and the victim of the wrong on the other hand. This framework justifies the award of restitutionary damages.

VIII   The Object of the Restitutionary Claim

As already intimated, the definition of restitution for wrongs as the legal response which aims to strip the agent of ill-gotten gains does not contain sufficient information to identify the application requirements. The formula is not even specific enough to delimit the object of the restitutionary measure. I have first examined the requirements of the claim: the irrelevance of the victim's loss and the direct, that is immediate, relationship of the wrongdoer's gain to the commission of a wrong. The relationship is 'immediate' because it is not

---

[54]   LD Smith, 'The Province of the Law of Restitution' (1992) 71 *Canadian Bar Rev* 672-699, 684-685.

[55]   RJ Sharpe and SM Waddams, 'Damages for Lost Opportunity to Bargain' [1982] 2 *OJLS* 290-297.

[56]   *Wrotham Park Estate Co Ltd v Parkside Homes Ltd* [1974] 1 WLR 798.

[57]   See ch 3, n 32 and text thereof, for a principled discussion of this doctrine and for the references to my next statements.

[58]   *T Mahesan S/O Thambiah v Malaysia Government Officer's Co-op Housing Society Ltd* [1979] AC 374 (PC). See ch 3, text to n 63.

mediated by an evaluation of the loss. At this point, the analysis moves on to the determination of the object of the claim.

According to Weinrib, 'in the case of alienation, the plaintiff can choose either the value of the thing alienated or the price the defendant received.'[59] Weinrib refers this alternative to the way in which his restitutionary damages are 'usually' computed. In chapter eight, I explained why, in my opinion, Weinrib's account does not deal with restitution, but with compensation for wrongs. Still, his statement paves the way to an important qualification of compensation. The different measures of compensation might give the – mistaken – impression that different legal responses, as opposed to methods of quantification, are in operation at the same time. Going back to the bicycle example, let us assume that the agent sells the bicycle for £150, which is more than its value of £100. The victim's loss, quantifiable in £100, can be nullified only by an award of compensatory damages. The qualification of the remaining £50 is more difficult. As £100 is tied to compensation, one might assume that restitutionary damages will be as high as the part of the gain which is not linked to the loss, which is £50. Therefore, if the victim claims in tort, he will obtain £100 as compensation and £50 as restitution. However, such analysis would come across the same difficulty which has been previously identified in Weinrib's and Edelman's accounts: by selling the bicycle, the agent makes a profit which falls within the '*dominium*' – as Edelman put it – of the victim. The price paid by the third party, £150, is an element of the victim's right wrongfully used by the agent. The wrongful exploitation of the right has deprived the victim of a possibility of gain which belonged to the victim. One avenue to quantify the patrimonial disadvantage is to see the damage in the claimant's lost opportunity to bargain with the third party. The loss originates in the violation of the victim's proprietary interest. This means that the £150 cannot be claimed through a restitutionary, but only through a compensatory, action. The courts will award £100 or £150 according to their quantification of the victim's loss.

As regards proper restitutionary damages, the subject-matter of a claim might not coincide with the enrichment of the defendant at the moment of the claim. For example, the agent might no longer be enriched, or he might be less enriched, at the point in time in which the victim raises his claim. There are two main possible scenarios. Either the victim recovers the entire gain, or he recovers only that part of the transfer of wealth which still enriches the defendant. Both possibilities are compatible with the legal system, although the second solution might be preferable. The necessity of delimiting a clear and strict ambit of application of the claim finds its reason, inter alia, in the risk of affecting too heavily non-intentional wrongdoers, for instance in the case of strict liability, in which it is immaterial whether the wrongdoer knew of the wrong and of the restitutionary duty attached to it. Furthermore, this solution would mirror what happens in compensation: normally, the victim can only require reparation of

---

[59]   Weinrib, *Restitutionary damages* 16.

any loss existing at the moment of the claim. As compensation and restitution have a specular structure,[60] it seems correct to keep the same legal structure for both responses.

The more restrictive option, which allows restitution of the still available enrichment, might create a problem if the agent wilfully reduces the amount of his enrichment, although such possibility is more of theoretical than of practical interest. This situation could be solved through a device similar to the one adopted by the German BGB. With regard to unjust enrichment, the German code grants the victim a compensatory claim for the loss caused by the defendant's intentional reduction of the gain.[61] Thus, if the agent intentionally or grossly negligently disposes of the enrichment, he is depriving the victim of what should belong to the victim; therefore the totally or partly useless restitutionary claim for wrongs could be substituted by a compensatory claim measured by the quantity of enrichment of which the agent divested himself.

IX   Election between Compensation and Restitution

My account is irreconcilable with the Law Commission proposal on the compatibility of restitution and compensation. The Commission favours what it considers to be the judicial approach, according to which the victim ought not to recover both full restitution and full compensation for a wrong.[62] This position rests upon the Privy Council judgment in *Tang Man Sit v Capacious Investments*,[63] in which, according to the Commission Report, Lord Nicholls construed the relationship between restitution and compensation as one between alternative and inconsistent remedies. The Commission overcomes the inconsistency of the remedies by propounding only a partial compatibility between restitution and compensation. Thus, if the agent has received a bribe of £1000 and has caused a loss of £2000 to the victim, he will be required to pay £2000. 'This might be justified as full compensation alone, but it could also be justified as full restitution (£1000) plus partial compensation (£1000).'[64] Birks raises a powerful objection against this approach: it does not appear to be inconsistent to allow full compensation along with full restitution, given that in the absence of loss – which is the position the victim would be in after having obtained full compensation – the victim could still obtain full restitution.[65]

The Commission is unhappy with a judicial solution which compels an election between remedies. Yet, its own compromise of granting only partial compensation and partial restitution just restates the question in another form. A

---

[60]   See section X in this chapter.
[61]   Paras 818 (4) and 819 BGB.
[62]   Law Commission (n 18) Part III para 1.68.
[63]   *Tang Man Sit v Capacious Investments Ltd* [1996] AC 514 (PC).
[64]   Law Commission (n 18) 1.70.
[65]   P Birks, 'Inconsistency between Compensation and Restitution' (1996) 112 *LQR* 375-378, 378.

similar approach characterises some academic analysis as well. Edelman, for instance, argues that compensatory, 'restitutionary' and 'disgorgement' awards cannot be obtained together. Examining the main responses of the law of damages, he observes: '[t]he highest in quantum of all of these remedies operates to serve the purposes of the others'.[66] As regards compensation and his disgorgement damages, Edelman's point is that '[t]he inconsistency arises from the fact that the higher of the two awards *in its effect* fulfils the purpose of the other award.'[67] For Edelman, this overlapping of effects is possible because 'each remedy *incidentally* performs the functions of the other remedies. To the extent that all damages remedies involve a subtraction from the wealth of the defendant, they are all punitive and all operate to deter.'[68] In the previous chapter, I have proposed an account of restitution for wrongs which shows the weaknesses of this approach from a normative perspective. But even from the viewpoint of legal analysis is such position untenable. The first spontaneous objection is that, if deterrence is linked to a subtraction from the wealth of the defendant, even nominal damages would have a deterrent and punitive function. Brought to its extreme conclusions, the last statement quoted implies that all responses eventually achieve the same result, albeit incidentally. Edelman accepts first that compensatory, 'restitutionary', 'disgorgement' and exemplary damages – to which one should add at least nominal damages– have a primary aim. Then he identifies a secondary aim. Finally, he reverses the relationship between primary and secondary aim: it is the secondary aim which determines the status of a legal response and its consistency with other legal responses. In reality, a mild form of deterrence is common to all responses of the law of damages – not only to those identified by Edelman. But this form of deterrence has nothing in common with the aim realised by the response. Edelman's reversion of the relationship between primary and secondary aim is irreconcilable with the principles of the law of obligations. Each response has one, and only one aim. Other, secondary aims do not realise the legal goals of the response according to the law of damages. Birks' objection mentioned above clarifies my point. Let me give you an example.

Victim V is a famous actress who has an intimate relationship with wrongdoer A. Once V and A split up, A agrees to write an article for a magazine describing his love story with V. The article falsely portrays V as a reckless and weird woman. The publication of the story secures A a gain of £1000. It also gives a new impulse to V's waning career. V is extremely glad of this development, has suffered no patrimonial loss and no negative feelings affect her health. If restitutionary damages were awarded, V would improve her financial situation by £1000.

We change the example a little, assuming that the publication of the article is a further blow to V's popularity, so that she loses a contract worth £1000.

---

[66]   *Edelman,* 246.
[67]   *Ibid* 248 n 18. Emphasis in the original.
[68]   *Ibid* 246. Italics in the original text. The remedies mentioned by Edelman are 'restitutionary', 'disgorgement', and exemplary damages.

According to the opinion which I reject,[69] V must here choose between compensation and restitution, so that she will not be able to obtain £2000 from A, but only £1000. In both variations of the case, A will get exactly the same sum of money although the situations are quite different. The similar treatment of different situations does not seem a result to which the legal system should aspire.

There are no objections of principle to a full level of compatibility between restitution and compensation. Staying with the Commission example, in the absence of external causes like contributory negligence, a reduction of compensation to £1000 has no sound theoretical basis. It is no explanation to qualify the other £1000 as restitution. Equally, there is no good reason for excluding restitution *in toto* when the £2000 is seen as a purely compensatory measure. The reduction of compensation or the alternative exclusion of restitution is not based upon any objective legal criterion. Either description would not circumvent the fact that the agent is able to keep the gain accruing to him from the wrong.

It is in my view arguable that the Commission's proposal has the judicial support to which the Report refers. The *Tang Man Sit* case,[70] for example, does not compel the conclusion suggested by the Law Commission. The parties had agreed to build jointly houses on a plot of land. On completion of the project, the defendant rented out all the houses in breach of a deed in which it bound itself to give a certain number of those houses to the claimant. One relevant issue concerned the compatibility of an account of the defendant's profits for breach of fiduciary duty with compensation for the loss of use and occupation. Lord Nicholls said:

> [T]here is an inconsistency between an account of profits, whereby for better or worse a plaintiff takes the money the defendant received from the use he made of the property, and an award of damages, representing the financial return the plaintiff would have received for the same period had he been able to use the property.[71]

Unlike the Law Commission, I do not infer from this passage that restitution and compensation are inconsistent. In chapter five, I analysed the account of profits for breach of fiduciary duty and came to the conclusion that different constructions are possible. The construction preferred in *Tang Man Sit* applies proprietary language. The use of this terminology indicates that the account of profits targets the loss of the victim, so that it must be alternative to other forms of quantification of the loss, not of the gain.[72] Therefore, the inconsistency mentioned by Lord Nicholls follows from the determination of the loss, rather than from the different aims of two legal responses.

---

[69]   This opinion enjoys good support among academic writers. See for instance D Friedmann, 'Restitution for Wrongs: The Measure of Recovery' (2001) 79 *Texas Law Review* 1879-1925, 1880-1882.

[70]   *Tang Man Sit v Capacious Investments Ltd* (n 64).

[71]   *Ibid* 520.

[72]   Ch 5, I A i.

My interpretation can draw support from a dictum by Lord Nicholls in *Kuwait Airways Corp v Iran Airways Co,*[73] His Lordship, analysing the damages available for conversion, said:

> But the wrongdoer may well have benefited from his temporary use of the owner's goods. It would not be right that he should be able to keep this benefit. The court may order him to pay damages assessed by reference to the value of the benefit he derived from his wrongdoing … In an appropriate case the court may award damages on this 'user principle' in addition to compensation for loss suffered. For instance, if the goods are returned damaged, the court may award damages assessed by reference to the benefit obtained by the wrongdoer as well as the cost of repair.[74]

Lord Nicholls refers expressly to the type of damages which were awarded in *A-G v Blake.*[75] There is little doubt that he is considering an award of restitutionary damages 'in addition' to what he considers the normal measure of damages, that is compensation.

X   The Neutrality of Restitution for Wrongs

If restitutionary damages are to be recognised, they ought to be recognised *in toto.* The fundamental question faced by the legal system concerns recognition or rejection. This is the core issue in the debate on restitution for wrongs. If restitutionary damages are accepted, their impact upon the system can be assessed on the different basis of policy considerations or of contrasting legal principles. This is not different from what happens in matters of compensation. Among all possible losses, the law distinguishes the compensable losses through the application of various legal tools such as causation and proximity. Similarly, among all possible gains, the law should develop the criteria to distinguish those gains which should be transferred to the victim. These legal tools do not question the existence of restitution, as they do not question the existence of compensation. Rather, they delimit the expansion of the application radius of the response.

This parallel between restitution and compensation is appropriate. Restitutionary damages mirror compensatory damages. Whereas the latter aim to place the victim in the same position in which he would be had the damaging event never occurred, restitutionary damages aim to place the agent in the same position in which the agent would be had the damaging event never occurred. From this point of view, restitution for wrongs has the same kind of neutral function which characterises compensation for wrongs: the agent is not worse off after the restitutionary transfer of wealth to the victim just as the victim is not better off after the compensatory transfer of wealth. Ideally, the victim ought to be in a position of neutrality as regards the choice between the position in which

---

[73]   *Kuwait Airways Corpn v Iran Airways Co (Nos 4 and 5)* [2002] 2 AC 883 (HL).
[74]   *Ibid* 1238.
[75]   *A-G v Blake* [2001] 1 AC 268, 278-280.

he was before the damaging event and the position in which he was after compensation. The agent ought to be in a position of neutrality before the same choice as regards restitution.

XI The *A Fortiori* Argument

The a fortiori argument has enjoyed wide consensus in the studies on restitutionary damages. It is often stated that, when the law allows punitive awards for wrongs, it must pave the way to restitutionary awards as well, for the latter are comprised in the former. This argument implies that punishment and restitution are distinguished by the magnitude of the award, rather than by the aim and the taxonomy which is behind the award itself. Authoritative statements both in the literature and from the judiciary support this point. Birks, for example, relies strongly on the a fortiori argument, applying the punitive reasoning in *Rookes v Barnard*[76] to restitution for wrongs. The Law Commission individuates a solid link between exemplary and restitutionary damages, which, if severed, in the Commission's view would lead to unacceptable results.[77] Lord Diplock in *Broome v Cassell*[78] saw in exemplary damages a function of prevention of unjust enrichment. Peter Jaffey considers that there are good reasons to explain why 'sometimes' restitution and punishment should be kept separated, whereas generally 'punishment encompasses disgorgement'.[79]

Mark Gergen has recently observed that '[g]enerally, a tort ought to be remedied through disgorgement only when it merits punishment'.[80] Gergen argues that it is possible to provide a utilitarian account of restitution for wrongs. This account would justify restitutionary damages as a deterrent in the way of punitive damages.[81] In his view,

> [u]nder the heading of restitution for wrongs, disgorgement is usually a remedy to punish wrongs and vindicate rights that exist and are enforced outside of the law of Restitution.[82]

The first function of restitution for wrongs, punishment, corresponds to the utilitarian approach. The second function, vindication, refers to non-utilitarian approaches like Weinrib's analysis of restitutionary damages. In this way, Gergen covers both the utilitarian and the non-utilitarian side and provides a clear-cut theory. The term 'usually' in the above quote is an indicator that not all constellations fit in this classification. Gergen acknowledges that there are cases of

---

[76] *Rookes* (n 4).
[77] See n 23.
[78] *Broome v Cassell* [1972] AC 1027. See ch 1, n 34.
[79] Jaffey (n 53) 375.
[80] MP Gergen 'What Renders Enrichment Unjust?' in (2001) 79 *Texas Law Review* 1927-1980, 1937.
[81] *Ibid* 1934.
[82] *Ibid* 1935.

breach of contract which do not deserve the 'punitive sanction of disgorgement'; and yet restitutionary damages are awarded. Therefore, the author concludes, a utilitarian explanation alone does not support a satisfactory theory of restitution for wrongs: such cases of restitution for wrongs depend 'on a moralistic view of breach of contract that no longer holds, if it ever did.'[83] Consequently, '[a]n unfortunate consequence of the denial of the moralistic view of breach is that we are without the conceptual tools to talk intelligently about these cases'.[84]

Gergen emphasises the fact that a utilitarian explanation alone fails to give a complete account of restitution for wrongs. He observes that a moral approach is necessary to be able to consider all different legal facets of restitutionary damages. Yet, he seems to think that the utilitarian explanation in terms of punishment holds true for the majority of the cases. If his thought has been correctly understood, this view is not completely convincing. From the perspective of legal theory, Gergen himself admits that the utilitarian theory can provide only a partial explanation. Indeed, he has to resort to non-utilitarian accounts to be able to cover a large area of application of restitution for wrongs. From the perspective of legal history, an explanation of restitutionary damages as having punitive content is simply incorrect. The historical evolution of this institution can be traced back to Roman law, which recognised *in primis* punishment and compensation for wrongs, leaving to restitution for wrongs only a niche, quite distinct from punishment for wrongs. From the perspective of legal taxonomy, an identification of punishment and restitution, with the latter being a mild variation of the former, is not sustainable. Restitution preserves the same function wherever it finds application: it compels one party to give up his enrichment to another party. This applies to wrongs, unjust enrichments, proprietary rights, and every other event or structure which triggers restitution.

The a fortiori argument must be rejected because it is simply wrong. My historical analysis has shown the truly independent origins of the two responses. Their theoretical underpinnings are very different. And even the subject-matter of the two claims cannot be compared, given that exemplary damages do not have that function of neutralisation which is typical of compensation and restitution. To link restitutionary damages to exemplary damages would prevent a full understanding of the nature and of the structure of restitution for wrongs.

XII   Conclusions

The want of coherence of some judicial constructions is not without some responsibility for the problems affecting most descriptive classifications of restitution for wrongs, as the studies by Birks and Jackman demonstrate. Yet, even more radical contributions on the judicial thought, like the one by Edelman, are

---

[83]   *Ibid* 1938.
[84]   *Ibid.*

not satisfactory because of their insufficient theoretical analysis. To comprehend the foundations of restitution for wrongs, I have extended my research beyond legal analysis to cover legal history, legal comparison, and philosophy. Its outcome indicates that restitution for wrongs is consistent with the existing structures of the law of damages in all jurisdictions under comparison. The mechanism of restitution mirrors the mechanism of compensation, although the former targets the agent of the wrong and the latter the victim. Restitution, like compensation, neutralises some aspects of the wrong: placed in front of a choice between the situation in which the agent was before the wrong was perpetrated and after restitution has been performed, the agent should be indifferent. This position of neutrality distinguishes restitution from punishment, which aims to place the agent in a worse status than the pre-wrong position.

What differentiates restitution from compensation is the relationship of each award with the victim's loss. Whenever the agent's gain is directly and necessarily connected with this loss, the response is compensatory, not restitutionary. Thus, the fact that I am enriched of the value of the book which I have wrongfully subtracted to you does not mean that you can claim restitution for wrongs. My gain is dependent on your loss and you can only eliminate my gain by compelling me to nullify your loss. But if I enrich myself by wrongfully enticing you to invest your money in my sinking business, mere compensation does not eliminate that part of my gain which is independent of your loss. In this case, a restitutionary award alone allows you to reach my gain.

A fundamental misunderstanding of the relationship between compensation and restitution is the cause of the taxonomical mistake which affects many studies. This mistake, which has its root in the application of the restitutionary model of unjust enrichment to the law of wrongs, is particularly evident in Edelman's analysis, where a measure of compensatory damages is treated as an instance of 'restitutionary' damages. Such model is, in its essence, a proprietary institution. The claimant seeks to restore the integrity of a proprietary interest which has been violated by the wrongdoer. When transferred into the context of the law of wrongs, this structure corresponds to compensation, not restitution. The existence of a proprietary bond indicates that the victim claims back a benefit which belongs to the victim and has been taken by the agent. This is not restitutionary reasoning.

10

Final Observations

I The Outcome of the Research

THE LAW COMMISSION describes restitutionary damages as the legal response which aims to strip the defendant of ill-gotten gains. Yet, this formula is of little avail for the understanding of their nature and function. I have tried to demonstrate that the concept at issue has been the object of terminological and classificatory misuse, for some awards regarded as restitutionary in reality have a compensatory function. Proprietary wrongs offer a clear instance of these pseudo-restitutionary damages. You have a beautiful villa with swimming pool. When you go on holiday for two weeks, you leave a set of spare keys with me, so that I can feed the dog. During this period, I organise lavish parties on your premises. The beautiful setting allows me to charge my guests and I am significantly better off once you are back than I was before, even considering the money I spent to restore the villa to pristine condition. I might even have made some improvements in the villa. Let us say that I had the leak in the pool repaired. Hence, once you come back, you are apparently in a better position than when you left.

Considering the alternatives before you, a reasonable answer to your legitimate dissatisfaction with my wrongful behaviour might be seen – and indeed, it has been seen by many academics – in an award of restitutionary damages: my conduct apparently caused no loss to you and I have obtained a benefit. However, if the court follows this avenue, it does not award restitution, but compensation. My gain is the consequence of the violation of your proprietary interest. With your claim, you are saying: 'The benefit which you obtained is mine!' But if the benefit is yours and I appropriated something which belongs to you, then your claim is for compensation, not for restitution. Your point is that the wealth which came to me should have stayed with you. Ernest Weinrib illustrates the idea behind your claim by observing that 'the potential for gain is an incident of the right that the wrongdoer violated.'[1] Clearly, this is no traditional compensatory award, for my loss is measured by your gain. But this particular method of

---

[1] Weinrib, *Restitutionary Damages* 37.

quantification does not affect the nature of the response, which remains compensatory. This line of reasoning has long been applied by the German judiciary[2] in cases of violations of intellectual property rights.

The influence of Aristotelian analysis can partly explain the reason why this award is not immediately recognised as compensatory. Aristotelian justice aims to obtain a balance between the more and the less. Aristotle made clear that the agent's gain does not necessarily have to be material: if I do not like you, wrongfully take your bicycle and damage it, you have a material loss, but I have only the satisfaction of seeing you in pain. What Aristotle did not expressly elucidate was the opposite situation: my behaviour has not caused any material loss to you, but has secured a material gain to me. From a theoretical perspective, there seems to be no ground to exclude that your loss, even if not material, has normative substance. From the perspective of legal analysis, however, the absence of a loss does not fit in the German model of the *Differenzhypothese*, according to which the damage is given by the difference in the assets of the victim between the pre-wrong and the post-remedy situation. A local variation of this model has been substantially accepted in England and Italy too.

For the court to award restitutionary damages, the wrongdoer's benefit must be independent of any loss, however measured, sustained by the claimant. The victim's claim will be: 'You benefited from a wrong against me and I want your benefit!' In this case, the wrongdoer does not retransfer to the victim what belonged to the victim in the first place because of some connection with the victim's violated right. Rather, the agent gives up to the victim the benefit obtained through the wrong – a benefit which would have neither gone nor belonged to the victim without the agent's intervention. I am aware that my position in the legal case against you is precarious. Losing the case would cost me a fortune. I bribe the judge to decide in my favour. If, as a consequence of my wrongful action, I win the case, I have caused a wrongful loss to you and you will have a compensatory claim against me. You might have a compensatory claim against the judge, but this is irrelevant to the present argument. Your compensatory claim cannot target the bribe obtained by the judge. Let us say for argument's sake that you bring the compensatory action against me and win. At this point, with no further actionable loss, you claim against the judge for restitution of his gain. There is no link between you and the gain beyond the fact that the gain is a consequence of the wrong of which you were the victim. If the court thinks that you, and not the bribed judge or any other wrongdoer, should obtain the sum which I paid to the judge, the court is awarding restitutionary damages.

This situation exemplifies the structure of restitution for wrongs. The benefit obtained by the wrongdoer qua agent of the wrong is awarded to the victim purely because the latter was on the weaker side of the wrongful relationship, not because the victim has been deprived of a patrimonial interest. The court weighs

---

[2]   Eg (1972) BGHZ 57 116, 118.

the position of the agent and the position of the victim and deems the latter to be more deserving than the former. Thus, behind the concept of restitution there is an evaluation of merit. The decision on the more deserving person to obtain the award between claimant and defendant is taken on the basis of the old Pomponian principle according to which 'it is just according to natural law that nobody become richer to the detriment and by the injury of another'.[3] In the context of restitution for wrongs, the concept of 'detriment of another' is construed in a loose sense. It refers to the idea that the claimant is the victim, that is the sufferer, of a wrong and that the defendant is the cause of the sufferance and has profited from the wrong. Once it is established that there is a relationship which links agent and victim to the wrong, it is just that the benefit goes to the person who has not perpetrated the wrong, instead of the person who is responsible for it.

Although compensation and restitution rest upon different principles, their legal structures mirror each other. Compensation places the victim in the pre-wrong position, whereas restitution places the agent in the pre-wrong position. The two structures are specular, a feature which characterises only compensation and restitution. For example, restitution and punishment are not similar from this perspective. The latter does not aim to place the agent in a pre-wrong position. The idea behind it is rather that the agent must be worse off after the punitive award than he was before the damaging event took place. This distinction is so fundamental that any description of restitution which applies punitive reasoning – the a fortiori argument – cannot reflect the nature of the two responses.

If restitution mirrors compensation, then it should be awarded whenever compensation is available to the claimant. No legal principle can justify the exclusion of restitution whilst at the same time accepting compensation. Still, the practical use of the two responses might well diverge. A legal system could recognise compensation and not restitution, or restitution only as an exceptional remedy. The basis for setting such boundaries, however, would have to be searched for in policy considerations, rather than in legal principle.

II The Chosen Avenue

The aforementioned conclusions follow from a wide-spectrum analysis. They are the result of a study which has combined legal comparison and legal theory. The German, the Italian, and the Roman legal systems have contributed to cast light upon the English law of damages. The comparison seems to suggest that the later recognition of the law of unjust enrichment in English law in comparison with civil law systems might have played a significant role in the shaping of restitution for wrongs in English law, which has been developed earlier than in the two other

---

[3] D 50. 17. 206 (Pomp): 'Iure naturae aequum est neminem cum alterius detrimento et iniuria fieri locupletiorem'.

jurisdictions. On the other hand, it has been demonstrated that even the more sophisticated systems of unjust enrichment do not normally provide an adequate answer to issues addressed by a restitutionary award for wrongs, so that even in such systems restitution for wrongs would close a gap, rather than simply increase the available legal tools.

The investigation of philosophy and legal theory has challenged the notion that legal responses for wrongs should only be compensatory. In fact, a Scholastic interpretation of the Aristotelian theory of justice which reads 'restitution' mainly as 'giving back' is likely to have played a major role in consolidating the pre-eminent position attributed to compensation by many studies on the theory of the law of damages. However, no Aristotelian tenet points to an exclusion of restitutionary damages.

I have dedicated much attention not only to the analysis of the results of my research, but also to the avenue which has paved the way to their attainment. To give an instance, in my opinion it is necessary to know the basic tenets of the Aristotelian theory of justice to be able to assess its relevance for restitution for wrongs and to counteract those accounts which link the victim's 'pain' to a patrimonial reduction. Similarly, to conclude that historical accidents have contributed to transform compensation into the main response of the law of damages, I had to show first that Roman law abandoned punishment for civil wrongs when the State took control of the criminal trial and that Aristotelian reasoning reached the modern courts of law through a series of passages which have sidelined non-compensatory responses.

III   Law of Obligations and Restitution for Wrongs

I have examined restitutionary damages on the basis of the premise that they need to be placed within the general context of the Roman partition of the law of obligations. This area of law is divided at least into the three main pillars of contract, tort/delict, and unjust enrichment. The difference between restitution for wrongs and restitution for unjust enrichment is not always clear. These legal responses might have some points of contact, but still remain different and independent remedies. Unjust enrichment does not require the perpetration of a wrong for its activation. The restitutionary response for unjust enrichment is the consequence of a transfer of wealth which normally – but there are important exceptions – is not sustained by an adequate cause. If I mistakenly transfer to you a sum of money which exceeds my debt, I shall be entitled to restitution for unjust enrichment even if your conduct was not wrongful. My claim rests upon the violation of my property interest in the sum of money which I erroneously transferred to you. By contrast, restitution for wrongs is a response to a wrongful behaviour of the agent which considers only the agent's gain, without any connection to the violation of a proprietary interest of the claimant. For this reason, the previous example of the mistaken overpayment cannot be solved through a restitutionary award for wrongs.

Part of the confusion is due to the fact that restitution for wrongs and restitution for unjust enrichment share the definition of restitution as a common element. In both cases, restitution is the legal response which consists in causing one person to give up to another a benefit received at his expense or its value in money. Thus, it is not the definition of restitution which is crucial, but rather what the claim is trying to achieve. The goal of restitution for wrongs is the deprivation of a benefit which is unrelated to the claimant's loss, whereas restitution for unjust enrichment affects a benefit which finds its justification in a patrimonial loss suffered the claimant. The aim of a claim for unjust enrichment is, therefore, often akin to compensation.

IV   The Comparative Perspective

Unlike English law, German and Italian law do not have the concept of a wrong. This has not been a problem for the legal comparison. It has been possible to work out a common definition of wrong which fits in all three jurisdictions considered. In the terminology of my research, a wrong is a breach of duty. It comprises torts, equitable wrongs, delicts, and breach of contract. On this basis, the comparative analysis has covered areas which, from civil law perspective, would be subject to a different classification.

The resistance to restitution for wrongs, or, more generally, the bias against non-compensatory awards, is a characteristic shared by all systems under comparison. The general view of the English judiciary on the law of compensation was stated by Lord Blackburn in his famous dictum in the *Livingstone* case:

> [W]here any injury is to be compensated by damages, in settling the sum of money to be given for reparation of damages you should as nearly as possible get at the sum of money which will put the party who has been injured, or has suffered, in the same position as he would have been in if he had not sustained the wrong for which he is now getting his compensation or reparation.[4]

This view was long considered as referring to the whole law of damages, as the definition of damages in *Cassell v Broome*[5] shows, according to which – one hundred years later – damages are still the pecuniary compensation for a wrong.[6] Only recently, English law has started to recognise that compensation is the main, but not the only legal response.[7] German law and Italian law follow a similar pattern. They both rely on the *Differenzhypothese*, which establishes that damages

[4]   *Livingstone v The Rawyards Coal Co* (1880) 5AC 25 (HL). But *Edelman*, 8-9, has convincingly argued that the decision in point did not close the doors to non-compensatory damages.
[5]   *Cassell & Co Ltd v Broome* [1972] AC 1027 (HL) 1070 (per Lord Hailsham).
[6]   *McGregor on Damages* (16th edn) para 1.
[7]   See the 17th edition of *McGregor on Damages*, para 12-002.

are the difference of the victim's assets between the pre-wrong and the post-remedy position. These formulae are principled, yet draw on policy considerations. The liability of the wrongdoer cannot be extended indefinitely. According to the 19th century doctrines, the boundary of liability was to be seen in the loss of the victim. However, there seems to be no reason why such boundaries could not have changed in the course of time, particularly given that an incompatibility of restitution for wrongs with the law of obligations could not be ascertained in this study. Any argument which excludes restitution because compensatory damages concern only compensation is caught in a vicious circle. The law of damages is not to be identified with the law of compensation, as the analysis of Roman law has shown. It does not appear that English, German or Italian law contains any unequivocal ban on restitutionary damages.

The legal comparison has mainly addressed the question of the level of integration of restitution for wrongs within the law of damages of the three jurisdictions. The positive identification of restitutionary structures for wrongs would provide a solid argument in favour of a high level of integration. One of the risks involved in this phase of the research was to be sidetracked by awards which seem restitutionary, but are compensatory. Intellectual property wrongs, for instance, tend to trigger a response which seizes the profit obtained through the violation. Thus, if I get hold wrongfully of the original plans of your new computing machine and brand it as mine, all three legal systems offer you a claim to get hold of my benefit. In Italy, this claim is exclusively for my unjust enrichment, but in England and Germany it can be based upon my wrong. The measure of the award is given by my profit. From this perspective, it could be said that the award is restitutionary. The German judiciary rejects this argument and states that it is only a different measure of compensation,[8] which is required by the peculiar nature of intellectual property wrongs. This interpretation is correct, for the claim is triggered by the violation of a proprietary interest, which means that the claimant is only seeking to obtain what is his.

On the other hand, the comparison has revealed that German law already applies a limited version of restitutionary damages through its *stellvertretendes Commodum* under para 285 (1) BGB. If I bind myself to sell my plot of land to you, but I sell it to a third party for a higher price, according to German law you do not have any proprietary interest which you can use to claim the plot back from the third party. You will be able to sue me but only up to the level of your loss. Yet, using the *stellvertretendes Commodum* you will also be able to compel me give up the profit which I obtained through my wrongful behaviour. This is a case of restitution for wrongs. However, this claim does not have the wide spectrum of application which the full recognition of restitutionary damages would imply. It could not be used, for example, if you and I contractually agreed on the registration of a right of passage on my land in your favour and I did not

---

[8]   (1993) BGHZ 119, 20 (*Tchibo/Rolex II* case).

register your right. If I sold the land at a higher price because there is no registered right of passage, you would have no action against me under para 285 (1) BGB.

In Germany, the idea of restitutionary damages is mainly an academic topic. In Italy, it is simply unknown. The different level of diffusion is partially explicable on the basis of the wider role which unjust enrichment plays in civil law systems and of the existence of mechanisms which are restitutionary for wrongs in the substance, but not in the name. It should be pointed out, however, that the expansion of this institution in English law is less advanced than academic discussion might indicate. *Attorney-General v Blake*[9] is a groundbreaking case because it changes the legal terminology by introducing a new legal concept. Yet, the judiciary has been busier restricting its impact than expanding its rationale. The limited availability of this response has been confirmed in many cases, such as *Experience Hendrix*.[10] This decision is particularly significant not only because it applies the *Blake* approach, but also because it rejects any attempt of expansion, such as the avenue proposed by the judiciary in *Esso v Niad*.[11] Notwithstanding the restrictive interpretation of the English courts and the modest success of the law of unjust enrichment in civil law as a substitute of restitution for wrongs, it cannot be denied that restitution for wrongs is recognised and applied in England, and not recognised or not applied in civil law. Even if, owing to the reasons given, the difference between common law and civil law is not as deep as the terminology indicates, still there is a difference, which guarantees English law more flexibility in the law of wrongs than its civilian counterparts. The English law of wrongs is more flexible because it can intervene in relation to broader spectrum of damages than civil law.

V   The Historical Perspective

Roman law has provided significant material of comparison. The analysis has shown that the often asserted identification of the law of damages with the principle of compensation is in reality unprincipled. In fact, classic Roman law was for a long time mainly punitive. Furthermore, there are some signals that the Roman law of wrongs might have allowed restitutionary awards to a limited extent. The primarily punitive character of the law of damages and the – arguable – presence of at least one instance of restitution for wrongs are important contributions to the understanding of modern legal systems. They corroborate the conclusion according to which there is no objection of legalistic nature to the adoption of restitutionary damages in the law of obligations. They also demonstrate that restitution for wrongs has a tradition which dates back to classical Roman law.

---

[9]   *A-G v Blake* [2001] 1 AC 268 (HL).
[10]   *Experience Hendrix LLC v PPX Enterprises Inc and E Chalpin* [2003] EWCA Civ 323 (CA).
[11]   *Esso Petroleum v Niad* (2001) WL 1476190.

The different origin and role played by punishment and restitution in Roman law confute the view according to which restitution finds application whenever punishment is available. Punishment and restitution have always been separate entities, with different requirements and different areas of application. There is no indication that any a fortiori argument has ever taken root in Roman law. Even the quantification of the damages is fundamentally different: the measure of punishment reflects the seriousness of the wrong, whereas the measure of restitution is established on the basis of the wrongdoer's enrichment. To the pragmatic Roman mentality the two responses were likely to share no common element.

The Roman structure of civil dispute resolution originally left the State out of the trial. The proceedings were exclusively dealt with by and between private parties. Damages were punitive, compensatory, and – maybe – restitutionary. In the context of the administrative centralisation which characterised the imperial period, the civil trial had to change if the State wanted to secure itself a larger degree of control over society. The transfer from a private to a State-controlled trial was smoothed by the adoption of the *cognito extra ordinem*, where for the first time a magistrate, and not a layman, presided the proceedings. The more traditional form of a private trial survived, but was limited to civil disputes which did not involve punishment. As a consequence of the State intromission into private matters, therefore, punishment fell exclusively into the public sphere, whereas compensation remained within the private sphere. This latter form of adjudication contains the seed of the modern civil trial, in which primarily compensation is awarded.

VI   The Philosophical Perspective

The theoretical analysis has integrated the historical data with a further element which is central to the understanding of the predominance of compensation at the expense of the non-compensatory responses: the success of the Aristotelian account of justice. The Thomistic interpretation of this account was extensively accepted by the Spanish moral theologians. The interest developed by the latter in legal questions accelerated the transfer from theology to law. The work of the *scholastici* played a major role in stimulating the interpretation of restitution as 'giving back' which has enjoyed great success in modern studies. This Scholastic interpretation might contribute to explain the difficulties encountered by theorists such as Weinrib and Coleman in their attempts to bring restitution under the roof of corrective justice. To be able to incorporate restitutionary damages within corrective justice, Weinrib must include within the restitution-yielding wrongs only those wrongful events which cause a proprietary loss to the victim. As has been seen, the ensuing awards seem restitutionary, but in reality they are compensatory.

In the face of those philosophical theories which place restitution for wrongs outside corrective justice, of which Coleman's 'restitutionary justice' is an excellent instance, I argue that restitutionary damages can be construed as corrective justice. I have proposed an account which establishes the parties as doer and sufferer of an injustice using, as Aristotle did, the concepts of gain and loss as having metaphorical value, for 'gain' can also be the feeling of satisfaction for having committed the wrong. Similarly, in my interpretation 'loss' can be a detriment of non-patrimonial nature. A detriment is a wrongful event which causes pain to the victim. Restitution for wrongs is justified by the principle which prohibits any enrichment through wrongdoing. The victim has a claim for restitution because the victim is more deserving than the wrongdoer and if the victim did not obtain the benefit nobody else would, given that the relationship created by the wrong involves only doer and sufferer.

The difficulties which trouble legal theory can be perceived even at the level of legal analysis. The latter struggles to identify those elements which qualify restitutionary damages as a legal response. The explanations which I have considered suffer two kinds of difficulties. Some authors, like Birks and Jackman, provide a descriptive account of the law. An obstacle to their analysis is the limited support which statutes and judiciary offer to their theories of restitution for wrongs. Thus, Birks falls into the trap of the a fortiori reasoning, justifying restitution where punishment can be awarded. Similarly, his test which distinguishes duties designed to prevent enrichment from non-restitution-yielding duties is not able to explain some important exceptions. Jackman's account has the added problem of lacking a satisfactory theoretical structure. Other theories, notably Edelman's approach, propound constructions which do not take the classification of the law of obligations into due consideration. This inconsistency invalidates their investigation from the outset. Edelman concurs with Weinrib and his construction is affected by the same problem: both authors classify as 'restitutionary damages' legal responses which in reality realise a compensatory aim.

That legal analysis has not managed to capture the nature of restitutionary damages should not surprise. Legal philosophy has not yet provided the necessary background structure to understand restitution for wrongs. Consequently, any attempt to identify the characteristics of restitutionary damages can rely only on the legal context within which this legal response operates. An expansion of the philosophical studies in this area, the first signs of which are already in sight, will have positive repercussions both at normative and at taxonomical level.

Bibliography

Monographs

Ackrill, JL (ed and transl), *Aristotle's Ethics* (London, Faber 1973)

Astone, F, *L'arricchimento senza causa* (Milano, Giuffrè 1999)

von Bar, C, *Gemeineuropäisches Deliktsrecht* (München, Beck 1996) vol 1

von Bar, C, *The Common European Law of Torts* (Oxford, Clarendon 2000) vol I

Birks, PBH, *An Introduction to the Law of Restitution* (revised edn) (Oxford, Clarendon 1989)

— *Textbook on Roman Law* (2nd edn) (London, Blackstone 1997)

— *Unjust Enrichment* (2nd edn) (Oxford, OUP 2005)

Browne, RW, *The Nicomachean Ethics of Aristotle* (London, Henry Bohn 1850)

Buckland, WW, *The Roman Law of Slavery* (London, CUP 1908, repr 1970)

Buckland, WW, McNair, AD, Lawson, FH, *Roman Law and Common Law – A Comparison in Outline* (2nd edn) (Cambridge, CUP 1952)

Burrows, A, *The Law of Restitution* (2nd edn) (London, Butterworths 2002)

— *Remedies for Tort and Breach of Contract* (3rd edn) (Oxford, OUP 2004)

Bydlinski, F, *System und Prinzipien des Privatrechts* (Wien, Springer 1996)

Coing, H, *Grundzüge der Rechtsphilosophie* (2nd edn) (Berlin, de Gruyter 1969)

— *Europäisches Privatrecht, Bd I, Älteres Gemeines Recht (1500 bis 1800)* (München, Beck 1985)

— *Europäisches Privatrecht, Bd II 19. Jahrhundert* (München, Beck 1989)

Coleman, J, *Risks and Wrongs* (Cambridge, CUP 1992)

Crisp, R (ed and transl), *Aristotle, Nicomachean Ethics* (Cambridge, CUP 2000)

Davies, B, *The Thought of Thomas Aquinas* (Oxford, Clarendon 1992)

di Majo, A, *La tutela civile dei diritti* (2nd edn) (Milano, Giuffrè 1993)

Edelman, J, *Gain-Based Damages* (Oxford, Hart 2002)

England, I, *The Philosophy of Tort Law* (Aldershot, Dartmouth 1993)

Esser, J, *Grundlagen und Entwicklung der Gefährdungshaftung* (2nd edn) (München, Beck 1969)

Finnis, J, *Aquinas* (OUP, Oxford 1998)

Fleming, JG, *The Law of Torts* (9th edn) (Sydney, Law Book Company 1998)

Goff, R and Jones, G, *The Law of Restitution* (6th edn) (London, Sweet & Maxwell 2002)

Gordley, J, *Foundations of Private Law* (Oxford, OUP 2006)

Grotius, H, *Le Droit de la Guerre et de la Paix* (J Barbeirac (trans), Amsterdam 1724)

Guarino, A, *Diritto privato romano* (12th edn) (Napoli, Jovene 2001)

Heuston, RFV and Buckley, RA, *Salmond and Heuston on the Law of Torts* (21st edn) (London, Sweet & Maxwell 1996)

Ibbetson, DJ, *A Historical Introduction to the Law of Obligations* (Oxford, OUP 1999)

Jaffa, JV, *Thomism and Aristotelianism* (Chicago, Univ of Chicago Press 1952)

Jaffey, P, *The Nature and the Scope of Restitution* (Oxford, Hart 2000)

Jhering, R von: *Abhandlungen aus dem römischen Recht* (Leipzig 1844, repr Aalen, Scientia 1981)

Kaser, M, *Das römische Privatrecht, 1. Abschnitt, Das Altrömische, das Vorklassische und das Klassiche Recht* (2nd edn) (München, Beck 1971)

— *Das römische Privatrecht, 2. Abschnitt, Die Nachklassischen Entwiklungen* (2nd edn) (München, Beck 1975)

Knowles, D, *The Evolution of Medieval Thought* (Luscombe and Brooke (eds), 2nd edn) (London, Longman 1988)

Lange, H, *Schadensersatz und Privatstrafe in der mittelalterlichen Rechtstheorie* (Münster/Köln, Böhlau 1955)

— *Schadensersatz* (2nd edn) (Tübingen, Mohr 1990) vol I

Larenz, K, *Lehrbuch des Schuldrechts, Band 1, Allgemeiner Teil* (14th edn) (München, Beck 1987)

Larenz, K and Canaris, C-W, *Lehrbuch des Schuldrechts. Band 2: Besonderer Teil, Halbband 2* (13th edn) (München, Beck 1994)

Liebs, D, *Die Klagenkonkurrenz im römischen Recht* (Göttingen, Vandenhoeck Ruprecht 1972)

Longo, G, *Contributi alla dottrina del dolo* (Padova, Cedam 1937)

McGregor, H, *McGregor on Damages* (17th edn) (London, Sweet & Maxwell 2003)

Meyer, H, *Ersatz und Erlösherausgabe* (Köln, Heymann 1999)

Moffat, G, *Trust Law – Text and Materials* (3rd edn) (London, Butterworths 1999)

Mommsen, F, *Beiträge zum Obligationsrecht II, Zur Lehre von dem Interesse* (Braunschweig, Schwetschke 1855)

Nicholas, B, *An Introduction to Roman Law* (Oxford, Clarendon 1962)

Nilstun, T, *Aristotle on Freedom and Punishment* (Lund, Studentlitteratur 1981)

Otte, G, *Das Privatrecht bei Francisco de Vitoria* (Köln/Graz, Böhlau 1964)

Pacchioni, G, *Elementi di diritto civile* (3rd edn) (Torino, UTET 1926)

Pernice, A, *Labeo* (2nd edn) (Halle, Niemeyer 1900) vol 2, abt 2.1

Pugliese, G, *Istituzioni di diritto romano* (Padova, Piccin 1985)

Reuter, D and Martinek, M, *Ungerechtfertigte Bereicherung* (Tübingen, Mohr 1983)

Rogers WVH, *Winfield and Jolowicz on Tort* (16th edn) (London, Sweet & Maxwell 2002)

Schlechtriem, P, *Schuldrecht Besonderer Teil* (6th edn) (Tübingen, Mohr 2003)

Schulz, F, *History of Roman Legal Science* (Oxford, Clarendon 1946)

Soto, D, *De Iustitia et Iure* (Antwerp 1567)

Stewart, JA, *Notes on the Nicomachean Ethics* (Oxford, OUP 1892) vol I

Stoll, H, *Haftungsfolgen im bürgerlichen Recht* (Müller, Heidelberg 1993)

Talamanca, M, *Istituzioni di diritto romano* (Milano, Giuffrè 1990)

Tettenborn, AM, *Law of Restitution in England and Ireland* (2nd edn) (London, Cavendish 1996)

Tettenborn AM (ed), *The Law of Damages* (London, LexisNexis UK 2003)

St Thomas Aquinas, *Summa Theologiae,* Blackfriars (ed) (London 1963)

—— *Commentary on Aristotle's Nicomachean Ethics* (CI Litzinger (trans), USA, Notre Dame 1993)

Thomas, JAC, *Textbook of Roman Law* (Amsterdam, North-Holland 1976)

Virgo, G, *The Principles of the Law of Restitution* (2nd edn) (Oxford, OUP 2006)

Vitoria, F de, *De Iustitia* (RP Beltran de Heredia (ed), Madrid, Medinaceli 1934) vol I

Weinrib, E, *The Idea of Private Law* (Cambridge Mass and London, Harvard University Press 1995)

Wieling, HJ, *Interesse und Privatstrafe vom Mittelalter bis zum bürgerlichen Gesetzbuch* (Köln/Wien, Böhlau 1970)

Wilburg, W, *Die Lehre von der ungerechtfertigten Bereicherung nach österreichischem und deutschem Recht* (Graz, Leuschner und Lubensky 1934)

Winfield, PH, *The Province of the Law of Tort* (Cambridge, CUP 1931)

Zimmermann, R, *The Law of Obligations* (Oxford, Clarendon 1996)

Articles and Book Chapters

Aertsen, JA, 'Aquinas's philosophy in its historical setting' in Kretzmann N and Stump E (eds), *The Cambridge Companion to Aquinas* (Cambridge, CUP 1993) 12-37

Andrews, N, 'Civil Disgorgement of Gains: the Temptation to do justice', in WR Cornish, R Nolan and J O'Sullivan (eds), *Restitution Past, Present and Future, Essays in Honour of Gareth Jones* (Oxford, Hart 1998) 155-162

Ankum, H, 'Actions by which we claim a thing (res) and a penalty (poena) in classical Roman law' (1982) 24 *Bullettino dell'Istituto di Diritto Romano* 15-39

Assmann, HD, 'Schadensersatz in mehrfacher Höhe des Schadens' [1985] *Betriebs-Berater* 15-25

Baker, JH, 'The History of Quasi-Contract in English Law' in WR Cornish, R Nolan, J O'Sullivan, *Restitution Past, Present and Future, Essays in Honour of Gareth Jones* (Oxford, Hart 1998) 37-56

Birks, PBH, 'Civil Wrongs: A New World' in *Butterworth Lectures 1990-1991* (London, Butterworths 1992) 55-112

—— 'Profits of Breach of Contract' (1993) 109 *LQR*, 518-521

—— 'Equity in the Modern Law: an Exercise in Taxonomy' [1996] *University of Western Australia Law Review*, 1-99

— 'Inconsistency between Compensation and Restitution' (1996) 112 *LQR*, 135-138
— 'The Concept of a Civil Wrong' in D Owen (ed), *Philosophical Foundations of Tort Law* (Oxford, Clarendon 1997) 31-51
— 'Restitution for Wrongs' in EJH Schrage (ed), *Unjust Enrichment – The Comparative Legal History of the Law of Restitution* (2nd edn) (Berlin, Duncker & Humblot 1999) 171-195
— 'Unjust Enrichment and Wrongful Enrichment' (2001) 79 *Texas Law Review* 1767-1794
Burrows, A, 'Reforming Exemplary Damages: Expansion or Abolition?' in PBH Birks (ed), *Wrongs and remedies in the Twenty-First Century* (Oxford, Clarendon 1996) 153-173
— 'Quadrating Restitution and Unjust Enrichment: A Matter of Principle?' (2000) 8 *Restitution Law Review* 257-269
Campbell, D, 'The Treatment of *Teacher v Calder* in *AG v Blake*' (2002) 65 *MLR* 256-269
Campbell, D and Wylie, P, 'Ain't No Telling (Which Circumstances are Exceptional)' [2003] 62 *CLJ* 605-630
Canaris, C-W, 'Gewinnabschöpfung bei Verletzung des allgemein Persönlichkeitsrechts' in A-J Ahrens (ed), *Festschift für E Deutsch zum 70. Geburstag* (Köln, Heymann 1999) 85-109
Cane, P, 'Markets and Morals in Contract and Tort' (1993) 13 *Legal Studies* 396-415
— 'The Anatomy of Private Law Theory: A 25th Anniversary Essay' (2005) 25 *OJLS* 203-217
Castronovo, C, 'Il danno all'ambiente nel sistema di responsabilità civile' in *La nuova responsabilità civile* (2nd edn) (Milano, Giuffrè 1997) 333-347
Coing, H, 'Zum Einfluß der Philosophie des Aristoteles auf die Entwicklung des römischen Rechts' (1952) 69 *Savigny Zeitschrift, romanistische Abteilung* 24-59
Coleman, J, 'The Practice of Corrective Justice' in D Owen (ed), *Philosophical Foundations of Tort Law* (Oxford, Clarendon 1995) 53-72
Dagan, H, 'Restitutionary Damages for Breach of Contract: An Exercise in Private Law Theory' (2000) 1 *Theoretical Inquiries in Law* 115-154
Edelman, J, 'Gain-Based Damages and Compensation' in A Burrows and Lord Rodger (eds) *Mapping the Law* (Oxford, OUP 2006) 141-160
Farnsworth, EA, 'Your Loss or My Gain? The Dilemma of the Disgorgement Principle in Breach of Contract' (1985) 94 *Yale Law Journal* 1339-1393
Feenstra, R, 'Grotius' Doctrine of Unjust Enrichment as a Source of Obligation: its Origin and its Influence in Roman-Dutch Law' in EJH Schrage (ed), *Unjust Enrichment – The Comparative Legal History of the Law of Restitution* (2nd edn) (Berlin, Duncker & Humblot 1999) 197-236
Flume, W, 'Der Bereicherungsausgleich in Mehrpersonenverhältnissen' (1999) *Archiv für die civilistische Praxis* 199, 1-37

Fox, D, 'Restitutionary Damages to Deter Breach of Contract' (2000) 60 *CLJ* 33-35

Friedmann, D, 'Restitution for Wrongs: the Basis of Liability' in WR Cornish, R Nolan and J O'Sullivan (eds), *Restitution Past, Present and Future, Essays in Honour of Gareth Jones* (Oxford, Hart 1998) 133-154

— 'Restitution for Wrongs: The Measure of Recovery' (2001) 79 *Texas Law Review* 1879-1925

Gergen, MP, 'What Renders Enrichment Unjust?' in (2001) 79 *Texas Law Review* 1927-1980

Giglio, F, 'A Systematic Approach to "Unjust" and "Unjustified" Enrichment' (2003) 23 *OJLS* 455-482

Goodhart, W, 'Restitutionary Damages for Breach of Contract' [1995] *Restitution Law Review* 3-14

Gordley, J, 'Tort Law in the Aristotelian Tradition' in DG Owen (ed), *Philosophical Foundations of Tort Law* (Oxford, Clarendon 1995) 131-158

— 'The Purpose of Awarding Restitutionary Damages: A reply to Professor Weinrib' (2000) 1 *Theoretical Inquiries in Law* 39-58

Gorla, G, 'Sulla cosiddetta causalità giuridica: "fatto dannoso e conseguenze"' *Rivista di diritto commerciale* 1951, I, 405-421

Graham, M, 'Restitutionary Damages: The Anvil Struck' [2004] 120 *LQR* 26-30

Hagen, H, 'Funktionale und dogmatische Zusammenhänge zwischen Schadens- und Bereicherungsrecht' in G Paulus, U Diederichsen and C-W Canaris (eds), *Festschrift Larenz zum 70. Geburstag* (München, Beck 1973) 867-884

Honoré, T, 'Responsibility and Luck' (1988) 104 *LQR* 530-553

Honsell, H and Harrer, F, 'Schaden und Schadensberechnung' [1991] *Juristische Schulung* 441-448

Jackman, IM, 'Restitution for Wrongs' (1989) 48 *CLJ* 302-321

Jaffey, P, 'Disgorgement for Breach of Contract' [2000] *Restitution Law Review* 578-587

Jones, G, 'The Recovery of Benefits Gained from a Breach of Contract' (1983) 99 *LQR* 443-460

Klimchuk, D, 'On the Autonomy of Corrective Justice' (2003) 23 *OJLS* 49-64

Köndgen, J, 'Gewinnabschöpfung als Sanktion unerlaubten Tuns' (2000) 64 *Rabels Zeitschrift* 661-695

Korsch, G, 'Der Anspruch auf das Surrogat' (1916) 114 *Archiv für die civilistische Praxis* 1-22, 9

Kramer, M, 'Of Aristotle and Ice Cream Cones: Reflections on Jules Coleman's Theory of Corrective Justice', in B Bix (ed), *Analyzing Law: New Essays in Legal Theory* (Oxford, Clarendon 1998) 163-180

Liebs, D, 'The History of the Roman *Condictio* up to Justinian' in N MacCormick and P Birks (eds), *The Legal Mind: Essays for Tony Honoré* (Oxford, OUP 1986) 163-184

MacCormack, G, 'The early History of the 'Actio de in Rem Verso' (Alfenus to Labeo)' in F Pastori et al (eds), *Studi in onore di Arnaldo Biscardi* (Milano, Giuffrè 1982) vol 2 319-339

Manthe, U, 'Beiträge zur Entwicklung des antiken Gerechtigkeitsbegriffes I, Die Mathematisierung durch Pythagoras und Aristoteles' (1996) 113 *Savigny Zeitschrift, romanistische Abteilung* 1-31

Markesinis, B, 'The Not so Dissimilar Tort and Delict' (1977) 93 *LQR* 78-123

McGregor, H, 'Restitutionary Damages' in P Birks (ed), *Wrongs and Remedies in the Twenty-First Century* (Oxford, Clarendon 1996) 203-216

McInnes, M, 'Disgorgement for Wrongs: An Experiment in Alignment' [2000] *Restitution Law Review* 516-546

- 'Account of Profits for Common Law Wrongs' in S. Degeling and J. Edelman, *Equity In Commercial Law* (Sydney, Thomson, 2005) ch 16

- 'Gain, Loss and the User Principle' [2006] Restitution Law Review 76-92

McKendrick, E, 'Taxonomy: Does It Matter?' in D Johnston and R Zimmermann (eds), *Unjust Enrichment, Key Issues in Comparative Perspective* (Cambridge, CUP 2002) 627-657

Motsch, R, 'Schadensersatz als Erziehungsmittel' [1984] *Juristische Zeitung* 211-221

Murphy, J, 'Noxious Emissions and Common Law Liability: Tort in the Shadow of Regulation' in J Lowry and R Edmunds (eds), *Environmental Protection and the Common Law* (Oxford, Hart 2000) 51-76

Nicholas, B, 'Unjust Enrichment and Subsidiarity' in F Santoro Passarelli and M Lupoi (eds), *Scintillae iuris: Studi in memoria di Gino Gorla* (Milano, Giuffrè 1994) vol III 2037-2045

Otte, G, 'Die Aristoteleszitate in der Glosse' (1868) 85 *Savigny Zeitschrift, romanistische Abteilung,*368-393

Owens, J, 'Aristotle and Aquinas', in Kretzmann and Stump (eds), *The Cambridge Companion to Aquinas* (Cambridge, CUP 1993) 38

Posner, RA, 'Wealth Maximisation and Tort Law: A Philosophical Inquiry', in DG Owen (ed), *Philosophical Foundations of Tort Law* (Oxford, Clarendon 1995) 99-111

Ratti, U, 'Il risarcimento del danno nel diritto giustinianeo' (1933) 41 *Bullettino dell'Istituto di Diritto Romano* 169-199

Rosengarten, J, 'Der Präventionsgedanke im deutschen Zivilrecht' [1996] *Neue Juristische Wochenschrift* 1935-1938

Rossetti, G, 'Problemi e prospettive in tema di "struttura" e "funzione" delle azioni penali private' (1993) 35 *Bullettino dell'Istituto di Diritto Romano* 343-394

Rotondi, G, '"Dolus ex delicto" e "dolus ex contractu" nelle teorie bizantine sulla trasmissibilità delle azioni', in *Scritti giuridici II* (Padova, Cedam 1922) 371-410

Samuel, G, 'English Private Law: Old and New Thinking in the Taxonomy Debate' (2004) 24 *OJLS* 335-362

Schlechtriem, P, 'Bereicherungsansprüche wegen Persönlichkeitsverletzung' in R Fischer (ed), *Festschrift für W Hefermehl zum 70. Geburtstag* (München 1976) 445-465

Schlechtriem, P, 'Some Thoughts on the Decision of the BGH concerning Princess Caroline of Monaco', in B Markesinis (ed), *Protecting Privacy – The Clifford Chance Lectures* (Oxford, OUP 1999) vol 4 131-138

Schlesinger, P, 'L'ingiustizia del danno nell'illecito civile' (1960) *Jus* 336-347

Schulz, F, 'System der Rechte auf den Angriffserwerb' (1909) 105 *Archiv für die civilistische Praxis* 1-488

Seitz, W, 'Prinz und Prinzessin – Wandlungen des Deliktsrechts durch Zwangskommerzialisierung der Persönlichkeit' [1996] *Neue Juristische Wochenschrift* 2848-2850

Sharpe, RJ and Waddams, SM, 'Damages for Lost Opportunity to Bargain' [1982] 2 *OJLS* 290-297

Siemes, C, 'Gewinnabschöpfung bei Zwangskommerzialisierung der Persönlichkeit durch die Presse' (2001) 201 *Archiv für die civilistische Praxis* 202-231

Smith, LD, 'The province of the Law of Restitution' (1992) 71 *Canadian Bar Review* 672-699

Virgo, G, 'Clarifying Restitution for Wrongs' [1998] *Restitution Law Review* 118-126

Voci, P, 'Azioni penali e azioni miste' (1998) 64 *Studia et Documenta Historiae et Iuris* 1-46

Watterson, S, 'An Account of Profits or Damages? The History of Orthodoxy' (2004) 24 *OJLS* 471-494

Weinrib, E, 'Understanding Tort Law' (1989) 23 *Valparaiso University LR* 485-526

— 'Restitutionary Damages as Corrective Justice' (2000) 1 *Theoretical Inquiries in Law* 1-37

— 'Punishment and Disgorgement as Contract Remedies' (2003) 78 *Chicago-Kent Law Review* 55-103

Winkel, L, 'Le droit romain et la philosophie grecque, quelques problèmes de méthode' (1997) 65 *Tijdschrift voor Rechtsgeschiedenis* 373-384

Wolf, JG, 'Barkauf und Haftung' (1977) 45 *Tijdschrift voor Rechtsgeschiedenis* 1-25

Worthington, S, 'Reconsidering Disgorgement for Wrongs' (1999) 62 *MLR* 218-240

Other Publications

Academia Scientiarum Borussica, *Vocabularium Iurisprudentiae Romanae* (Berlin 1939)

Alff, R, '§ 281', in *Das bürgerliches Gesetzbuch – RGRK* (12th edn) (Berlin 1976)

Beltramo, M, Longo, G and Merryman, JH (tr), *The Italian Civil Code* (New York, Oceana 1969)

Bianca, CM, 'Dell'inadempimento delle obbligazioni, Art 1218-1229', in A Scialoja and G Branca (eds), *Commentario del Codice civile* (2nd edn) (Bologna-Roma, Zanichelli 1979)

Brasiello, B, 'Delicta', in *Novissimo Digesto italiano* (Torino, UTET 1968) 377-379

Cendon, P, *Commentario al Codice civile* (Torino, UTET 1991)

Cian, G and Trabucchi, A, *Commentario breve al Codice civile* (5th edn) (Padova, Cedam 1997)

Crawford MH (ed), *Roman Statutes* (London, Institute of Classical Studies 1996) vol II

Creifelds, C, *Rechtswörterbuch* (14th edn) (München, Beck 1997)

Emmerich, V, '§ 279-283', in *Münchener Kommentar zum Bürgerlichen Gesetzbuch* (4th edn) (München, Beck 2001)

Franzoni, M, 'Dei fatti illeciti, Art 2043 – 2059', in A Scialoja and G Branca (eds), *Commentario del Codice Civile* (2nd edn) (Bologna-Roma, Zanichelli 1993)

Ghidini, G, *Della concorrenza sleale*, in P Schlesinger (ed), *Il codice civile – Commentario* (Milano, Giuffrè 1994)

Goren, SL, *The German Civil Code* (revd edn) (Littleton, Colorado, Rothman 1994)

Grothe, H, '§ 346', in Bamberger and Roth (eds), *Kommentar zum Bürgerlichen Gesetzbuch* (München, Beck 2001)

Hager, J, '§§ 823-825', in *J von Staudingers Kommentar zum Bürgerlichen Gesetzbuch mit Einführungsgesetz und Nebengesetzen* (13th edn) (Berlin 1999)

Law Commission, *Aggravated, Exemplary and Restitutionary Damages* (Law Com No 247 1997)

Lieb, M; '§§ 812-822', in *Münchener Kommentar zum Bürgerlichen Gesetzbuch* (4th edn) (München, Beck 2004)

Löwisch, M, '§281', in *J von Staudingers Kommentar zum Bürgerlichen Gesetzbuch mit Einführungsgesetz und Nebengesetzen* (13th edn) (Berlin 1995)

Mertens, H-J, '§§ 823-829', in *Münchener Kommentar zum Bürgerlichen Gesetzbuch* (3rd edn) (München, Beck 1997)

Monateri, PG, 'Le Fonti delle Obbligazioni, 3, La Responsabilità Civile', in R Sacco (ed), *Trattato di Diritto Civile* (Torino, UTET 1998)

Mugdan, B (ed), *Die gesamten Materialien zum Bürgerlichen Gesetzbuch für das Deutsche Reich* (Berlin 1899, repr Aalen, Scientia 1979)

Oetker, H, '§§ 249-255', in *Münchener Kommentar zum Bürgerlichen Gesetzbuch* (4th edn) (München, Beck 2001)

Palandt, O (ed), *Bürgerliches Gesetzbuch* (7th edn) (München, Beck)

Pugliatti, S, 'Alterum non laedere', in *Enciclopedia del Diritto* (Milano, Giuffrè 1958) vol 2 93-108

Rescigno, P, 'Ripetizione dell'indebito', in *Novissimo Digesto italiano* (Torino, UTET 1968) vol 15 1223-1237

Schäfer, K, '§§ 823-832', in *J von Staudingers Kommentar zum Bürgerlichen Gesetzbuch mit Einführungsgesetz und Nebengesetzen* (12th edn) (Berlin 1985)

Schiemann, G, '§§ 249-254', in *J von Staudingers Kommentar zum Bürgerlichen Gesetzbuch mit Einführungsgesetz und Nebengesetzen* (13th edn) (Berlin 2005)

Scognamiglio, R, 'Illecito (Diritto vigente)' in *Novissimo Digesto Italiano* (Torino, UTET 1962) vol 8 164-173

Seiler, H-H, '§667', in *Münchener Kommentar zum Bürgerlichen Gesetzbuch* (3rd edn) (München 1997)

Trimarchi, P, 'Illecito (Diritto privato)', in *Enciclopedia del Diritto*, Vol 20, (Milano, Giuffrè 1970) 90-112

Wang, CH, *The German Civil Code* (London, Stevens 1907)

Watson, A (tr), Mommsen T, Krueger P (eds), *The Digest of Justinian* (Philadelphia, Univ of Pennsylvania 1985)

Wendehorst, C, '§ 818' in Bamberger/Roth, *Kommentar zum Bürgerlichen Gesetzbuch* (München, Beck 2003)

Wittmann, R, '§ 667' in *J von Staudingers Kommentar zum Bürgerlichen Gesetzbuch mit Einführungsgesetz und Nebengesetzen* (13th edn) (Berlin 1994)

Youngs, R, *Sourcebook on German Law* (reprd, London, Cavendish 1998)

Index